YO-ABE-445

230.59   Introduction to
I8   Puritan theology

DATE			
NOV 17 1980			
DEC 11 1995			

INTRODUCTION TO
Puritan
Theology
A READER

EDWARD HINDSON, EDITOR
FOREWORD BY JAMES I. PACKER

A CANON PRESS BOOK

BAKER BOOK HOUSE
Grand Rapids, Michigan

The text for the Puritan writings included in this volume comes from the following sources:

BAXTER, RICHARD. "The True Catholic, and Catholic Church Described; and the Vanity of the Papists, and All Other Schismatics, That Confine the Catholic Church to Their Sect, Discovered and Shamed." In *The Practical Works of the Rev. Richard Baxter, with a Life of the Author, and a Critical Examination of His Writings.* 23 vols. London: James Duncan, 1830. 16:283-370 (pages included in the excerpt in this book, 283-99, 307).

BUNYAN, JOHN. "A Holy Life the Beauty of Christianity, or, An Exhortation to Christians to Be Holy." In *The Entire Works of John Bunyan.* Edited by Henry Stebbing. 4 vols. Toronto: Virtue, Yorston & Co., 1859? 3:294-332 (312-17).

CHARNOCK, STEPHEN. "Discourse V: On the Eternity of God." In *Discourses upon the Existence and Attributes of God.* 2 vols. New York: Robert Carter, 1873. 1:276-309 (276-93).

DOWNAME, GEORGE. "Bellarmine's Eight Allegations to Prove Justification by Inherent Righteousness, Answered." In *A Treatise of Justification: Wherein Is First Set Down the True Doctrine in the Causes, Effects, Fruits, [and] Consequences of It, According to the Word of God. And Then All Objections and Cavils of the Adversaries to God's Free Justification by Grace Are Answered and Confuted, Especially [Those] of Robert Bellarmine, Jesuit and Cardinal.* London: Felix Kyngston, 1633. Pp. 227-42.

EDWARDS, JONATHAN. "The Portion of the Wicked" and "The Portion of the Righteous." In *The Works of President Edwards, with a Memoir of His Life.* 10 vols. New York: S. Converse, 1829-1830. 8 (1830): 195-279 (195-201, 203, 205-11, 227-28, 236, 239-40, 242, 244-46, 248-50, 271).

HOPKINS, SAMUEL. "The Cause, Nature, and Means of Regeneration." In *The Works of Samuel Hopkins, D.D., . . . with a Memoir of His Life and Character.* 3 vols. Boston: Doctrinal Tract and Book Society, 1852. 3:543-78 (543-55, 560-69, 571-78).

JEWEL, JOHN. "A Treatise of the Holy Scriptures, Gathered out of Certain Sermons . . . Preached at Salisbury, Anno Domini 1570." In *Various Tracts and Extracts from the Works of John Jewell, with a Memorial of His Life.* The Fathers of the English Church, or, A Selection from the Writings of the Reformers and Early Protestant Divines, of the Church of England, vol. 7. London: John Hatchard, 1811. Pp. 419-79 (419-29, 454-63, 465-68, 472-73, 476-79).

MANTON, THOMAS. "Man's Impotency to Help Himself out of His Misery." In *The Complete Works of Thomas Manton, D.D.* Edited by Thomas Smith et al. 22 vols. London: James Nisbet, 1870-1875. 5 (1871): 475-84.

OWEN, JOHN. "An Answer to the Twentieth Chapter of the Book Entitled, *The Universality of God's Free Grace,* etc. [Written by Thomas More and Published in 1643], Being a Collection of All the Arguments Used by the Author Throughout the Whole Book to Prove the Universality of Redemption." In *The Death of Death in the Death of Christ.* In *The Works of John Owen, D.D.* Edited by William H. Goold. 24 vols. Edinburgh: T. and T. Clark, 1862. 10:368-403 (368-94, 403).

PERKINS, WILLIAM. "A Golden Chain, or, The Description of Theology: Containing the Order of the Causes of Salvation and Damnation, According to God's Word: A View Whereof Is to Be Seen in the Table Annexed." In *The Works of That Famous and Worthy Minister of Christ, in the University of Cambridge, M. W. Perkins.* 3 vols. Cambridge: John Legate, 1608-1613. 1: insert between pp. 10 and 11.

PRESTON, JOHN. "God's Name and Attributes: The First Sermon." In *Life Eternal, or, A Treatise of the Knowledge of the Divine Essence and Attributes. Delivered in 18 Sermons . . .* 4th ed. London: E. P., 1634. 1:1-29 (1-22).

USSHER, JAMES. "Immanuel, or, The Mystery of the Incarnation of the Son of God." In *A Body of Divinity, or, The Sum and Substance of Christian Religion . . . Whereunto Is Adjoined a Tract Entitled "Immanuel, or, The Mystery of the Incarnation of the Son of God."* London: Thomas Downes and George Badger, 1649. Pp. [1-24] (1-9, 14-24).

To
Dr. John Gerstner
a lover of the Puritans and
an able practitioner of their principles

Contents

Foreword

What was Puritanism? Much ink gets spilled over that question, and no wonder; Puritanism was so many-sided and diversified a movement (and *movement* is the right word, for it was constantly developing) that no neat formula can embrace all that was there. The facts about the word *puritan* are clear enough. It was coined early in Elizabeth's reign, possibly by Roman Catholics in derision at English Protestants, possibly by separatists in pride at having withdrawn from defiling associations (there is some evidence for both possibilities). Defenders of the church establishment at once began to hurl it at would-be reformers as an insult, implying schismatic tendencies, while others used it as a term of abuse for the godly generally, along with "precisian," "gehennian" (hell-fire man!), and similar choice language. Under the Stuarts, theologians were called Puritans for opposing Arminianism. After 1642, according to Richard Baxter, "puritan" was replaced in all contexts by "presbyterian," spoken with similar venom and innuendo. But these facts yield no clear definition of the movement to which the word *puritan* was for two generations applied; only by inspection can its real nature be discerned. So any definition offered at this point of time will be selective, interpretive, and persuasive, reflecting an overall view of the movement's total scope and ingredients. Adequate judgment of this is not, however, easy.

English historians often speak of the "puritan century"—the century, that is, during which the Puritans made the running—and date it from the return of the Marian exiles in 1559 or the appearance of the word *puritan* in 1564 to the Great Ejection of Puritan pastors from the reestablished church in 1662, after which twenty-five years of persecution broke Puritanism as a national force. But American Puritanism (which is only English Puritanism exported in the persons of colonists in the twenties and thirties of the seventeenth century) maintained itself as a religious and cultural norm into the eighteenth century, when it was rejuvenated into Calvinistic revivalism by Jonathan Edwards, a Puritan born out of due time, and so gained strength to continue as an influence into the nineteenth century. Taking account of both sides of the Atlantic, one will see Puritanism as spanning two centuries at least.

In England Daniel Neal's *The History of the Puritans* (1732-1738), written as a nonconformist apologia, fixed the image of Puritanism as essentially a movement of ecclesiastical protest, the main aim of which was to amend the established order. Recently, however, English and American scholars have taken note of the literature of Puritan piety and ethics, and it is now seen that church reorganization was only part of what the Puritans were after. The truth is that, inheriting the medieval vision of the solidarity of Christian society (*corpus Christianum*), the Puritans saw and felt the unity of life to a degree that moderns find hard to grasp. Their vision of reality was not fragmented; they did not need to argue the point that Christian concern may not be limited to church order or the welfare of individuals, but must embrace both together, along with the politics, economics, and culture of nations, for they took this as axiomatic. Therefore they spent their strength trying to insure that "holiness to the Lord" could be written in letters of gold over every part of life and relationship—the nation-church's faith and order, the personal state and conduct of each citizen-worshiper, and the goals and standards of all community activities. These areas of concern were not seen as a hierarchy of priorities, but as a complex of coordinates. This breadth and unity of Puritan concern is mirrored in the title of Richard Baxter's million-word epic, *A Christian Directory: or, A Sum of Practical Theology, and Cases of Conscience. Directing Christians, How to Use Their Knowledge and Faith; How to Improve All Helps and Means, and to Perform All Duties; How to Overcome Temptations, and to Escape or Mortify Every Sin. In Four Parts. I. Christian Ethics (or Private Duties). II. Christian Economics (or Family Duties). III. Christian Ecclesiastics (or Church Duties). IV. Christian Politics (or Duties to Our Rulers and Neighbours)* (written 1664/5, published 1673). It was this unity of concern, together with the attractiveness and, indeed, authority of the "serious" preaching, devotion, and discipline which it bred, that held together within the movement episcopalians, presbyterians, and congregational independents of both baptist and pedobaptist principles; despite their in-fighting about church order and other doctrinal problems, they were at one on the kind of persons and nations they wanted to see in Britain and America, and this gave them a family feeling that went deeper than all their domestic disputes.

For Professor Hindson, Puritanism is the name for a stream of theological conviction that ran through both Old and New England, taking into its flow persons who in their own lifetime were not called Puritans at all. Conventional persons might raise their eyebrows at finding in an anthology of Puritan writing extracts from three Anglican bishops (Jewel, Downame, Ussher) and Samuel Hopkins, Jonathan Edwards's controversial disciple who lived into the nineteenth century. But Dr. Hindson discerns in all these authors common ways of thinking—a common appeal to Scripture, with a common hermeneutic; a common Augustinianism, deep and doxological, regarding sin and grace; a common Calvinism, Bezan in method and style, on the details of soteriology; a common view of general revelation, natural theology, and the place of reason in theological construction; and a common concern to be "experimental"—that is, to show how we may prove God's Word true in our own experience. There is, I think, no reason whatever to doubt that if the authors from whom Dr. Hindson made his selections could have been consulted, they would have thought it entirely right for them to appear in each other's company, as exponents of a single school of thought.

Not, indeed, that all the detailed positions stated in these extracts were unanimously held within that school of thought. Not all the Reformed Augustinians of Britain and America in the Puritan period embraced (for instance) the Bezan supralapsarianism of Perkins's chart in the "Golden Chains," or the crushing rigor of John Owen's polemic against the idea of indefinite (that is, ineffective) redemption. Nor does this selection cover all that the Puritans had to say, or thought, important. Their ethics, their sabbatarianism, their views of faith, assurance, and what Thomas Hooker called "the soul's preparation for Christ," their thoughts (not unanimous) about God's plan of history and the public return of Jesus Christ are all matters demanding attention before we have the measure of Puritan theology—not to mention their quite extraordinary insight into conscience and its problems, and the magisterial pastoral anthropology that guided them in their cure of souls. But it would be churlish to complain of not being given more when we have already been given so much. Professor Hindson's selections have a double value. They are a valuable resource for understanding the Puritan theological mind, and they constitute a pioneer venture in identifying the Reformed Augustinian stream of thought in the English-speaking world over a period of two centuries. From both standpoints it is a pleasure to commend them to the study of those who care for these things.

There is a further reason for joy when Augustinian material of this caliber is made available in our day. It does not seem possible to deny that the Puritans (using the word in the broad and inclusive sense that Professor Hindson gives it) were strongest just where evangelical Christians today are weakest, and their writings can give evangelicals more real help that those of any other body of Christian teachers, past or present, since the days of the apostles. This is a large claim, but there is a solid basis for it. Consider the characteristics of Puritan Christianity. Here were men of outstanding intellectual power, in whom the mental habits fostered by sober scholarship were linked with a flaming zeal for God and a minute acquaintance with the human heart. All their work reveals this unique fusion of gifts and graces. Their appreciation of God's sovereign majesty was profound; their reverence in handling His Word was deep. They understood the ways of God with men, the glory of Christ the Mediator, and the work of the Spirit in the believer and the church, as richly and fully as any since their day. Nor was their knowledge a mere theoretical orthodoxy. They sought to "reduce to practice" (their own phrase) all that God taught them. They yoked their consciences to Scripture, disciplining themselves to demand a theological, as distinct from a merely pragmatic, justification for everything they did. They saw the church, the family, the state, the arts and sciences, the world of commerce and industry, along with the personal world and involvements of each individual, as so many spheres in which the Creator and Lord of all things must be served and glorified.

Then, too, knowing God, they also knew man. They saw him as essentially a noble being, made in God's image to rule God's world, but now tragically brutified and brutalized by sin. In the light of God's law, lordship, and holiness, they saw sin in its threefold character: as transgression and guilt; as rebellion and usurpation; and as uncleanness, corruption, and inability for good. Seeing these things and knowing as they did the ways and means whereby the Spirit brings sinners to faith and new life in Christ, and leads saints to grow up into their Savior's image by growing downwards into humility and an increasing dependence on grace, the Puritans became superb pastors in their own day. By the same token, they can, though dead, yet speak to us for our guidance and direction.

For we evangelicals need help. Where the Puritans called for order, discipline, depth, and thoroughness, our temper is one of casual haphazardness and restless impatience. We crave for stunts, novelties, entertainments; we have lost our taste for solid study, humble self-examination, disciplined meditation, and unspectacular hard work in our callings and in our prayers. Again, where Puritanism had God and His glory as its unifying center, our thinking revolves round ourselves as if we were the hub of the universe. The hollowness of our vaunted biblicism becomes apparent as again and again we put asunder things God has joined. Thus, we concern ourselves about the individual but not the church, and about witness but not worship. In evangelizing, we preach the gospel without the law and faith without repentance, stressing the gift of salvation and glossing over the cost of discipleship. No wonder so many who profess conversion fall away! Then, in teaching the Christian life our habit is to depict it as a path of thrilling feelings rather than of working faith, and of supernatural interruptions rather than of rational righteousness; and in dealing with Christian experience we dwell constantly on joy, peace, happiness, satisfaction, and rest of soul with no balancing reference to the divine discontent of Romans 7, the fight of faith of Psalm 73, or any of the burdens of responsibility and providential chastenings that fall to the lot of a child of God. The spontaneous jollity of the carefree extrovert comes to be equated with healthy Christian living, and jolly extroverts in our churches are encouraged to become complacent in carnality, while saintly souls of less sanguine temperament are driven almost crazy because they cannot bubble over in the prescribed manner. Whereupon they consult their pastor, and he perhaps has no better remedy than to refer them to a psychiatrist! Truly, we need help, and the Puritan tradition can give it. If Dr. Hindson's selections encourage students and pastors to dig more deeply into these Augustinian mines of spiritual lore, the church will benefit enormously. It is much to be hoped that this is the effect his book will have.

J. I. Packer
Associate Principal
Trinity College
Bristol, England

Preface

The theological writings of the Puritans for too long have been neglected by contemporary theologians and studied only by students of literature. Only recently has interest in the theological content of the Puritans' works revived, and it is to encourage this that the present symposium has been compiled. Its purpose is to acquaint the general reader, as well as the more advanced student of theology, with various leading writers on the several subjects of systematic theology. The selections are intended to represent not a consistent expression of theology, but basic Puritan teaching on various matters. Writers included here represent the best authors on certain subjects as well as a wide range of affiliations—Anglican, Presbyterian, Congregationalist, Baptist, and nonconformist.

The edited selections in this volume conform to the printed texts listed on the copyright page, varying only in these respects: subheadings have been inserted into nine of the articles (the subheads all reflect the authors' explicit outlines); Scripture references have been put into a consistent form, with abbreviated book titles following the same rules throughout, with book numbers always being in capital roman numerals, and with chapter and verse numbers always being separated by colons; footnotes that were keyed to letters are now keyed to numbers; quotation marks that followed British style have been Americanized; and archaic *s*'s, of necessity, have been modernized. Of the twelve selections, eight are based on nineteenth-century critical texts, four on original seventeenth-century texts. The latter, of course, reflect more archaic spellings.

The author expresses his sincere appreciation to former professors in historical theology—John Gerstner, John W. Montgomery, and Robert Culver—whose instruction and guidance have been invaluable to this project. Dr. Gerstner first called my attention to many of these selections and is a great lover of the Puritans and their theology. A word of thanks also is due to: Gordon Cross, dean of Trinity Graduate School of Theology (Florida) for serving as my advisor in the original development of this project as a research thesis; Donna, my devoted wife, for typing the entire manuscript and for the patience that has made this book possible; Iain Murray, editor of Banner of Truth Trust, for reviewing the manuscript and making helpful suggestions; Peter H. Lewis, for supplying two of the illustrations; Arthur Kuschke, librarian at Westminster Theological Seminary, for helping to secure original Puritan works; Martha Aycock, reference librarian at Union Theological Seminary (Virginia), also for helping to secure Puritan works; and Allan Fisher, a project editor at Baker Book House, for his work on, and great personal interest in, this book.

OMNIA AD DEI GLORIAM!

1

Introduction to the Puritans

Puritanism never designated a particular group or denomination of Christians, but those preachers and laymen who held certain spiritual convictions that transcended confessional boundaries. It was more a religious term than an ecclesiastical label. Puritanism began as a reform movement within the Anglican church of England during the late sixteenth century.[1] It was not initially an attempt to split the church, but to continue to reform a church which the Puritans saw as still too much like Roman Catholicism.

Ernest F. Kevan noted that in the ecclesiastical realm the Puritans believed in maintaining the national church, but also in reforming it more extensively[2] in line with the true evangelical and apostolic heritage of the New Testament.[3] The Reformation of the sixteenth

---

1. An excellent discussion, including definitions, appears in Perry Miller and Thomas H. Johnson, *The Puritans,* 1:1-12. This work, though, deals mainly with New England Puritanism and refers only in a limited way to the English divines.

2. *The Grace of Law: A Study in Puritan Theology,* p. 17. This work is a fine discussion of the place of moral law in sanctification, as viewed by the Puritans.

3. This concept is best recognized and developed in Philip Edgcumbe Hughes, *Theology of the English Reformers.* Unlike those who discuss Puritanism from a merely social standpoint, Hughes recognized the spiritual and theological importance of the movement. The social historians are often baffled by the Puritans' emphasis on spiritual experience.

century involved the rediscovery of divine grace and Scriptural authority, and the Puritans recognized that the fruit of the Reformation (the evangelical church) was the outgrowth of its roots (*sola fide* and *sola Scriptura*). Thus Puritanism became a doctrinal movement.[4] It involved a rediscovery of God's sovereignty and Christ's all-sufficiency. It, like the Continental Reformation, was a revival of Augustinianism and Biblical theology. At the core of Puritan sentiment was an intense disgust for the Roman Catholic emphasis on man's ability to merit his own salvation.

The "early" Puritans strongly opposed High Church notions, a conflict which intensified and came to the fore in the early seventeenth century. The Act of Uniformity of 1662 ejected hundreds of Puritan preachers from the Anglican Church, making Puritanism a nonconformist movement. Puritanism matured later in New England and lasted until the end of the eighteenth century. Thus Puritanism touched men of God in many denominations and became the basis of modern-day evangelicalism.

In an age when the evangelical church is being challenged and threatened on every side, it is necessary to reconsider the doctrinal truths that are its root and foundation.[5] If it is to survive the ecumenical milieu of our day, orthodoxy must stand on the Reformation principle of *sola Scriptura*. One of the failures of many evangelical preachers today is their lack of doctrinal preaching. A. N. Martin commented that modern evangelicals suffer from a mentality that regards doctrine and theology as a medieval hobgoblin![6] This mentality accuses theologians of obscuring the truth of Scripture instead of clarifying it. The express purpose of doctrinal preaching is to place particular truths in the framework of the whole counsel of God. It involves exegesis and exposition that lead to a philosophically and apologetically sound orthodoxy. It does not isolate truth from experience, but applies truth to experience. To the Puritan preacher truth had no relevance except in its practical application to the believer's life.

---

4. This theme is developed in William Childs Robinson, *The Reformation: A Rediscovery of Grace*. Robinson criticized American preachers who fail to appreciate the Reformers' doctrine, saying that without doctrinal roots there is no evangelical church.

5. The current struggle is examined in Francis A. Schaeffer, *The Church at the End of the 20th Century* (Chicago: Inter-Varsity, 1970). Schaeffer called the conservative church back to its historic doctrine and practice.

6. *What's Wrong with Preaching Today?* (London: Banner of Truth, 1970), pp. 16, 17. Martin traced the failures of modern preaching to deficiencies in the preacher's devotional life and in the content of his messages.

Puritan Piety

Only with the rise of modern theology has theological study returned to entangled, abstract minutia.[7] The loss of absolute truth has resulted in the loss of absolute morals. The importance of theology has been minimized by existentialism. Truth as truth is no longer important to the modern theologian, and unfortunately this attitude is affecting many contemporary evangelicals. When doctrine deteriorates, methods of evangelism and standards of conduct do too. The Puritan preacher constantly applied doctrinal truth to the practice and ethics of the individual Christian.[8]

As Miller showed, the Puritan was not the gaunt, lank-haired kill-joy in a black hat that historians long thought him to have been.[9] He was a colorful individual with a sense of humor and a deep sense of spiritual devotion to God. A seventeenth-century contemporary of the Puritans described them as ones who honored God above all else and who believed that the best Christians should be the best husbands, wives, parents, children, masters, and servants, so that the doctrine of God might be glorified and not blasphemed.[10]

William Perkins, an early Puritan, was the most eminent theologian of Cambridge, and his "Golden Chain" of the decrees of predestination and damnation is included in this reader. Yet he also was the father of English casuistical divinity.[11] William Ames recounted his experience of hearing Perkins lecture at Cambridge and noted that he "instructed them soundly in the truth, stirred them

---

7. One example is Paul Tillich, *Systematic Theology*, 3 vols. (Chicago: University of Chicago, 1969). His philosophy of history reduces his theology to meaningless "jibberish." His ontological blunder was to make "being" equal everything and thus nothing! Critiques of Tillich are Kenneth Hamilton, *The System and the Gospel: A Critique of Paul Tillich* (New York: Macmillan, 1963); and John Warwick Montgomery, "Tillich's Philosophy of History," *Themelios* 4 (1967): 28-41.

8. This fact is being rediscovered today more than ever before in this century. See two Methodist works: Gordon Stevens Wakefield, *Puritan Devotion: Its Place in the Development of Christian Piety;* and Robert C. Monk, *John Wesley: His Puritan Heritage.* The latter traces Wesley's use of various Puritan books, some of which he even republished! On the Puritan influence on Baptist preacher Charles Haddon Spurgeon, see Ernest W. Bacon, *Spurgeon: Heir of the Puritans* (Grand Rapids: Eerdmans, 1968).

9. *The Puritans,* 1:2, 3.

10. John Geree, *The Character of an Old English Puritan or Nonconformist* (London, 1646).

11. Wakefield, *Puritan Devotion,* p. 6.

up effectually to seek after godlinesse . . . that they might promote true Religion unto God's glory, and others' salvation."[12]

As hope for the complete purification of the Church of England dimmed, the Puritans became theologians of the Christian life. Kevan said, "They mounted the pulpit, and undertook the task of creating a new understanding of spiritual things in a nation that had not fully awakened to the full implications of the Scriptural principles of the Reformation."[13] The weakness of the Anglican church was due not to weakness in the Reformation, but to the Anglicans' failure to comply fully with the principles of the Reformation. Fundamentalism is an outgrowth of Puritanism and has its love for pure doctrine, but most fundamentalists have little appreciation or even awareness of the English Reformers to whom they owe so much.[14]

The genius of Puritan theologians was that they were preachers first and theological writers secondly. Their written works were mainly edited versions of their sermons.[15] Because of their emphasis upon application of doctrine to the Christian life, their writings generally came to be designated as "practical divinity." They were not "ivory-tower" theologians, but preachers of God's grace who were determined to meet the needs of men.

The term *puritan* was contemptuously given the movement by High Church Anglicans who thought the Puritans narrow-minded hypocrites (just as the term *fundamentalist* is often applied today by those who oppose fundamentalism).[16] The ungodly are often quicker to condemn the godly than vice versa.

Puritan devotion is a model of Christian piety. Despite their strong stand for doctrinal purity, Puritan ministers led their flocks gently, always concerned to deliver Christians from the devices of Satan

---

12. *Conscience, with the Power and Cases Thereof,* preface. Ames became a famous casuist in his own right.

13. *The Grace of Law,* p. 19.

14. This is due in part to the early dispensational view that the church of Sardis (Rev. 3) represents the Reformation period in church history. The Sardis church was alive but dead; only a few had believed. Thus many fundamentalists have underestimated seriously the importance of the Reformation. The English Reformers, however, were anything but worldly and "dead."

15. William Haller, *The Rise of Puritanism,* pp. 10-25.

16. Puritan Robert Bolton actually resented the name *puritan. True Happiness* (London, 1611), p. 132. An example of contemporary disdain for the term *fundamentalism* is Bernard Ramm's definition of it as "anti-intellectual," "anti-cultural," "obscurantist," and "separatist." *A Handbook of Contemporary Theology* (Grand Rapids: Eerdmans, 1966), p. 48.

and to warn unbelievers to rest in Christ alone.[17] Richard Greenham and his son-in-law, John Dod, were known for their ability to explain the gospel to the most simple souls in their own terminology and expressions. The Puritans loved God and the truth; they were not Pharisees. They denounced extremists and fanatics (enthusiasts).[18] Their spiritual piety was sincere, resulting from their commitment to Biblical doctrine.

The key to Puritan devotion was discipline. The Christian life is a disciplined life, not a happy-go-lucky one. Too many contemporary evangelicals have missed this principle entirely, and so our churches stumble after the truth and grab at falsehoods. On every hand voices are calling for a reevaluation of doctrine, ethics, and methods. Why? We have neglected doctrine, and this has affected our piety and devotion adversely.

At the core of Puritan sentiment was an absolutely authoritative Scripture. The Word of God governed and disciplined their lives. The great transformation of the Reformation was caused by the release of the Word of God from the clerical chain. The Reformation could not be stopped because numerous lives had been transformed by the power of the Word of the living God.[19] Thomas Cranmer wrote: "... this book is the Word of God, the most precious jewel, the most holy relic that remaineth upon earth."[20]

The Puritans' interest in the Word of God included an emphasis on the law of God. The moral law retains its authority over disciples—disciplined believers—and it is useful in convicting men of their sin and showing them that their only hope is the grace and mercy of God. The Puritans, then, strongly opposed antinomianism (those who claim the Christian has no obligation to keep the moral law). The Puritans even considered the civil law in Scripture to be their "primary law book."[21]

Kevan felt that the authority of the law in the believer's life is

---

17. Cf. the depth of compassion in Thomas Brooks, *Precious Remedies Against Satan's Devices* (London, 1652). On every page Brooks pleaded with great compassion with his readers.

18. Cf. Richard Alleine, *Vindiciae Pietatis* (London, 1664), pp. 1-12.

19. See examples of conversions in *Theology of the English Reformers*, pp. 12-15.

20. In John Strype, *Memorials of Archbishop Cranmer*, 3 vols. (London: Oxford University, 1954), 3:385.

21. Cf. discussion in John D. Eusden, *Puritans, Lawyers, and Politics in Early Seventeenth-Century England*, p. 120.

central to the Puritan concept of the Christian life.[22] True devotion to Christ involves obedience to the moral law of God. The Puritans never taught that this obedience is a basis for salvation, but that it is the inevitable result of a man's heart and will having been regenerated by God. The Puritans criticized the antinomians for their failure to distinguish properly between justification and sanctification, discerning that the doctrine of the antinomians too frequently becomes their practice.[23]

Thus the Puritans emphasized the practical use of the law: to restrain sin, to lead men to Christ, and to direct the believer's conduct. In this they closely followed the teaching of Calvin,[24] who had urged that the law be preached to show the sinner his great failure and need and to encourage the believer to strive for holiness and integrity.[25]

The Puritan wanted to live as godly as possible, not—as with so many professing Christians today—as worldly as possible. Cranmer wrote, "True faith doth ever bring forth good works."[26] Only true righteousness is evidence that one's faith and repentance are true. Edwin Sandys wrote, "The duty which we owe Him again is in holiness and righteousness of life continually to serve Him."[27] The twentieth-century church greatly needs to recover and reemphasize this truth in order to restore the dynamic power of Christianity to pulpits and homes. Sandys wrote again: "If the fear of God were planted in our hearts, . . . we would not live in such careless security as we do; the gospel would take better effect in us, and bring forth more plentiful fruit; we would at the length cast away impiety and worldly concupiscence, and live a sober, just, and godly life; . . . the

---

22. *The Grace of Law*, p. 22. He cited several important Puritan refutations of antinomianism: Samuel Rutherford, *A Free Disputation Against Pretended Liberty of Conscience* (London, 1649); Rutherford, *A Survey of the Spiritual Antichrist* (London, 1648); Thomas Bedford, *An Examination of the Chief Points of Antinomianism* (London, 1646); Samuel Bolton, *The True Bounds of Christian Freedom* (London, 1645); Henry Burton, *The Law and the Gospel Reconciled* (London, 1631); George Downame, *An Abstract of Duties Commanded in the Law of God* (London, 1620); Thomas Gataker, *Antinomianism Discovered and Confuted* (London, 1652); Robert Traill, *A Vindication of the Protestant Doctrine Concerning Justification* (London, 1692).

23. Cf. John Sedgwick, *Antinomianism Anatomized* (London, 1643), p. 29.

24. *Institutes of the Christian Religion* (Geneva, 1559), 2.7.12. See also Ronald S. Wallace, *Calvin's Doctrine of the Christian Life* (Grand Rapids: Eerdmans, 1959), pp. 141-47.

25. *Institutes*, 3.19.2.

26. "Homily of Faith," in *Works*, ed. John Edmund Cox, 2 vols. (Cambridge: University, 1844, 1846), 2:140.

27. Quoted in Hughes, *Theology of the English Reformers*, pp. 80, 81.

ministers would be more diligent in feeding of the flock, the people more ready to hear the voice of the shepherd. . . ."[28]

Sanctification is the immediate work of the Holy Spirit in the believer's life, but the outworking of it involves being disciplined by the Word of God. John Jewel commented: "We are children of God, the brethren of Christ, and heirs of the everlasting kingdom, we are Christian men, we profess God's Gospel; let us therefore remember that we must walk as becometh the servants of Christ: we must live like the professors of God's holy Gospel."[29] This passionate devotion to holy living was intended not to earn salvation but to express sonship, the believer's destiny in Christ.

Puritan piety contrasted greatly with that of Catholicism. The latter, based on Neo-Platonism, identifies three stages in the Christian life: purgation, illumination, and union. For the Puritan, union with Christ was not the end of the Christian life but the beginning! Thus, "all spiritual life and holiness is treasured up in the Fulness of Christ, and communicated to us by Union with him; therefore, the accomplishing of Union with Christ is the first work of saving Grace in our hearts."[30] Again, we modern-day evangelicals must recapture these truths if we are to stand the flood of ecumenism that minimizes the differences between Protestant and Catholic doctrine. Love of Christ and faithfulness to His truth were the sterling qualities of Puritan piety.

Puritan Doctrine

The greatness of Puritanism was its fidelity to the Word of God as the only source of true doctrine and right practice. But it was not merely a religious creed; it was a philosophy of life that integrated man's whole being with the teaching of Scripture. Thus Puritans did not fear science, logic, and philosophy, but sought to bring the Word of God to bear on each discipline. They believed that God can be glorified in every area of academic pursuit. They believed Scripture to be in harmony with reason and science, refusing to allow mere rationalism to overrule the Word of God.[31] They considered Scripture the fountain of all reasonable truth and sought to discern "reality" in relation to what the Scripture taught. They did

---

28. *Sermons,* ed. John Ayre (Cambridge: University, 1842), p. 280.

29. *Works,* ed. John Ayre, 4 vols. (Cambridge: University, 1845-1850), 2:1056ff.

30. Walter Marshall, *The Gospel Mystery of Sanctification,* 8 vols. (London, 1692), 1:69.

31. Cf. John Cotton, *A Practical Commentary upon the First Epistle General of John* (London, 1656), p. 8.

not, therefore, avoid natural theology as do most modern theologians.[32] They saw the truth of God as the only reasonable answer to man's needs. Despite their strong belief in fallen man's total depravity, the Puritans believed they should show the sinner the unreasonableness of his unbelief and pray that the Holy Spirit would enlighten him with the truth.[33]

When man discards the truth of God, he also throws away the only possible basis for law, justice, education, and philosophy. He is left with only an empty and meaningless universe, and his only options are self-preservation and self-gratification. Francis Schaeffer said that the only way to reach twentieth-century man is through the truth that the Reformers grasped so well: faith and reason are a unity.[34] The truth of God is unreasonable only to the unbelieving heart and mind. Christianity's answer to the despair of modern man is that unified, rational truth is available if one will submit to God's truth. "It is true that man will have to renounce his rationalism," wrote Schaeffer, "but then . . . he has the possibility of recovering his rationality."[35]

In the matter of doctrine we may safely say that the Puritans were Calvinists. Their view of life was theocentric, directed and controlled by God's Word. J. I. Packer noted that the basic principle of Calvinism is the Biblical principle that "salvation is of the Lord."[36] Thus the Puritans emphasized the activity of God in salvation: election by the Father, redemption by the Son, and effectual calling by the Holy Spirit. It is totally unfair, though, to label them hyper-Calvinists, for they made a full and free offer of Christ to sinners and urged them to seek Him.[37] Cheap sentimentalizing had no place in Puritan

---

32. Cf. chapter 2.

33. It is in this vein that Schaeffer analyzed the current trend of modern philosophical thought away from reason and toward the despair of existentialism. *Escape from Reason* (Chicago: Inter-Varsity, 1968), pp. 42-45. He traced the loss of meaning and purpose in contemporary thought and life to the abandonment of any rational hope in finding the real meaning of man's existence. He called contemporary man back to the truth of Scripture. Ibid., pp. 80-87.

34. Ibid., p. 82.

35. Ibid.

36. "Introductory Essay," in John Owen, *The Death of Death in the Death of Christ* (London: Banner of Truth, 1963), p. 4. This essay provides a guideline to Owen's teaching on the limited atonement.

37. *Hyper-Calvinism* is that form of Calvinism that forbids the use of evangelism and missions to reach unbelievers. But advocates of this view forget that the same God who ordained the *result* (salvation by God's sovereign grace) also ordained the *means* (the fervent preaching of the gospel to sinners and inviting them to trust Christ as Savior) in order to bring it to pass.

theology. The Puritans were not afraid to preach the clear truth of God as it is expressed in the Word of God. The Puritan preacher considered his ministry a solemn calling from God not to be treated lightly. Because the interpretation of Scripture is an abstruse art to be studied thoroughly and employed cautiously, the Puritans strongly opposed the "enthusiast" methods of the Quakers, who subordinated faith and reason to passion and emotion. John Cotton wrote: "Though knowledge is no knowledge without zeal, zeal is but a wilde-fire without knowledge."[38]

Puritanism was a healthy combination of orthodox faith and fervent devotion, two elements which were separated by the stepchildren of the Puritans—unitarianism and revivalism. The unitarians replaced Scripture with reason alone as their authority and completely secularized religion; the revivalists overemphasized emotion. The Great Awakening of the 1740s was still essentially Puritan, but revivals in the nineteenth century discarded most vestiges of authentic Puritanism,[39] including the concept of a trained ministry.[40] In their defense, however, the revivalists' love for Christ kept them from unitarian rationalism, but not from such doctrinal errors as perfectionism and adventism. Fundamentalism is heir to both the Puritans' emphasis on doctrinal purity and the revivalists' enthusiastic piety. The balance between these two strains determines the fundamentalist's denominational affiliation.

Evangelicalism is in a state of uncertainty and confusion today. Packer wrote: "In such matters as the practice of evangelism, the teaching of holiness, the building up of the local church ... the exercise of discipline, there is evidence of widespread dissatisfaction with things as they are and of equally widespread uncertainty as to the road ahead."[41] Packer traced the problem to the loss of the Biblical doctrines proclaimed by the Reformers. The doctrinally "watered-down" gospel of our day fails to produce deep reverence, deep repentance, deep humility, a spirit of worship, and concern for the

---

38. *Christ the Fountain of Life* (London, 1651), p. 145.

39. Miller and Johnson, *The Puritans,* 1:3-5. Cf. J. Edwin Orr, *The Second Evangelical Awakening* (London: Marshall, Morgan and Scott, 1964), pp. 117-20. On the social influence of revivalism see Timothy L. Smith, *Revivalism and Social Reform* (New York: Harper, 1965).

40. B. B. Warfield, *Perfectionism* (Philadelphia: Presbyterian and Reformed, 1931), pp. 101ff.

41. "Introductory Essay," p. 1. This confusion is apparent in the speculations in Carl F. H. Henry, *Frontiers in Modern Theology* (Chicago: Moody, 1966), pp. 120-42.

church. "It fails to make men God-centered in their thoughts and God-fearing in their hearts."[42]

The result is that worldliness has crept into many conservative churches and affected doctrine, ethics, and even music. Doctrinal reevaluation is widespread among evangelicals who are no longer certain what they believe. Relativistic morality is producing a morality more lax than the church has ever known. Charles Woodbridge identified the problem as an attitude of toleration of doctrinal error.[43]

The Puritans, like the fundamentalists, insisted on separation from doctrinal error. Both groups have been called separatists by their opponents. The Puritans were firmly committed to the inspired and authoritative Word of God. They believed man fell in Adam, was totally depraved, and could not save himself; he needed a Savior. Christ gave His sinless blood to cleanse man from his sin and set him free from his bondage to it. Salvation is all of grace and man in no way can earn or merit it. He is saved by God sovereignly moving on his behalf.

The Puritans were preachers, not abstract theologians. They studied the Word of God carefully and thoroughly and then opened its truth to their listeners. They were powerful preachers because they preached that God is able to save man from his sin. They opposed the Roman Catholic concept of man's free will and his cooperation with God in salvation. Cranmer preached: "It is not that I take away your sins, but it is Christ only; and to him only I send you for that purpose, renouncing therein all your good virtues, words, thoughts, and works, and putting your trust in Christ."[44]

William Tyndale, who gave his life that we might have the Scripture in the English language, said of sovereign grace: "... the right faith springeth not of man's fantasy, neither is it in any man's power to obtain it; but it is altogether the pure gift of God poured into us freely, ... without deserving and merits, yea, and without seeking for of us ... [it] is ... God's gift and grace, purchased through Christ."[45] Hugh Latimer, the converted priest, preached that God must first love us and open our eyes to the truth in Christ so that we may receive him: "So you see, as touching our salvation, we must not go to working to think to get everlasting life with our own doings.

---

42. "Introductory Essay," p. 1.

43. *The New Evangelicalism* (Greenville: Bob Jones University, 1969), pp. 13-16.

44. *Works*, 2:131.

45. *Works*, ed. Henry Walter, 3 vols. (Cambridge: University, 1848-1850), 1:53.

No, this were to deny Christ. Salvation and remission of sins, is His gift, His own and free gift."[46]

How can reading the Puritans benefit the evangelical church today? It can encourage us to reaffirm the doctrines of Scripture in our pulpits. We need not proclaim every detail of Puritan theology, but certain of its emphases are essential.

One is the necessity and nature of true repentance. Men need to be seriously warned to turn from their sin. The apostle Paul preached that men "should repent and turn to God and do works meet for repentance" (Acts 26:20). The sinner must turn from his sin, his own righteousness, Satan, and the world.[47] Such repentance will leave little room for envying the world and bringing it into the church.

Second, the true Christ must be presented to the sinner. Our passion is not for numbers but for the broken hearts of dying men. Too often fundamental preachers have been sidetracked into extensive discussions of Biblical numerology, the Bible and science, "the gospel in the stars," and extreme interpretations of Biblical prophecies.[48] We have preached against the heresy of liberalism, and rightly so, but we have neglected the positive preaching of the person of Christ. Christ needs to be preached from the Gospels where His earthly life is revealed and from the doctrines of Christology where His nature and atonement shine forth. Joseph Alleine wrote: "The unsound convert takes Christ by halves. He is all for the salvation of Christ, but he is not for sanctification. . . . the sound convert takes a whole Christ, and takes Him for all intents and purposes, without exceptions, without limitations, without reserve."[49]

These selections from Puritan writings are offered in the hope that the reader will discern the Puritans' deep trust in the Word of God and that contemporary evangelicals will refocus upon the doctrinal truths of Scripture. For with soundness of doctrine and fervency of devotion, the church of Christ shall be the church triumphant and the very gates of hell shall not prevail against it.

SOLI DEO GLORIA

---

46. Ibid., 1:419, 420.

47. Joseph Alleine, *An Alarm to the Unconverted* (London: Banner of Truth, 1964), pp. 37-42.

48. These extremes are criticized in John J. Davis, *Biblical Numerology* (Grand Rapids: Baker, 1968).

49. *An Alarm to the Unconverted*, p. 45.

John Preston
1587-1628

2

Natural Theology

John Preston became a noted Puritan divine of great position. He was born in Heyford, Northamptonshire, and was educated at King's College and Queen's College of Cambridge University. He became tutor and fellow of Queen's College and later chaplain to Prince Charles. He preached extensively at Lincoln's Inn and Trinity Church in Cambridge.

His fame spread rapidly through his daily lectures, his Sunday sermons, and a series of debates with the famous Arminian, Richard Montague. Preston argued the Calvinistic doctrine of election with great ability and persuasiveness. He became a popular preacher and powerful writer, but he wore himself out with his extensive labors and died at age forty-eight. To the warnings of his friends he had replied: "Our life, like iron, consumes with rust, as much without as by employment.... seven years in the life of some men are as much as seventy in others."

His written works were never completely collected, though William Tennent published an abridgment of them in 1658. Preston's main works were *The New Covenant* (1629), *The Breastplate of Faith and Love* (1630), *Life Eternal* (1631), *The Saint's Daily Exercise* (1633), *The Saint's Qualifications* (1634), *Sermons Before His Maj-*

esty (1637), *Doctrines of the Saint's Infirmities* (1638), *Fulness of Christ for Us* (1640), *Thesis de Gratiae Convertendis Irresistibilitate* (1652), *Riches of Mercy to Men in Misery* (1658).

In this essay Preston discusses natural theology, a subject that the Puritan writers did not overlook. He begins with some very helpful definitions of the science of theology. His divisions of the system of theology follow those of Calvin. He deals here with the testimony of God in creation and reason, and he discusses man's conscious awareness of God and his innate desire for eternity. He shows, however, that this testimony only becomes evident by faith that terminates in the reality of its object (God). In contrast to many modern theologians who maintain that "faith" invents its own objects, Preston shows that "faith doth not believe things imaginary." His discussion is lively and vivid as well as very practical.

:::

Hebrevves 11:6—*Hee that commeth to God, must beleeve that God is, and that hee is a rewarder of them that seeke him.*

Having undertaken to goe thorow the whole body of *Theologie,* I will first give you a briefe definition of the thing it selfe, which we call *Divinitie,* it is this;

It is that heavenly Wisedome or forme of wholesome words, revealed by the Holy Ghost, in the Scripture, touching the knowledge of God, and of our selves, whereby wee are taught the way to eternall life.

I call it *[heavenly wisedome]* for, so it is called, I *Cor.* 2:13. *The wisedome which wee teach, is not in the words, which mans wisedome teacheth, but which the Holy Ghost teacheth.* So likewise the Apostle in another place calls it, *The forme of wholesome wordes;*[1] that is, that Systeme, or comprehension of wholesome Doctrine delivered in the Scripture.

Now it differs from other Systemes, and bodies of Sciences:

1 Because it is revealed from above; all other knowledge is gathered from things below.

2 Againe, all other Sciences are taught by men, but this is taught by the *Holy Ghost.*

3 All other knowledge is delivered in the writings of men, but this is revealed to us in the holy Word of *God,* which was written by GOD himselfe, though men were the mediat pen-men of it; therefore, I adde that, to distinguish it from all other Sciences; that, *It is*

---

1. II Tim. 1:13.

*not revealed by men, but by the Holy Ghost, not in bookes written
by men, but in the holy Scriptures.*

In the next place I adde the object, about which this wisedome is
conversant, it is, *the knowledge of God, and of our selves.* And so
it is likewise distinguished from all other knowledge, which hath
some other object. It is the knowledge of *God,* that is, of *God,* not
simply considered, or absolutely, in his Essence, but as hee is in
reference and relation to us.

And againe, it is not simply the knowledge of our selves, (for
many things in us belong to other Arts and Sciences) but as we
stand in reference to *God;* so that these are the two parts of it, the
knowledge of *God,* in reference to us; and of our selves, in reference
to him.

Last of all, it is distinguished by the end, to which it tends, which
it aimes at, which is to *teach us the way to eternall life:* And therein
it differs from all other Sciences whatsoever; for they onely helpe
some defects of understanding here in this present life: for where
there is some failing or defect, which common reason doth not help,
there, arts are invented to supply and rectifie those defects; but
this doth somewhat more, it leads us the way to eternall life: and
as it hath in it a principle above all others, so it hath an higher
end than others; as the wel-head is higher, so the streames ascend
higher than others. And so much for this description, what this summe
of the Doctrine of Theologie is.

The parts of it are two:

1 Concerning *God.*

2 Concerning our *selves.*

Now concerning *God,* 2 things are to be known:

1 That he is; $\Big\}$ both these are set downe
2 What he is; in the Text.

1 That *God* is, wee shall finde that there are two waies to prove
it, or to make it good to us:

1 By the strength of naturall reason.

2 By faith.

That we doe not deliver this without ground, look in the first of
the *Romans, v.* 20. *For the invisible things of him, that is, his eternall
power and God-head, are seene by the creation of the world, being
considered in his workes, so that they are without excuse.* So likewise,
Acts 17:27, 28. the Apostle saith, that they should *seeke after the Lord,
if happily they might grope after him, and finde him: for hee is not
farre from every one of us: for in him wee live, move, and have our*

being: That is, by the very things that we handle and touch, we may know that there is a *God;* and also, by our owne life, motion and being, wee may learne that there is a Deitie, from whence these proceed: For the Apostle speaketh this to them, that had no Scripture to teach them. So likewise, *Acts* 14:17. *Neverthelesse, he hath not left himselfe without witnesse, in giving us fruitfull seasons:* As if those did beare witnesse of him that is, those workes of his in the creatures. So that you see, there are two waies to come to the knowledge of this, that *God* is; One, I say, is by naturall reason: Or else, to make it more plaine, we shall see this in these two things:

1 There is enough in the very creation of the world, to declare him unto us.

2 There is a light of the understanding, or reason, put into us, whereby we are able to discerne those characters of GOD stamped in the creatures, whereby we may discerne the *invisible things of God, his infinite power and wisdome;* and when these are put together, that which is written in the creature, there are arguments enough in them, and in us there is reason enough, to see the force of those arguments, and thence we may conclude, that there is a *God,* besides the arguments of Scripture, that wee have to reveale it. For, though I said before, that Divinity was revealed by the *Holy Ghost,* yet there is this difference in the points of *Theologie:* Some truths are wholly revealed, and have no foot-steps in the creaturs, no prints in the creation, or in the works of *God* to discerne them by, and such are all the mysteries of the *Gospel,* and of the *Trinitie:* other truths there are, that have some *vestigia,* some Characters stamped upon the creature whereby we may discerne them, and such is this which we now have in hand, that, *There is a God.* Therefore we will show you these two things:

1 How it is manifest from the creation.

2 How this point is evident to you by faith. . . .

Seeing in Creation That God Exists

Now for the first, to explicate this, that, *The power and God-head is seen in the creation of the world.*

Besides those Demonstrations else-where handled, drawne from the Creation in generall, as from:

1 The sweet consent and harmony the creatures have among themselves.

2 The fitnesse and proportion of one unto another:

3 From the reasonable actions of creatures, in themselves unreasonable.

4 The great and orderly provision, that is made for all things.

5 The combination and dependance that is among them.

6 The impressions of skill and workmanship that is upon the creatures. All which argue that there is a *God*.

There remaine three other principall arguments to demonstrate this: The consideration of the *Originall of all things* which argues that they must needs be made by *God,* the maker of heaven and earth; which we wil make good to you by these three particulars:

If man was made by him, for whom all things are made, then it is certaine that all other things were made also. For the argument holds; If the best things in the world must have a beginning then surely those things that are subserving, and subordinate to them, must much more have a beginning.

Now that man was made by him, consider but this reason;

The father that begets, knows not the making of him; the mother that conceives, knowes it not, neither doth the formative vertue, (as we call it) that is, that vigour which is in the materials that shapes, and fashions, and articulates the body in the wombe, that knowes not what it doth. Now it is certaine, that he that makes any thing, must needs know it perfectly, and all the part of it, though the stander by may be ignorant of it. As for example; he that makes a statue, knowes how every particle is made, he that makes a Watch, or any ordinary worke of Art, he knowes all the junctures, all the wheeles, and commissures of it, or else it is impossible that hee should make it: now all these that have a hand in making of man, know not the making of him, nor the Father, nor the mother, nor that which we call the formative vertue, that is, that vigour which is in the materials, which workes and fashions the body, as the Work-man doth a statue, and gives severall limbs to it, all these know it not: therefore he must needs bee made by *God,* and not by man. See how the Wise-man to this purpose reasons, *Ps.* 94:9. *Hee that made the eye, shall hee not see? hee that made the eare, shall not he heare? &c.* that is, he that is the maker of the engines, or organes, or senses, or limbes of the body, or hee that is maker of the soule, and faculties of it, it is certaine that he must know, though others doe not, the making of the body and soule, the turnings of the will, and the windings of the understanding. Now none of those three know it, neither the father nor mother, nor that formative vertue, for they are but as pensils in the hand of him that doth all; as the pensill knowes not what it doth, though it drawes all, it is guided by the hand of a skilfull Painter, else it could doe nothing, the Painter onely knoweth what hee doth; so that formative vertue, that vigour that formes the body of a man that knowes no more what it doth than the pensill doth, but he in whose hand it is, who sets it on worke, it is he that gives vigour, and vertue to that seed in the wombe, from whence the body is raised, it is he that knowes it, for it is he that makes it. And this is the first particular by which wee prove that things were made and had not their originall form themselves. The second is.

If things were not made, then it is certaine, that they must have a being from themselves: Now to have a being from it selfe, is nothing else but to be *God:* for it is an inseparable propertie of *God* to have his being from himselfe. Now if you will acknowledge, that the creatures had a being of themselves, they must needs bee *Gods;* for it belongs to him alone, to have a being of himselfe, and from himselfe. The third follows, which I would have you chiefly to marke.

If things have a being from themselves, it is certaine then that they are without causes; as for example; That which hath no efficient cause, (that is) no maker, that hath no end. Looke upon all the workes made by man (that we may expresse it to you;) take an house, or any worke, or instrument that man makes; therefore it hath an end, because he that made it, propounded such an end to himselfe; but if it have no maker, it can have no end: for the end of any thing is that which the maker aimes at; now if things have no end, they could have no forme: for the forme and fashion of every thing ariseth only from the end, which the maker propounds to himselfe; as for example, the reason, why a knife hath such a fashion, is because it was the end of the maker, to have it an instrument to cut with: the reason why an axe or hatchet hath another fashion, is, because it might be an instrument to chop with; and the reason why a key hath another fashion different from these, is, because the maker propounded to himselfe another end in making of it; namely to open lockes with; these are all made of the same matter, that is, of iron, but they have divers fashions, because they have severall ends, which the maker propounds to himself. So that, if there be no ends of things, there is no forme, nor fashion of them, because the ground of all their fashions, is their severall end. So then, we will put them all together; if there be no efficient, no maker of them, then there is no end, and if there be no end, then there is no forme nor fashion, and if there be no forme, then there is no matter, and so consequently, they have no cause; and that which is without any cause, must needs bee *God,* which I am sure none dares affirme; and therefore they have not their being of themselves.

But besides that negative argument, by bringing it to an impossibility, that the creatures should be *Gods,* we will make it plaine by an affirmative argument, that all the creatures have an end.

For looke upon all the creatures, and we shall see that they have an end; the end of the Sunne, Moone and Starres is, to serve the Earth; and the end of the Earth is, to bring forth Plants, and the end of Plants is, to feed the beasts: and so if you looke to all particular things else, you shall see that they have an end, and if they have an end, it is certaine, there is one did ayme at it, and did give those creaturs those severall fashions, which those severall ends did require: As for example, What is the reason, why a horse hath one fashion, a dog another, sheepe another, and oxen another? The reason is plaine, an horse was made to runne, and to carry men; the oxen to plow; a dogge to hunt, and so of the rest. Now this cannot be without an author, without a maker, from whom they have their beginning. So likewise this is plaine by the effects; for this is a sure rule, Whatsoever it is, that hath no other end, but it selfe, that seekes to provide for its owne happinesse, in looking no further than it selfe; and this is onely in *God,* blessed for ever; hee hath no end but himselfe, no cause above himselfe, therefore he lookes onely to himselfe, and therein doth his happinesse consist. Take any thing that will not goe out of its owne spheare, but dwels within its owne compasse, stands upon its owne bottome to seek its happinesse, that thing destroys it selfe; looke to any of the creatures, and let them not stirre out of their owne shell, they perish there. So, take a man that hath no further end than himselfe, let him seeke himselfe, make himselfe his end in all things he doth, looke onely to his own profit and commodity, such a man destroyes himselfe: for he is made to serve *God,* and men, and therein doth his happinesse consist, because that he is made for such an end: take those that have beene serviceable to *God,* and men, that have spent themselves in serving *God,* with a perfect heart, we see that such men are happie men; and doe wee not finde it by experience, that those that have gone a contrary way, have destroyed themselves? And this is the third particular.

If things had no beginning, if the world was from eternity, what is the reason there are no Monuments of more ancient times, than there are? For if wee consider what eternity is, and what the vastnesse of it is, that when you have thought of millions of millions of yeeres, yet still there is more beyond: if the world hath been of so long continuance, what is the reason, that things are but, as it were, newly ripened? what is the reason, that things are of no greater antiquity than they are? Take all the Writers that ever wrote, (besides the Scripture) and they all exceed not above foure thousand yeeres; for they almost all agree in this, that the first man, that had ever any history written of him, was *Ninus*, who lived about *Abrahams* time, or a little before; *Trogus Pompeius,* and *Diodorus Siculus* agree in this. *Plutarch* saith, that *Theseus* was the first, before him there was no history of truth, nothing credible; and this is his expression: Take the Histories of times before *Theseus,* and you shall find them to be like skirts, in the Maps, wherein you shall find nothing but vast Seas. *Varro* one of the most learned of their Writers, professeth, that before the Kingdome of the *Sicyonians,* which begun after *Ninus* time, nothing was knowne to be certaine, and the beginning of that was doubtfull and uncertaine. And their usuall division of all history, into fabulous, and certaine, by Historians, is well knowne to those that are conversant in them; and yet the Historians that are of any truth, began long after the Captivitie in *Babylon;* for *Herodotus,* that lived after *Esthers* time, is counted the first that ever wrote in Prose, and he was above eight hundred yeeres after *Moses* time. For conclusion of this, we will onely say, that which one of the ancientest of the *Roman* Poets, drawing this conclusion from the argument we have in hand, saith, If things were from eternitie, and had not a beginning;

> *Cur supra bellum Thebanum & funera Troje*
> *Non alias alii quoque res cecinere Poeta?*

If things were from eternitie, what is the reason, that before the Theban and Trojan warre, all the ancient Poets, and ancient Writers did not make mention of any thing? Doe you thinke if things had beene from eternity, there would be no monuments of them, if you consider the vastnesse of eternity, what it is? So likewise for the beginning of Arts and Sciences; what is the reason that the originall of them is knowne? why were they no sooner found out? why are they not sooner perfected? Printing, you know, is a late invention; and so is the invention of Letters: take all Sciences, the ancientest, as *Astrologie* and *Philosophie,* as well as the *Mathematicks;* why are their Authors yet knowne, and we see them in the blade, and in the fruit? So for the *Genealogies* of men (for that I touch, because it is an argument insinuated by *Paul,* when hee disputed with the Heathens, *Acts* 17:26. *That God hath made of one blood all mankind*) you see evidently how one man begets another, and hee another, &c. and so goe and take all the *Genealogies* in the Scripture, and in all other historiographers, we shall see, that they al come to one Well-head. Now, I aske, if the world was from eternity, what is the reason, that there is but one fountaine, one blood whereof we are all made? Why should they not be made all together? Why was not the earth peopled together, and in every Land a multitude of inhabitants together, if they had been from eternity, and had no beginning?

The second principall Head, by which wee will make this good to you, that *there is a God* that made heaven and earth, is the testimony of *God* himselfe. There is a double testimony; one is the written testimony, which wee have in the Scripture; the other is, that testimony, which is *written in the hearts of men*.

Now, you know that all Nations doe acknowledge a *God*, (this we take for granted) yea, even those that have been lately discovered, that live, as it were, disjoyned from the rest of the world, yet they all have, and worship a *God*; those Nations discovered lately by the *Spaniards*, in the *West Indies*, and those that have been discovered since; all of them, without exception, have it written in their hearts, that *there is a God*. Now the strength of the argument lies in these two things:

1 I observe that phrase used, *Rom.* 2:15. It is called *a law written in their hearts*. Every mans soule is but (as it were) the table or paper, upon which the writing is; the thing written is this principle that wee are now upon, that *there is a God*, that made heaven and earth: but now who is the Writer? surely it is *God*, which is evident by this, because it is a general effect in the heart of every man living, and therefore it must come from a generall cause: from whence else shall it proceed? no particular cause can produce it; if it were, or had beene taught by some particular man, by some sect, in some one Nation or Kingdome, in one age; then, knowing the cause, we should see that the effect would not exceed it, but when you find it in the hearts of all men, in all nations and ages; then you must conclude, it was an universall effect, written by the generall Author of all things, which is *God* alone; and so consequently, the Argument hath this strength in it, that it is the testimony of *God*.

2 Besides, when you see every man looking after a *God*, and seeking him, it is an argument that there is one, though they doe not find him: it is true, they pitch upon a false *god*, and goe the wrong way to seek him, yet it shewes that there is such a Deity. For as in other things when we see one affect that which another doth not; as to the eye of one, that is beautifull which is not to another, yet all affecting some beauty; it is an argument that beauty is the generall object of all: & so in tast & other senses. So when

we see men going different waies, one worshipping one *God,* one another, yet all conspiring in this, to worship a *God,* it must needs argue that there is one: for this law ingraven in every mans heart, you will grant it is a worke of Nature at least, and the workes of Nature are not in vaine; even as, when you see the fire to ascend above the aire, it argues that there is a place where it would rest, though you never saw it; and as (in winter) when you see the Swallowes flying to a place, though you never saw the place, yet you must needs gather that there is one which nature hath appointed them, and hath given them an instinct to flie unto, and there to be at rest, so when you see in every mans soule such an instigation to seek *God* though men never saw him, and the most go the wronge way to seeke him, and take that for *God* which is not, yet this argues there is a Deitie which they intend. And this is the third.

The last argument is taken from the soule of man, *the fashion of it. and the immortalitie of it.*

First, *God* is sayd to have *made man after his owne Image;* he doth not meane his body, for that is not made after the Image of *God,* neither is it only that holinesse which was created in us and now lost: for then he would not have sayd *Gen.* 9:6. *He that sheds mans bloud, by man shall his bloud bee shed, for in the Image of* GOD *made he man.* The principall intent of that place is (for ought I can see or judge, the Scripture speaking of the natural fashion of things, and not of the supernaturall graces) to expresse that *God* hath given a soule to man, that carries the Image of God, a likenesse to the Essence of God immateriall, immortall, invisible; for there is a double Image of *God* in the soule, one in the substance of it, which is never lost; another is the supernaturall grace, which is an Image of the knowledge, holinesse, and righteousnesse of *God;* and this is utterly lost. But the soule is the Image of the essence of *God* (as I may so speake) that is, it is a spirit immateriall, immortall, invisible, as he is, hath understanding and will, as he hath; he understands all things, and wils whatsoever he pleaseth. And you see an expression of him in your owne soule, which is an argument of the Deity.

Secondly, besides the immortality of the soule, which argues it came not from any thing here below, but that it hath its originall from *God; it came from God, and to God it must returne;* that is, it had not any beginning here, it had it from him, and to him againe it must returne. For what is this body, wherein the soule is? it is but the case of the soule, the shell and sheath of it; therefore the soule useth it but for a time, and dwels in it, as a man dwels in a house while it is habitable, but when it is growne ruinous, he departeth: the soule useth the body, as a man doth a vessell, when it is broken he laies it aside; or as a man doth an instrument, whilest it will be serviceable to him; but when it is no longer fit to play upon, he casts it aside; so doth the soule as it were lay aside the body: for it is but as a garment that a man useth, when it is worne out, and threed-bare, he casts it off: so doth the soule with the body. And for the further proofe of this, and that it depends not on the body, nor hath its originall of it, or by it; consider the great acts of the soule, which are such as cannot arise from the temper of the matter, bee it never so curious: As the discourse of the soule from one generall to another; the apprehension of so high things as *God* and Angels; the devising of such things as never came into the senses; for though it be true, that sounds & colours be carried into the understanding by the senses, yet to make pictures of these colours, and musicke of these sounds, this is from the understanding with in: So the remembrance of things past; observing the condition of things, by comparing one with another. Now, looke upon bruitbeasts, we see no actions but may arise from the temper of the matter; according to which their fancie and appetite are fashioned; though some actions are stronger than others, yet they arise not aboue the Wellhead of sense: all those extraordinary things which they are taught to doe, it is but for their food, as Hawks; and some Pigeons it is reported, in *Assyria* that they carry Letters from one place to another, where they use to have food; so other beasts that act dancing, and such like motions, it is done by working on their senses: but come to man, there are other actions of his understanding and will in the soule. It is true indeed, in a man there are fancy and appetite, and these arise from the temper of the body; therefore as the body hath a different temper so there are severall appetites, disposition and affections; some men longs after one thing, some after another, but these are but the several turnings of the sensuall appetite, (which is also seene in beasts) but come to the higher part of the soule, the actions of the will and understanding of man, and they are of an higher nature; the acts which they doe have no dependence upon the body at all. Besides, come to the motions of the body; the soule guides and moves the body; as a Pilot doth a ship, now the Pilot may be safe, though the ship be split upon the Rock.) Looke on beasts, they are led wholly as their appetite carries them, and they must goe that way; therefore they are not ruled, as a Pilot governs a ship: but in men, their appetites would carry them hither, or thither, but the will saith no, and that hath the understanding for its counseler. So that the motions of the body arise not from the diversity of the sensuall appetites, as in all other creatures, but of the will and understanding; for the soul depends not upon the body, but the acts of the body depend upon it: therefore when the body perisheth, the soule dies not; but, as a man that dwels in a house, if the house fall, hee hath no dependence on it, but may goe away to another house; so the soule hath no dependence upon the body at all; therefore you must not think that it doth dye when the body perisheth.

Besides, the soule is not worne, it is not weary, as other things are; the body is weary, and the spirits are weary; the body weares, as doth a garment, till it be wholly worne out: now, any thing that is not weary, it cannot perish; and, in the very actions of the soule it selfe there is no wearinesse, but whatsoever comes into the soule perfects it, with a perfection naturall to it, & it is the stronger for it; therefore it cannot be subject to decay, it cannot weare out, as other things doe, but the more notions it hath, the more perfect it is: the body, indeed, is weary with labour, and the spirits are wearie, but the soule is not weary, for in the immediate acts thereof, it workes still, even when the body sleepeth: Looke upon the actions of the soule, and they are independent, and as their independencie growes, so the soule growes younger and younger, and stronger and stronger, *senescens juvenescit,* and is not subject to decay, or mortality: as you see in a Chicken, it growes still, and so the shell breakes, and falls off: so is it with the soule, the body hangs on it but as a shell, and when the soule is growne to perfection, it falls away, and the soule returnes to the Maker.

Believing That God Exists

The next thing that I should come to, is to shew you how this is made evident by faith. When a man hath some rude thoughts of a thing, and hath some reason for it, hee then begins to have some perswasion of it; but when (besides) a man wise and true, shall come and tell him it is so, this addes much strength to his confidence: for when you come to discerne this *God-head,* and to know it by reasons from the creatures, this may give you some perswasions; but when one shall come and tell you of the Scripture, made by a wise and true *God,* that is so indeed; this makes you confirmed in it. Therefore the strength of the argument by faith, you may gather after this manner: I beleeve the Scriptures to bee true and that they are the word of *God;* now this is contained in the Scriptures, that *God made heaven and Earth;* therefore I beleeving the Scriptures to be the Word of *God,* and whatsoever is contained in them, my faith layes hold upon it also, and so my consent growes strong and firme, that there is a *God:* After this manner you come to conclude it by faith. For what is faith? Faith is but when a thing is propounded to you even as an object set before the eye, there is an habit of faith within, that sees it what it is; for faith is nothing else, but a seeing of that which is: for though a thing is not true because I beleeve it is so, yet things first are, and then I beleeve them. Faith doth not beleeve things imaginary, and such as have no ground; but whatsoever faith beleeves, it hath a being, and the things we beleeve doe lye before the eyes of reason, sanctified and elevated by the eye of faith; therefore *Moses,* when he goes about to set downe the Scripture, doth not proue things by reason, but propounds them, as, *In the beginning* GOD *made the Heaven and Earth;* he propounds the object, and leaves it to the eye of faith to looke upon. For the nature of faith is this: *God* hath giuen to man an understanding facultie, (which we call, Reason) the object of which is all the truths that are delivered in the world, and whatsoever hath a being. Now take all things that wee are said to beleeve, and they also are things *that are,* which are the true objects of the understanding and reason. But the understanding hath objects of two sorts:

1 Such as we may easily perceive, as the eye of man doth the object that is before him.

2 Such as wee see with more difficulty, and cannot do it, without something above the eie to elevate it: As the candle and the bignesse of it, the eye can see; but to know the bignesse of the Sunne, in the latitude of it, you must have instruments of art to see it, and you must measure it by degrees, and so see it: so is it here, some things wee may fully see by reason alone, and those are such as lye before us, and them wee may easily see: but other things there are, that though they are true, yet they are more remote, and further off; therefore they are harder to bee seene; and therefore wee must have something to helpe our understanding to see them. So that indeed, Faith is but the lifting up of the understanding, by adding a new light to them and it: and therefore they are said to be *revealed,* not because they were not before, as if the revealing of them gave a being unto them; but even as a new light in the night discovers to us that which we did not see before, and as a prospective glasse reveales to the eye, that which we could not see before, and by its owne power, the eye could not reach unto: So that the way to strengthen our selves by this argument, is to beleeve the Scriptures, and the things contained in them. . . .

John Jewel
1522-1571

3

Scripture

An Oxford graduate and an Anglican bishop, John Jewel was one of the outstanding Puritan leaders in the English Reformation. He was born at Buden in Devon County on 24 May 1522. Jewel, one of the earliest Puritans, received a B.A. in 1541. He became a tutor and lecturer of rhetoric and privately taught the Reformed principles of the Scripture to his students until Edward VI came to the throne in 1546. Jewel then made an open declaration of his Protestant faith and became a close friend of the Reformer Peter Martyr, who was then visiting Oxford.

On the accession of Queen Mary in 1553, Jewel was one of the first forced to flee for his life. Eventually he joined English exiles in Frankfurt, Germany, and became more vocal in his criticism of the Roman Church. From Frankfurt he went to Strasbourg, France, and Geneva, Switzerland. In Geneva he resided with Peter Martyr. In 1559 Mary died and Jewel returned to England, and in 1560 he was appointed bishop of Salisbury. From this time onward he wrote extensively in defense of the Reformed faith. Years of study then came to fruition in his *Apologia pro Ecclesia Anglicana,* translated into English in 1562 as *An Apology in Defence of the Church of England.*

Jewel's labors and previous exiles led to an early death—at age forty-nine. He was known for great piety and a warm concern for the poor. His writings included controversial titles: *A Defence of the "Apology"* (1565) and *A View of a Seditious Bull Sent into England by Pope Pius V in 1569.* He also produced *An Exposition upon the Two Epistles to the Thessalonians* (1583), *A Treatise of the Holy Scriptures* (1582), and *A Treatise of the Sacraments* (1583). Jewel's essay on the Scriptures explains first the divine origin of the Bible and its power to change man's heart; then, the pleasure the Word of God gives to the believer; and finally, the reverence to be accorded God's Word. Though some of his discussion may lack the vividness of later Puritan writings, Jewel presents very well the age-old temptation to substitute man's authority for Scripture's. He refers to the Pharisees, various heretics, and Roman Catholics. Liberal and neo-orthodox theologians, who also tend to put man's authority above Scripture's, would do well to heed Jewel's admonitions.

Among all his creatures in heaven or earth, God hath not made any like unto the sun in the firmament, the beams whereof are beautiful and pleasant, and do give comfort in all places to all things. It rejoiceth the whole, and relieveth the sick; it causeth birds to sing, fishes to play, cattle to stir, worms to creep, grass to grow, and trees to bring fruit; it reneweth the face of the whole earth.

Yet a blind man hath no pleasure in the beauty thereof, because he is blind, and cannot see it; yet a dead man hath no warmth by the heat thereof, because he is dead, and feeleth it not.

Adam was placed in Paradise in perfect estate, and in the company of God's angels; God walked and did talk with him. He heard the voice, and beheld the presence of God. The rivers yielded waters abundantly, the trees brought him food of life. He had plenty without travail; he had pleasures, joy, and his heart's desire.

But Adam was unthankful; he knew not God, the worker of his happiness; he knew not the place in which he was; he knew not his own estate and blessedness; therefore the wrath of the Lord grew against him; he fell into the snares of the devil, he became mortal, and returned to dust.

What nation in all the world so happy as Israel? they were delivered by a mighty hand out of Egypt, from the tyranny of Pharaoh, from service and villainy. Their children were no more slain before their faces. They passed through the bottom of the sea, as upon dry land. When they were hungry, there went forth a wind from the Lord, and brought them quails from the sea, and manna was given them from heaven to eat; when they thirsted, the rocks opened and poured out water, that they and their beasts might drink.

In battle they were mighty and strong, no power was able to stand against them. The Lord went before them by day in a pillar of a cloud, to lead them the way; and by night in a pillar of fire, to give them light. When they called upon the Lord, he heard them. When they trusted in him, they were not confounded.

But they grew unmindful of all these mercies, and murmured against the Lord, and against his servants; therefore God raught forth his hand against them. He sware in his wrath that they should not enter into his rest. He sent his angel, and destroyed them in the wilderness.

Even so fareth it with all such which regard not the word of their salvation; because they have ears and hear not, nor will understand with their hearts, the fury of the Lord shall be kindled against them. The Prophet saith in the name of God to Israel (Jer. 7:25), "I have sent unto them all my servants the Prophets, yet would they not hear me, nor incline their ear."

And (II Esd. 9:31), "Behold, I sow in my law in you, that it may bring forth fruit in you. But our fathers which received the law kept it not; neither observed thine ordinances, neither did the fruit of thy law appear. For they that received it perished, because they kept not the thing that was sown in them." Samuel telleth Saul (I Sam. 15:26), "Thou hast cast away the word of the Lord, and the Lord hath cast away thee."

Again, Jeremiah saith (6:10), "How do ye say we are wise, and the law of the Lord is with us? They have rejected the word of the Lord, and what wisdom is in them?" Again, "Unto whom shall I speak, and admonish, that they may hear? Behold, their ears are uncircumcised, and they cannot hearken; behold, the word of the Lord is unto them as a reproach, they have no delight in it; I will cause a plague to come upon this people, even the fruit of their own imaginations; because they have not taken heed unto my words, nor to my law, but cast it off."

After this sort doth God shew the cause why his word taketh not place in us, because we are wilful, and will not hear it, nor receive it, nor take delight in it, nor let the fruit thereof appear, but reject it, and make it a reproach, and cast it away from us; and therefore is it that the Lord doth cast us away; that we are unwise; that we please ourselves with our own devices, and follow our own imaginations, and perish, because we have not understanding to hear the instruction of the Lord's word, but like ignorant men disallow it, and cast it behind the back.

The consideration hereof moveth me to say somewhat of the Holy Scriptures, which are the bright sun of God; which bring light unto our ways, and comfort to all parts of our life, and salvation to our souls; in which is made known unto us our estate, and the mercy of God in Christ our Saviour witnessed.

That we may the better see the path which we have to walk in; my meaning is, truly, and plainly, and shortly, to shew you what authority and majesty the word of God beareth; then, what profit we may reap by it; also, how needful it is, that we be well instructed in the Holy Scriptures; and what pleasure and delectation a Christian conscience may find in them; and lastly, whether they be dark and doubtful, or plain and easy for your understanding: that when we know the majesty and authority of the word, and what comfort and profit God giveth us by it, we deprive not ourselves thereof by our unthankfulness, nor close up our eyes that we see it not; but hear it in reverence and in fear, that it may be fruitful in us, and we receive it not in vain.

God's Word Is Authoritative

The Scriptures are the word of God. What title can there be of greater value? What may be said of them to make them of greater authority, than to say, "The Lord hath spoken by them? that they came not by the will of men, but holy men of God spake as they were moved by the Holy Ghost?" (II Peter 1:21) At the word of proclamation of an earthly prince we stand up and vail our bonnets, and give good heed to it; we are bound so to do, it is our duty: such honour belongeth to the powers that are placed to rule over us; for they are ordained of God. And whosoever resisteth them, resisteth the ordinance of God.

If we should have a revelation, and hear an angel speak unto us, how careful would we be to mark, and remember, and be able to declare the words of the angel! yet is an angel but a glorious creature, and not God. And what is a king? great and mighty, yet mortal and subject to death: his breath departeth, and his name shall perish. Both he and his word, his power and his puissance, shall have an end.

But the word of the Gospel is not as the word of an earthly prince. It is of more majesty than the word of an angel. The Apostle saith

(Heb. 2:2), "If the word spoken by angels was steadfast, and every transgression and disobedience received a just recompense of reward, how shall we escape if we neglect so great salvation which at the first began to be preached by the Lord, and was confirmed unto us by them that heard him?"

God saith, by the prophet Isaiah (55:11), "My word shall accomplish that which I will, and it shall prosper in the thing whereto I sent it." And the same Prophet saith (11:8), "The word of God shall stand for ever." And "It is more easy that heaven and earth pass away, than that one tittle of the law should fail," saith our Saviour (Luke 16:17). For it is the word of the living and almighty God, of the God of Hosts, which hath done whatsoever pleased him both in heaven and in earth.

By this word he maketh his will known. "I have not spoken of myself (saith Christ, John 12:49); but the Father which sent me gave me a commandment what I should say, and what I should speak." And again (John 15:22), "If I had not come and spoken unto them, they should not have had sin, but now have they no cloak for their sin." No man hath seen God at any time. He is invisible, no eye can reach unto him. The only begotten Son which is in the bosom of his Father, he hath declared him; he hath shewed us the throne of grace, that we may seek for mercy, and find grace in time of need; he hath disclosed unto us the will of his Father; he hath left unto us, and ordained that we should hear his holy word.

This word the angels and blessed spirits used when they came down from heaven to speak unto the people; when they came to the blessed Virgin, and to Joseph, and to others, they spake as it was written in the Prophets, and in the Scriptures of God; they thought not their own authority sufficient, but they took credit to their saying, and authority to their message out of the word of God.

This word the Prophets vouched and alleged to the people. Albeit they were sanctified in their mothers' womb; albeit God had endued them with his heavenly Spirit; although a seraphim came unto one of them and touched his mouth with a hot coal; albeit he saw the Lord sitting upon an high throne; yet they would not speak as of themselves, but only in the name of the Lord; for thus they use to say, The Lord hath spoken. This is the word of the Lord. Hear what the Lord saith. Saint Paul, albeit he was taken up into the third heaven, and into paradise, and heard words that are not lawful for man to utter, yet he wrote not his own words to the churches of Rome, of Corinth, and Thessalonica, and of other places, but delivered them which he had received, and taught them according to the Scriptures.

This word is the true manna; it is the bread which came down from heaven; it is the key of the kingdom of heaven; it is the savour of life unto life; it is the power of God unto salvation. In it God sheweth unto us his might, his wisdom, and his glory. By it he will be known of us. By it he will be honoured of his creatures. Whatsoever truth is brought unto us contrary to the word of God, it is not truth, but falsehood and error; whatsoever honour done unto God, disagreeth from the honour required by his word, it is not honour unto God, but blasphemy.

As Christ saith (Matt. 15:9), "In vain they worship me, teaching for doctrines men's precepts." By Isaiah God saith, "Who required this at your hands?" And by Jeremiah (7:22), "I spake not unto your fathers, nor commanded them, when I brought them out of the land of Egypt, concerning burnt offerings and sacrifices. But this thing commanded I them, saying, Obey my voice, and I will be your God, and ye shall be my people; and walk ye in all the ways which I have commanded you, that it may be well unto you."

Again (Jer. 23:28), "What is the chaff to the wheat? saith the Lord. What are your dreams to be weighed with the truth of God? Search the Scriptures. In them ye shall learn to know me, and how you should worship me; in them ye shall find everlasting life. The words of the Lord are pure words, as the silver tried in the furnace; there is no filth nor dross remaining in them; they are the storehouse of wisdom, and of the knowledge of God; in respect whereof, all the wisdom of this world is but vain and foolish.

Numa Pompilius, king of the Romans, Lycurgus, king of Lacedemon, and Minos, king of Creta, were wise men, and of great government; they devised laws to rule the people, and bare them in hand, that they were taught by revelation, that so their ordinances might win the more credit, and be established for ever. But where are they now? Where is Numa, Minos, or Lycurgus? Where be their books? What is become of their laws?

They were unwise, and had no knowledge nor understanding of God; they and their laws are dead, and their names forgotten. But the law of God came from heaven indeed. God wrote it with his finger, it is the fountain of all wisdom, and therefore shall it continue for ever, and never have an end.

Here let us behold the great power and work of God. When Moses received the law, God himself came down in person, with thousand thousands of angels; the air was darkened at his presence, the Mount stood all covered with fire, the earth shook, the heavens thundered, the people stood afar off, and fled for fear, and said unto Moses, "Talk thou with us, and we will hear; but let not God talk with us, lest we die." This was the first proclaiming and publishing of the law; such force and credit God gave to his word, and warranted himself to be the Lord.

Since that time, so many thousand years are already passed. In the mean time, the people of Israel were oppressed by tyrants, were spoiled and chased out of their country; first, by Nebuchadnezzar into Babylon; after that, by Antiochus into Syria; and lastly, were as vagabonds driven from country to country.

Their city Jerusalem was sacked, their houses overthrown, their temple razed, and not a stone left upon a stone; their library destroyed, their books burnt, the tabernacle lost, the covenant broken. No vision, no revelation, no comfort for the people left; nor prophet, nor priest, nor any to speak in the name of the Lord.

In all those times of decays, of sackings, of darkness, and of misery, what was done with the word of God? It was wickedly burnt by Jehoiakim, king of Juda; and Antiochus burnt the books of the law, and cut them in pieces. No man durst be known to have them, and avouch the having; so thought they utterly to deface the glory of God, and abolish all remembrance of his laws.

Then came the Pharisees; they drowned the word of God with their traditions; they took away the key of knowledge, and entered not in themselves, but forbad them that came in. After them came heretics; they denied some one part, and some another part of Scripture. They razed, blotted, corrupted, and altered the word of God; of the word of God they made it their own word, or, which is worse, they made it the word of the devil.

By the space of so many thousand years, the word of God passed by so many dangers of tyrants, of Pharisees, of heretics, of fire, and of sword, and yet continueth and standeth until this day, without altering or changing one letter. This was a wonderful work of God, that having so many and so great enemies, and passing through so many and so great dangers, it yet continueth still, without adding or altering of any one sentence, or word, or letter. No creature was able to do this, it was God's work.

He preserved it, that no tyrant should consume it; no tradition choke it; no heretic maliciously should corrupt it. For his name's sake, and for the elect's sake, he would not suffer it to perish; for in it God hath ordained a blessing for his people, and by it he maketh covenant with them for life everlasting. Tyrants, and Pharisees,

49

and heretics, and the enemies of the cross of Christ, have an end, but the word of God hath no end.

No force shall be able to decay it. The gates of hell shall not prevail against it. Cities shall fall; kingdoms shall come to nothing; empires shall fade away as the smoke; but the truth of the Lord shall continue for ever. Burn it, it will rise again; kill it, it will live again; cut it down by the root, it will spring again. "There is no wisdom, neither understanding nor counsel against the Lord." (Prov. 21:30)

God's Word Is Profitable

Let us behold the nations and kingdoms which sometimes professed Christ, and are now heathenish; Illyricum, Epirus, Peloponnesus, Macedonia, and others. Again, let us behold such kingdoms and countries, which were in times past heathenish, and knew not God; as England, Ireland, Rome, Scotland, and divers other.

They were all without the Gospel, without Christ, without God, and without hope of life. They worshipped idols, even the work of their own hands. To them they appointed priests for their service, days and places for the people to resort together to worship them.

Here in England, Paul's church in London was the temple of Diana; Peter's church in Westminster was the temple of Apollo. In Rome, they had the temple of the great god Jupiter, and in Florence the temple of Mars; and in other places they had temples dedicated to other idols.

Jupiter, Mars, Apollo, and Diana were unclean spirits and filthy devils; yet gave they thanks to them for their peace and prosperity, prayed to them in war and in misery, and commended unto them their wives, their children, themselves, the safe keeping and custody of their souls. They built gorgeous churches and chapels; set up images of silver and gold to them; prayed, lifted up their hands, did sacrifice, and offered up their children to them.

A horrible thing to say, yet true it is, the darkness of those times were such, that men slew their own children, and offered them up to idols. They said, Great is Jupiter, great is Apollo, and great is Diana of the Ephesians. These are the gods of our fathers; our fathers trusted in them; they made us, and have defended us, and have given us victory against our enemies. Whosoever denied them were thought worthy to die.

Thus were the kings, and the princes, and the people persuaded, and so continued they by the space of some thousand years, without controlment or contradiction. They had great props of antiquity, universality, and consent—antiquity of all times; universality of all places; consent of all the people. So strongly and so mightily were they founded, who would think such a religion, so ancient, and so universal, and so defended by common consent, should ever possibly be removed?

But when the fulness of time came, God sent forth his word, and all was changed. Errors fell down, and truth stood up; men forsook their idols, and went to God. The kings, and priests, and people were changed; the temples, and sacrifices, and prayers were changed; men's eyes and hearts were changed. They forsook their gods, their kings, their priests; they forsook their antiquity, customs, consent, their fathers, and themselves.

What power was able to work these things? What emperor by force ever prevailed so much? What strength could ever shake down so mighty idols from their seat? What hand of man could subdue and conquer the whole world, and make such mighty nations confess they had done amiss? This did the Lord bring to pass by the power of his word and the breath of his mouth.

This was it that led captivity captive, and threw down every high thing that lifted itself up against the Lord, and brought all powers under subjection unto the Lord. It is the image, the power, the arm, the sword, and the glory of God. It is mighty, of great force and virtue, of authority and majesty, because it is the word of God; therefore the glory thereof is great. . . .

Knowledge of God's Word Is Necessary

Now it followeth, that we consider how necessary and needful it is for us to be guided by the word of God, in the whole trade of our life. The word of God is that unto our souls, which our soul is unto our body. As the body dieth when the soul departeth, so the soul of man dieth, when it hath not the knowledge of God. "Man liveth not by bread only, but by every word that proceedeth out of the mouth of God." (Deut. 8:3)

Behold, saith God (Amos 8:11), "I will send a famine in the land, not a famine of bread, nor a thirst of water, but of hearing the word of the Lord." Their tongue shall wither, their heart shall starve, they shall die for hunger. (Isa. 59:10) "They shall wander from sea to sea; and from the north unto the east shall they run to and fro to seek the word of the Lord, and shall not find it. They shall stumble at noon-day, as at the twilight; they shall grope for the wall like the blind, and truth shall fall in their streets."

For how shall they be saved, unless they call on the name of the Lord? "How shall they call on Him, in whom they have not believed? how shall they believe in Him, of whom they have not heard? and how shall they hear without a preacher? and how shall they preach except they be sent?" (Rom. 10:14) Chrysostom therefore saith, "Neither can it be, I say it cannot be, that any man shall attain to salvation, except he be always occupied in spiritual reading." The wise man saith (Prov. 24:18), "Where there is no prophecy, the people decay."

When the Scriptures are not opened, when there is none that can edify, and exhort, and comfort the people by the word of God, they must needs perish; for they know not the way in which they should walk; they know not whom to honour, nor upon whose name they should call; they know neither what to believe, nor what to do. Hell hath enlarged itself, and hath opened his mouth without measure; and they that are wilful and ignorant, and the children of darkness, go down into it.

They become thrall and captives unto Satan; their heart is bound up; they understand nothing; their eyes are shut up, they can see nothing; their ears are stopped up, they can hear nothing; they are carried away as a prey into hell, because they have not the knowledge of God.

So doth Christ tell the Sadducees (Matt. 22:29), "Ye are deceived, because you know not the Scriptures, nor the power of God." Thus he teacheth, that error is the child of ignorance. The cause why you are so deceived, is because you know not the Scriptures; you have hated the light, and loved darkness; you have neither known the Father nor me. He that knoweth not the truth of God, knoweth not God.

Herein, in this case, there is no plea of ignorance. Ignorance will not excuse us. Chrysostom saith, "Thou wilt say, I have not heard the Scriptures. This is no excuse, but a sin." Again he saith, "This is the working of the devil's inspiration; he would not suffer us to see the treasure, lest we should get the riches; therefore he counselleth us, that it utterly availeth us nothing to hear the laws of God, lest that upon the hearing he may see our doing follow."

Gregory saith, "Whoso know not the things that pertain unto the Lord, be not known of the Lord." Origen also giveth reason of this practice of Satan: "Unto the devils it is a torment above all kinds of torment, and a pain above all pains, if they see any man reading the word of God, and with fervent study searching the knowledge of God's law, and the mysteries and secrets of the Scriptures.

Herein standeth all the flame of the devils; in this fire they are tormented, for they are seized and possessed of all them that remain in ignorance."

Carneades, a philosopher, was wont to say of his master and reader, Chrysippus, If it had not been for Chrysippus, I never had been any body; he was my master and teacher; he made me learned; whatsoever I have, I have it of him. How much better may we use the like words of the Scripture, and say, Unless it were for the word of God, our wisdom were nothing, and our knowledge were nothing. Whatsoever we have, we have it by the word. Without it, our prayer were no prayer; without it, our sacraments were no sacraments; our faith were no faith; our conscience were no conscience; our church were no church. Take away the light of the sun, and what remaineth but darkness? Heaven and earth are darkened. No man can see his way, or discern the things about him; even so, if the word of God be taken away, what remaineth, but miserable confusion and deadly ignorance?

When the Philistines had shorn the hairs of Samson, they fell upon him, took him, bound him, and plucked out his eyes; they danced about him, and made scorn and games of him. We are Samson; the strength of our hairs is the knowledge of the will of God; it is laid up in our heads, in the highest and principal part of us; if that be shorn off, if we be kept from hearing, reading, and understanding of the word of God, then will error, superstition, and all wickedness, get the upper hand, and fall upon us, and bind us, and pluck out our eyes, and make scorn of us, and utterly destroy us.

When the people of Jerusalem were besieged, and wanted food to eat, they fed on rats and mice, and many unwholesome and filthy things. A woman was driven for want of meat to do a cruel part upon her own child; she took her own babe, which was the fruit of her own body, killed it, cut it in pieces, dressed it, and fed upon it: a loathsome meat, especially for a mother to eat her own child. But she was driven to it by extremity and hunger; it was so cruel a thing to lack wherewith life might be preserved.

Even so fared it with us and our fathers, after it pleased God to take away his Gospel, and to send a famine of hearing the word of the Lord. We were driven to eat those things which were loathsome and horrible to behold; we were driven to feed upon our own children, even the fantasies and vanities of our heart. There was no substance in them, they could not feed us.

In this case were the children of Israel, when they grew weary of the word of God, and left the ordinances set down unto them.

God had no pleasure in them, their prayers and sacrifice were not accepted. "I cannot suffer (saith the Lord, Isa. 1:13, 12) your new moons, nor sabbaths, nor solemn days. Who hath required this of your hands?"

In such case were the Scribes and Pharisees, when they forsook to be guided by the word of God, and took away the key of knowledge; they fed upon their own devices, they neglected the commandments and will of God, and followed their own traditions; therefore Christ reproved them (Matt. 15:7): "O hypocrites, Isaiah prophesied well of you, saying, This people draweth near unto me with their mouth, and honoureth me with their lips, but their heart is far off from me. But in vain they worship me, teaching for doctrines men's precepts."

Therefore if we seek to know the sacraments of the church, what they are; if we would be instructed in the sacrament of baptism, or in the sacrament of the body and blood of Christ; if we would learn to know our Creator, and to put the difference between the Creator and a creature; if we desire to know what this present life is, and what is that life which is to come; if we would believe in God, and call upon the name of God, and do worship unto God; if we would be settled in perfect zeal and true knowledge; if we would have an upright conscience towards God; if we would know which is the true church of God, it is very needful that we hear the word of God. There is no other word that teacheth us unto salvation.

God's Word Blesses Us

Now it remaineth we speak of the delectation and pleasure which the word of God giveth. The word of God is full of sad and grave counsel, full of the knowledge of God, of examples of virtues, and of correction of vices, of the end of this life, and of the life to come. These are the contents of the word of God. These things (say you) are great and weighty of themselves, there is no vanity or pleasure in them.

They are great and weighty, I grant; and because they are so weighty, they be the more worthy, that we hear them. But we must take a delight and settle our fancy, that it may like of the weight and greatness. They were unto the Prophet David, "more sweet than honey and the honeycomb." If we taste them with such an affection as he did, we shall feel and see the great, and weighty, and heavenly pleasure which is in them.

Many are delighted in the stories of Julius Caesar, of Alexander the Great, of mighty and victorious princes; they have pleasure to read of their wars, of their victories, and of their triumphs; and many take their pleasure in travel to far countries, to see the divers fashions and behaviour of men.

If it were possible we might stand upon such a hill, from which we might at once see all parts of the world, the cities and towns, and mountains, and forests, and castles, and gorgeous buildings, and all the kings and princes of the world, in their princely estate; if we might see the variety of the whole world, how some live quietly in peace, others are turmoiled in war, some live in wealth, others in poverty and misery; some rise, others fall; to see and behold so great variety of things, it cannot be but it would delight us.

Such a hill, from whence we may take views of so great variety, such a story in which we may read of noble princes, of their wars and victories, is the word of God. Upon this hill you may at once behold all the works of his hands, how he made heaven and earth, the sun and the moon, the sea and floods, the fishes in the water, the fowls in the air, and the beasts in the field. Upon this hill you may stand and see his angels, and his archangels, and blessed spirits, how some of them fell, and some continued in glory; how God hath sent them in message, how they have come down from heaven to serve the sons of men.

Here you may read of the wars of the God of Hosts; how he hath pitched his tents in the midst of his people, and hath gone before them, and fought for them; how the Amorites and Canaanites were rooted out; how the Amalekites were overthrown by the lifting up of Moses' hands in prayer; how the wall of Jericho fell down flat at the sound of a trumpet, and the shouting of the people; and how one hundred and eighty-five thousand Assyrians were slain in one night by the hand of one angel, when God raught out his hand from heaven to give victory to his people.

Here may you see how God plagued and overcame his enemies; how he drowned Pharaoh in the Red Sea, and his horses, and men, and chariots, all together. Here may you see Nebuchadnezzar, a mighty prince, so bereft of his wits, that he forsook his palaces, and the company and order of men, and lived in the fields after the manner of beasts. Here may you see how God struck king Antiochus and king Herod with filthy diseases, and caused lice to eat their flesh; how he sent down fire and brimstone from heaven, and destroyed Sodom and Gomorrah for their sins; how he made the earth open, and swallow up Dathan and Abiram; how king Uzziah was stricken with leprosy, and carried from the temple, and cut off from his kingdom.

What stories of any princes or people in any age can report unto us so strange battles, so mighty conquests, so wonderful deliverance in extremities, so dreadful subduing of the enemies, as the hand of God hath wrought, and the story of the Scriptures declareth unto us?

This word also sheweth the goodness and mercy of God towards the people which put their trust in him; how he made them terrible to their enemies; how he made their enemies their footstool; how he led them safe through the Red Sea; how he sent his angel to go before them, and guide them; how he gave them water out of a rock, and rained down bread from heaven; how he brought them into a land that flowed with milk and honey, and sware unto them, that he would be their God, and they should be his people.

In this word are to be seen wonderful and strange works of God, such as are beyond the course of nature, and pass the reason of man: that the sea parted, and stood on both sides as a high wall; that at the word of Joshua the sun stood still, and went not on his course. Hezekiah spake the word, and required it, and the sun went back ten degrees. At the word of Elias, fire came down from heaven to consume his sacrifice.

Here may you see an ass open his mouth, and speak and reprove his master; three servants of God walk in a hot burning furnace without hurt; Daniel in the den among lions, and not devoured; Peter in the raging sea, and not drowned; lepers cleansed, the lame to go, the dumb to speak, the deaf to hear, the blind to see, the dead to rise out of their graves and live; simple and unlearned men to speak in strange tongues; the devil to go out of the possessed, and to say, I know thou art Christ the Son of God.

Here may you see twelve poor silly men, without spear, or sword, or force, make conquest and win the whole world. No power could repress them, no might could withstand them. It is reckoned a great matter for a king or a nation to yield submission unto another king or nation. It must therefore be a matter of great wonder to see all kings throw down their maces, and all people to yield before so few, so simple, so unarmed; and to acknowledge they embraced lies, and lived in ignorance; and that these twelve are the servants of the Highest; and to see how God hath chosen the foolish things of this world, to overthrow the wise; and the weak things of this world, to confound the mighty things: such force did God give to their words. He made them the sons of thunder; they shook the foundations of the world; they threw down whatsoever stood against them.

Here you may see the fight of God's elect children; how they patiently suffered afflictions in their bodies, rather than they would deny the truth of God; they gave their backs to the scourge, their necks to the sword, their bodies to the fire. No tyrant, no menacings, no rack, no torment, no sword, no death could remove them from the love of the Gospel which they had received.

The more of them were cut down, the more did spring up; the more were killed, the more were left alive. Augustine saith, "They were bound, and shut up, and racked, and burnt, and yet were increased." This is the victory that hath overcome the world. For the Lord answered (St. Paul, II Cor. 12:9), "My power is made perfect through weakness." It liveth in death; it is made whole and sound by wounds and stripes; it is increased by those means whereby men destroy it.

Jacob saw a ladder stand upon the earth, and the top of it reach up into heaven, and the angels of God go up and down by it. This was but a dream and vision in his sleep; yet when he awoke, he took pleasure and comfort of this vision.

We have not only the delight of this with Jacob, but we have other far greater visions. We see Isaiah beholding the Lord as he sat upon an high throne; we see Paul taken up into the third heavens; we see the glory of God appear, and hear the voice which came out of the cloud, saying (Matt. 17:5), "This is my well-beloved Son, in whom I am well pleased; hear him."

We see Jesus Christ, the Son of God, born of a virgin, and how "he made himself of no reputation, and took on him the form of a servant, and was made like unto man, and was found in shape as a man; that he humbled himself, and became obedient unto the death, even the death of the cross." (Phil. 2:7) We hear him cry with a loud voice, "My God, my God, why hast thou forsaken me?" We hear him say, "Father, forgive them, for they know not what they do." And, "Father, into thine hands I commend my spirit." (Luke 23:34)

Here we may see the sun to be darkened, that the moon giveth no light; the earth to shake, the rocks to cleave asunder, the vail to rent, the graves to open, and Christ rise from the dead, and go up into heaven, and sit at the right hand of his Father.

Here may we see the overthrow of "Babylon, which made all nations to drink of the wine of the wrath of her fornication" (Rev. 14:8): how she is destroyed with the breath of God's mouth. Here we behold the resurrection of the dead, and four-and-twenty elders sit before God on their seats, and the Ancient of days sit upon his throne, and the judgment-seat, and the books opened, and all flesh appear before him; and how some are taken into everlasting life, and some are sent into everlasting death.

What tongue is able to express these pleasures and delights which are laid open to us in the word of God? . . .

Thus have I performed promise, and simply and homely opened those four things which I took in hand. I have declared what weight and majesty the word beareth; what huge harvest of profit we may reap by it; how needful it is for us travelling through the wilderness of this life, and what repast and pleasure we may find in it.

God's Word Is Understandable

But all this notwithstanding, some take exception, and say, the Scriptures are dark and doubtful, the matters are deep, the words are hard, few can understand them. One taketh them in this sense, another in a sense clean contrary. The best learned cannot agree about them; they are the occasion of many great quarrels. John seeth this book sealed with seven seals, and an angel preaching with a loud voice, "Who is worthy to open the book, and to loose the seals thereof?" (Rev. 5:2) No man can open it, no man can read it. St. Peter saith (II Peter 3:16), "Among the Epistles of Paul, some things are hard to be understood, which they that are unlearned and unstable, pervert as they do all other Scriptures unto their own destruction." And St. Paul saith (I Tim. 6:16), "God dwelleth in the light that none can attain unto," whom man never saw, neither can see.

Therefore, although the majesty be never so weighty, the profit, the necessity, and the pleasure never so great, yet it is not good for the people to read them. Pearls must not be cast before swine, nor the bread of the children unto dogs. Thus they say. Indeed the word of God is pearls, but the people are not swine.

They may not read them (say some); they are not able to wield them; the Scriptures are not for the people. Hereof I will say something, and a word or two of the reverence and fear, with which we ought to come to the hearing of them. . . .

God saith (Deut. 30:11), "This commandment which I command thee this day is not hid from thee, neither is it far off. It is not in heaven, that thou shouldest say, Who shall go up for us to heaven, and bring it us, and cause us to hear it, that we may do it? Neither is it beyond the sea, that thou shouldest say, Who shall go over the sea for us, and bring it us, and cause us to hear it, that we may do it? But the word is very near thee, even in thy mouth, and in thy heart, for to do it." Thou needest not run hither and thither, nor wander over the sea, nor beat thy brains in searching what thou shouldest do, or by what means thou mayest live uprightly. The word and commandment of God will teach thee sufficiently.

The Prophet David saith (Ps. 19:8), "The commandment of the Lord is pure, and giveth light unto the eyes." And (Ps. 119:105), "Thy word is a lantern unto my feet, and a light unto my paths." Thy word is not dark, it is a light unto my path, it giveth light unto the eyes. What is clear, if the light be dark? or what can he see, which cannot see the light?

Human knowledge is dark and uncertain; philosophy is dark, astrology is dark, and geometry is dark. The professors thereof oftentimes run a-muck; they lose themselves, and wander they know not whither; they seek the depth and bottom of natural causes, the change of the elements, the impressions in the air, the causes of the rainbow, of blazing stars, of thunder and lightning, of the trembling and shaking of the earth, the motions of the planets, the proportion and the influence of the celestial bodies.

They measure the compass of heaven, and count the number of the stars; they go down, and search the mines in the bowels of the earth; they rip up the secrets of the sea. The knowledge of these things is hard; it is uncertain; few are able to reach it; it is not fit for every man to understand it.

But the holy Spirit of God, like a good teacher, applieth himself to the dulness of our wits; he leadeth not us by the unknown places of the earth, nor by the air, nor by the clouds; he astonisheth not our spirits with natural vanities; he writeth his law in our hearts; he teacheth us to know him and his Christ; he teacheth us (Titus 2:12), that we should "deny ungodliness and worldly lusts, and that we should live soberly, and righteously, and godly in this present world"; he teacheth us to look "for the blessed hope and appearing of the glory of the mighty God, and of our Saviour Jesus Christ." This matter is good, and it is plain; the words are plain, and the utterance is plain.

Chrysostom saith, "Therefore hath the grace of the Holy Spirit disposed and tempered them so, that publicans, and fishers, and tentmakers, shepherds, and the Apostles, and simple men, and unlearned, might be saved by these books; that none of the simpler sort might make excuse by the hardness of them; and that such things as are spoken might be easy for all men to look on; that the labouring man, and the servant, the widow woman, and whosoever is most unlearned, may take some good, when they are read. For they whom God ever from the beginning endued with the grace of his Spirit, have not gathered all these things for vain glory, as the heathen writers use, but for the salvation of the hearers."...

As for the wisest and learned men in matters of this world, they have not always proved the readiest and most willing to set forth the glory of God: they have not been the meetest scholars for this school. Who were they that resisted Moses and Aaron, the servants of God? Not the people, but the wisest and best learned in Egypt. Who were they that stood against Elias? Not the people, but the learned and wise men, and the prophets and priests of Baal. Who were they that stoned and killed the Prophets? Not the people, but the chiefest and wisest in Israel.

Who were they that resisted Christ and his Gospel, and sought to deface the glory of God? Not the people, but the Scribes, and Pharisees, and high-priests, and all the troop of their clergy. They called Christ a deceiver, and Beelzebub, a companion of publicans and harlots; they laid in wait every where to entrap him, they sued him to death.

St. Paul saith for conclusion in this matter (I Cor. 1:19), "It is written, I will destroy the wisdom of the wise, and will cast away the understanding of the prudent. Where is the wise? where is the Scribe? where is the disputer of this world? Hath not God made the wisdom of this world foolishness? For seeing the world by wisdom knew not God, in the wisdom of God, it pleased God by the foolishness of preaching, to save them that believed. Brethren, you see your calling, how that not many wise men after the flesh, not many mighty, not many noble, are called, but God hath chosen the foolish things of the world to confound the wise; and God hath chosen the weak things of the world to confound the mighty things, and vile things of the world, and things which are despised, hath God chosen."

Mark, saith he, how mercifully God hath dealt with you. Few of the learned sort, few such as are counted wise, embrace the Gospel with you, or join with you in faith, or keep you company. God hath let them be deceived in their wisdom; they take themselves to be wise, and yet are become fools, and contrary to worldly judgment. God hath made you, which were weak and simple, and of no reputation, wise and righteous, and sanctified and redeemed in Christ Jesus. And Christ saith (Matt. 18:3), "Except ye be converted, and become as little children, ye shall not enter into the kingdom of heaven."...

Therefore Christ said (Matt. 11:25), "I give thee thanks, O Father, Lord of heaven and earth, because thou hast hid these things from the wise and men of understanding, and hast opened them unto babes," even to such as have no learning, which rejoice in nothing but in thee. The wise and learned of the world cannot hear them, cannot see them; but they to whom it pleased thee to give understanding. It is thy mercy. Flesh and blood cannot reach the knowledge of thy will. The Spirit of the Father hath revealed it.

Christ saith (John 10:3, 5), "My sheep hear my voice, and I know them, and they follow me; they will not follow a stranger." My people are simple as sheep, they are rude, and know not what they do; yet they know my voice, and follow me; they know their shepherd from a thief; they follow not the call and voice of a stranger. So we see that God chaseth no man away from hearing his word; he loatheth not the poor, because of his poverty; he refuseth him not, for he is the God of the poor, they be his creatures.

St. Augustine saith, "Almighty God, in the Scriptures, speaketh as a familiar friend, without dissimulation, unto the hearts both of the learned and of the unlearned." He abaseth himself, and speaketh to their capacity; for his will is, that all should come to the knowledge of the truth, and be saved.

God's Word Is to Be Revered

Now let us consider with what fear and reverence we ought to come to the hearing or reading of the word of God. "The angel of the Lord appeared unto Moses in a flame of fire, out of the midst of a bush." (Exod. 3:2) When Moses turned aside to see, God said unto him, "Come not hither, put thy shoes off thy feet, for the place whereon thou standest is holy ground."

Again, when God had appointed to speak unto the people from Mount Sinai, he said to Moses, "Go unto the people, and sanctify them to-day and to-morrow, and let them wash their clothes, and let them be ready on the third day; for the third day the Lord will come down in the sight of all the people upon Mount Sinai." (Exod. 19:10)

The word of the Lord is the bush, out of which issueth a flame of fire. The Scriptures of God are the mount, from which the Lord of Hosts doth shew himself. In them God speaketh to us; in them we hear the words of everlasting life. We must be sanctified, and wash our garments, and be ready to hear the Lord. We must strip off all our affections; we must fall down before him with fear; we must know who it is that speaketh; even God the maker of heaven and earth; God the Father of our Lord Jesus Christ; God which shall judge the quick and the dead, before whom all flesh shall appear.

This word is holy. Let us take heed into what hearts we bestow it. Whosoever abuseth it, shall be found guilty of high trespass against the Lord. We may not receive it to blow up our hearts, and wax proud with our knowledge; we may not use it to maintain debate and contention; we may not use it to vaunt ourselves, or to make show of our cunning.

The word of God teacheth lowliness of mind; it teacheth us to know ourselves. If we learn not humility, we learn nothing. Although we seem to know somewhat, yet know we not in such sort as we ought to know.

The Scriptures are the mysteries of God; let us not be curious; let us not seek to know more than God hath revealed by them: they are the sea of God; let us take heed we be not drowned in them: they are the fire of God; let us take comfort by their heat, and warily take heed they burn us not. They that gaze over-hardly upon the sun, take blemish in their eyesight.

When the people of Israel saw the manna in the desert, they said, *Man Hu?* what is this? So they reasoned of it when they took it up in their hands, and beheld it. They asked one another what good it would do. The Scriptures are manna, given to us from heaven, to feed us in the desert of this world. Let us take them, and behold them, and reason of them, and learn one of another what profit may come to us by them; let us know that they are written for our sake, and for our learning, that through patience and comfort of the Scriptures we may have hope. They are given us to instruct us in faith, to strengthen us in hope, to open our eyes, and to direct our going.

If we withhold the truth in unrighteousness, if we know our master's will, and do it not; if the name of God be ill spoken of through us, the word of God shall be taken away from us, and given to a nation which shall bring forth the fruits thereof. God shall send us strong delusions, that we shall believe lies; our own heart shall condemn us, and we shall be beaten with many stripes.

Therefore we ought diligently to give heed to those things which we hear, we must consider of them, we must chew the cud. "Every beast that cheweth not the cud is unclean" (Lev. 11:3-8), and not fit for the sacrifice. Let us be poor in spirit, and meek in heart; let us be gentle, as becometh the lambs of Christ, and as his sheep; let us hear his voice, and follow him; let us be of a contrite spirit, and tremble at the words of God; let us, when we know God, glorify him as God.

So shall God look upon us; so shall the spirit of wisdom, and understanding, and of counsel, and of knowledge, and of the fear of God, rest upon us; so shall we be made perfect to all good works; so shall we rejoice in his salvation, and with one mouth glorify God, even the Father of our Lord Jesus Christ.

Stephen Charnock
1628-1680

4

God

Stephen Charnock, who was born in London, in 1642 entered Emmanuel College, Cambridge, and there was converted. His public ministry began in Southwark, London, after receiving his B.D. from the university. In 1650 he earned a fellowship at New College, Oxford, where he associated with Thomas Goodwin and John Howe. He became chaplain in 1655 to Henry Cromwell, governor of Ireland. He earned his reputation in Dublin, where his preaching without notes greatly impressed his listeners. With the coming of the Restoration, he lost his position and lived in London in semiretirement until his death. For a short time he was joint pastor with Thomas Watson of the church at Crosby Hall.

Charnock published only one sermon in his lifetime, his greatest works being published after his death. *A Discourse of Divine Providence* was published in 1680 and followed in 1682 by *On the Existence and Attributes of God*. His complete works were published in nine volumes in 1815 with a biography prefixed by Edward Parsons. Charnock's style was lofty and sublime. He wrote of God's attributes in a declarative, nonspeculative manner. He set forth the divine attributes as qualities (not impersonal abstractions) observable in God's dealings with men. He was grave without being dull and thorough without being wearisome.

In this section on the eternity of God, Charnock develops a thorough outline of his subject. His primary concern here is the extension of God's duration. In typically Puritan style he concludes the treatise with a section on the "use" of the doctrine, which is as valuable as the foregoing exposition because it shows how God is interested in applying doctrine to the life of the believer. Charnock points out, for example, the great psychological value of this doctrine, turning man's attention from temporal materialistic values to eternal verities.

Psalm 90:2—Before the mountains were brought forth, or ever thou hadst formed the earth and the world, even from everlasting to everlasting, thou art God.

The title of this psalm is a prayer; the author, Moses. Some think not only this, but the ten following psalms, were composed by him. The title wherewith he is dignified is, "The man of God," as also in Deut. 33:1. One inspired by him to be his interpreter, and deliver his oracles; one particularly directed by him;[1] one who as a servant did diligently employ himself in his master's business, and acted for the glory of God;[2] he was the minister of the Old Testament, and the prophet of the New.[3]

There are two parts of this psalm. 1. A complaint of the frailty of man's life in general (v. 3-6); and then a particular complaint of the condition of the church (v. 8-10). 2. A prayer (v. 12). But before he speaks of the shortness of human life, he fortifies them by the consideration of the refuge they had, and should find in God (v. 1): "Lord, thou hast been our dwelling-place in all generations." We have had no settled abode in the earth, since the time of Abraham's being called out from Ur of the Chaldees. We have had Canaan in a promise, we have it not yet in possession; we have been exposed to the cruelties of an oppressing enemy, and the incommodities of a desert wilderness; we have wanted the fruits of the earth, but not the dews of heaven. "Thou hast been our dwelling-place in all generations." Abraham was under thy conduct; Isaac and Jacob under thy care; their posterity was multiplied by thee, and that under their oppressions. Thou hast been our shield against dangers, our security in the times of trouble; when we were pursued to the

1. Coccei *in loc.*

2. Austin *in loc.*

3. Pareus *in loc.*

Red Sea, it was not a creature delivered us; and when we feared the pinching of our bowels in the desert, it was no creature rained manna upon us. Thou hast been our dwelling-place; thou hast kept open house for us, sheltered us against storms, and preserved us from mischief, as a house doth an inhabitant from wind and weather; and that not in one or two, but in all generations. Some think an allusion is here made to the ark, to which they were to have recourse in all emergencies. Our refuge and defence hath not been from created things; not from the ark, but from the God of the ark. Observe,

1. God is a perpetual refuge and security to his people. His providence is not confined to one generation; it is not one age only that tastes of his bounty and compassion. His eye never yet slept, nor hath he suffered the little ship of his church to be swallowed up, though it hath been tossed upon the waves; he hath always been a haven to preserve us, a house to secure us; he hath always had compassions to pity us, and power to protect us; he hath had a face to shine, when the world hath had an angry countenance to frown.[4] He brought Enoch home by an extraordinary translation from a brutish world; and when he was resolved to reckon with men for their brutish lives, he lodged Noah, the phoenix of the world, in an ark, and kept him alive as a spark in the midst of many waters, whereby to rekindle a church in the world; in all generations he is a dwelling-place to secure his people here, or entertain them above. His providence is not wearied, nor his care fainting; he never wanted will to relieve us, "for he hath been our refuge," nor ever can want power to support us, "for he is a God from everlasting to everlasting." The church never wanted a pilot to steer her, and a rock to shelter her, and dash in pieces the waves which threaten her.

2. How worthy is it to remember former benefits, when we come to beg for new. Never were the records of God's mercies so exactly revised, as when his people have stood in need of new editions of his power. How necessary are our wants to stir us up to pay the rent of thankfulness in arrear! He renders himself doubly unworthy of the mercies he wants, that doth not gratefully acknowledge the mercies he hath received. God scarce promised any deliverance to the Israelites, and they, in their distress, scarce prayed for any deliverance; but that from Egypt was mentioned on both sides, by God to encourage them, and by them to acknowledge their confidence in him. The greater our dangers, the more we should call to mind God's former kindness. We are not only thankfully to acknowledge the

---

4. Theodoret *in loc.*

mercies bestowed upon our persons, or in our age, but those of former times. "Thou hast been our dwelling-place in all generations." Moses was not living in the former generations, yet he appropriates the former mercies to the present age. Mercies, as well as generations, proceed out of the loins of those that have gone before. All mankind are but one Adam; the whole church but one body. In the second verse he backs his former consideration. 1. By the greatness of his power in forming the world. 2. By the boundlessness of his duration: "From everlasting to everlasting." As thou hast been our dwelling-place, and expended upon us the strength of thy power and riches of thy love, so we have no reason to doubt the continuance on thy part, if we be not wanting on our parts; for the vast mountains and fruitful earth are the works of thy hands, and there is less power requisite for our relief, than there was for their creation; and though so much strength hath been upon various occasions manifested, yet thy arm is not weakened, for "from everlasting to everlasting thou art God."[5] Thou hast always been God, and no time can be assigned as the beginning of thy being.[6] The mountains are not of so long a standing as thyself; they are the effects of thy power, and therefore cannot be equal to thy duration; since they are the effects, they suppose the precedency of their cause. If we would look back, we can reach no further than the beginning of the creation, and account the years from the first foundation of the world; but after that we must lose ourselves in the abyss of eternity; we have no cue to guide our thoughts; we can see no bounds in thy eternity. But as for man, he traverseth the world a few days, and by thy order pronounced concerning all men, returns to the dust, and moulders into the grave. By mountains, some understand angels, as being creatures of a more elevated nature; by earth, they understand human nature, the earth being the habitation of men. There is no need to divert in this place from the letter to such a sense. The description seems to be poetical, and amounts to this: he neither began with the beginning of time, nor will expire with the end of it; he did not begin when he made himself known to our fathers, but his being did precede the creation of the world, before any created being was formed, and any time settled.[7] "Before the mountains were brought forth," or before they were begotten or born; the word being used in those senses in Scripture; before they stood up higher than the rest of the earthly

---

5. ‏אל‎ , strong.

6. Amyrald *in loc.*

7. Ἄναρχος καὶ ἀτελεύτητος, Theodoret *in loc.*

mass God had created. It seems that mountains were not casually cast up by the force of the deluge softening the ground, and driving several parcels of it together, to grow up into a massy body, as the sea doth the sand in several places; but they were at first formed by God. The eternity of God is here described,

1. In his priority: "Before the world."
2. In the extension of his duration: "From everlasting to everlasting thou art God." He was before the world, yet he neither began nor ends; he is not a temporary, but an eternal God; it takes in both parts of eternity, what was before the creation of the world, and what is after; though the eternity of God be one permanent state, without succession, yet the spirit of God, suiting himself to the weakness of our conception, divides it into two parts; one past before the foundation of the world, another to come after the destruction of the world; as he did exist before all ages, and as he will exist after all ages. Many truths lie couched in the verse.

1. The world hath a beginning of being: it was not from eternity, it was once nothing; had it been of a very long duration, some records would have remained of some memorable actions done of a longer date than any extant. 2. The world owes its being to the creating power of God: "Thou hast formed it" out of nothing into being; Thou, that is, God; it could not spring into being of itself; it was nothing; it must have a former. 3. God was in being before the world: the cause must be before the effect; that word which gives being, must be before that which receives being. 4. This Being was from eternity: "From everlasting." 5. This Being shall endure to eternity: "To everlasting." There is but one God, one eternal: "From everlasting to everlasting, thou art God." None else but one hath the property of eternity; the gods of the heathen cannot lay claim to it.

Doct. God is of an eternal duration. The eternity of God is the foundation of the stability of the covenant, the great comfort of a Christian. The design of God in Scripture is, to set forth his dealing with men in the way of a covenant. The priority of God before all things begins the Bible: "In the beginning God created" (Gen. 1:1). His covenant can have no foundation, but in his duration before and after the world:[8] and Moses here mentions his eternity, not only with respect to the essence of God, but to his federal providence; as he is the dwelling-place of his people in all generations. The duration of God forever is more spoken of in Scripture than his eternity, *à parte ante,* though that is the foundation of all the comfort we can

8. Calv. *in loc.*

take from his immortality: if he had a beginning, he might have an end, and so all our happiness, hope and being would expire with him; but the Scripture sometimes takes notice of his being without beginning, as well as without end: "Thou art from everlasting" (Ps. 93:2); "Blessed be God from everlasting to everlasting" (Ps. 41:13); "I was set up from everlasting" (Prov. 8:23): if his wisdom were from everlasting, himself was from everlasting: whether we understand it of Christ the Son of God, or of the essential wisdom of God, it is all one to the present purpose. The wisdom of God supposeth the essence of God, as habits in creatures suppose the being of some power or faculty as their subject. The wisdom of God supposeth mind and understanding, essence and substance. The notion of eternity is difficult; as Austin said of time,[9] if no man will ask me the question, what time is, I know well enough what it is; but if any ask me what it is, I know not how to explain it; so may I say of eternity; it is easy in the word pronounced, but hardly understood, and more hardly expressed; it is better expressed by negative than positive words. Though we cannot comprehend eternity, yet we may comprehend that there is an eternity; as, though we cannot comprehend the essence of God what he is, yet we may comprehend that he is; we may understand the notion of his existence, though we cannot understand the infiniteness of his nature; yet we may better understand eternity than infiniteness; we can better conceive a time with the addition of numberless days and years, than imagine a Being without bounds; whence the apostle joins his eternity with his power; "His eternal power and Godhead" (Rom. 1:20); because, next to the power of God, apprehended in the creature, we come necessarily by reasoning, to acknowledge the eternity of God. He that hath an incomprehensible power must needs have an eternity of nature; his power is most sensible in the creatures to the eye of man, and his eternity easily from thence deducible by the reason of man. Eternity is a perpetual duration, which hath neither beginning nor end; time hath both. Those things we say are in time that have beginning, grow up by degrees, have succession of parts; eternity is contrary to time, and is therefore a permanent and immutable state; a perfect possession of life without any variation; it comprehends in itself all years, all ages, all periods of ages; it never begins; it endures after every duration of time, and never ceaseth; it doth as much outrun time, as it went before the beginning of it: time supposeth something before it; but there can be nothing be-

---

9. Confes. lib. ii. Confes. 14.

fore eternity; it were not then eternity. Time hath a continual succession; the former time passeth away and another succeeds: the last year is not this year, nor this year the next. We must conceive of eternity contrary to the notion of time; as the nature of time consists in the succession of parts, so the nature of eternity in an infinite immutable duration. Eternity and time differ as the sea and rivers; the sea never changes place, and is always one water; but the rivers glide along, and are swallowed up in the sea; so is time by eternity.[10] A thing is said to be eternal, or everlasting rather, in Scripture,

1. When it is of a long duration, though it will have an end; when it hath no measures of time determined to it; so circumcision is said to be in the flesh for an "everlasting covenant" (Gen. 17:13); not purely everlasting, but so long as that administration of the covenant should endure. And so when a servant would not leave his master, but would have his ear bored, it is said, he should be a servant "forever" (Deut. 15:17); *i.e.*, till the jubilee, which was every fiftieth year: so the meat-offering they were to offer is said to be "perpetual" (Lev. 6:20); Canaan is said to be given to Abraham for an "everlasting" possession (Gen. 17:8); when as the Jews are expelled from Canaan, which is given a prey to the barbarous nations. Indeed circumcision was not everlasting; yet the substance of the covenant whereof this was a sign, viz. that God would be the God of believers, endures forever; and that circumcision of the heart, which was signified by circumcision of the flesh, shall remain forever in the kingdom of glory: it was not so much the lasting of the sign, as of the thing signified by it, and the covenant sealed by it: the sign had its abolition; so that the apostle is so peremptory in it, that he asserts, that if any went about to establish it, he excluded himself from a participation of Christ (Gal. 5:2). The sacrifices were to be perpetual, in regard to the thing signified by them; viz. the death of Christ, which was to endure in the efficacy of it: and the passover was to be "forever" (Exod. 12:24), in regard of the redemption signified by it, which was to be of everlasting remembrance. Canaan was to be an everlasting possession, in regard of the glory of heaven typified, to be forever conferred upon the spiritual seed of Abraham.

2. When a thing hath no end, though it hath a beginning. So angels and souls are everlasting; though their being shall never cease, yet there was a time when their being began; they were nothing before they were something, though they shall never be nothing again, but shall live in endless happiness or misery. But that properly is

---

10. Moulin. God. 1, Ser. 2, p. 52.

eternal that hath neither beginning nor end; and thus eternity is a property of God.

In this doctrine I shall show, I. How God is eternal, or in what respects eternity is his property. II. That he is eternal, and must needs be so. III. That eternity is only proper to God, and not common to him with any creature....

The Manner of God's Eternity

I. How God is eternal, or in what respects he is so. Eternity is a negative attribute, and is a denying of God any measures of time, as immensity is a denying of him any bounds of place. As immensity is the diffusion of his essence, so eternity is the duration of his essence; and when we say God is eternal, we exclude from him all possibility of beginning and ending, all flux and change. As the essence of God cannot be bounded by any place, so it is not to be limited by any time: as it is his immensity to be everywhere, so it is his eternity to be alway. As created things are said to be somewhere in regard of place, and to be present, past, or future, in regard of time; so the Creator in regard of place is everywhere, in regard of time is *semper*.[11] His duration is as endless as his essence is boundless: he always was and always will be, and will no more have an end than he had a beginning; and this is an excellency belonging to the Supreme Being.[12] As his essence comprehends all beings, and exceeds them, and his immensity surmounts all places; so his eternity comprehends all times, all durations, and infinitely excels them.[13]

1. God is without beginning. "In the beginning" God created the world (Gen. 1:1). God was then before the beginning of it; and what point can be set wherein God began, if he were before the beginning of created things? God was without beginning, though all other things had time and beginning from him. As unity is before all numbers, so is God before all his creatures. Abraham called upon the name of the everlasting God (Gen. 21:33) the eternal God.[14]—It is opposed to the heathen gods, which were but of yesterday, new coined, and so new; but the eternal God was before the world was made. In that sense it is to be understood; "The mystery which was kept secret since the world began, but now is made manifest, and

11. Gassend.

12. Crellius de Deo, c. 18, p. 41.

13. Lingend Tom. II. p. 496.

14. אל צדלם.

by the scriptures of the prophets, according to the command of the everlasting God, make known to all nations for the obedience of faith" (Rom. 16:26). The gospel is not preached by the command of a new and temporary god, but of that God that was before all ages: though the manifestation of it be in time, yet the purpose and resolve of it was from eternity. If there were decrees before the foundation of the world, there was a Decreer before the foundation of the world. Before the foundation of the world he loved Christ as a Mediator; a fore-ordination of him was before the foundation of the world (John 17:24); a choice of men, and therefore a Chooser before the foundation of the world (Eph. 1:4); a grace given in Christ before the world began (II Tim. 1:9), and therefore a Donor of that grace. From those places, saith Crellius, it appears that God was before the foundation of the world, but they do not assert an absolute eternity; but to be before all creatures is equivalent to his being from eternity.[15] Time began with the foundation of the world; but God being before time, could have no beginning in time. Before the beginning of the creation, and the beginning of time, there could be nothing but eternity; nothing but what was uncreated, that is, nothing but what was without beginning. To be in time is to have a beginning; to be before all time is never to have a beginning, but always to be; for as between Creator and creatures there is no medium, so between time and eternity there is no medium. It is as easily deduced that he that was before all creatures is eternal, as he that made all creatures is God. If he had a beginning, he must have it from another, or from himself; if from another, that from whom he received his being would be better than he, so more a God than he. He cannot be God that is not supreme; he cannot be supreme that owes his being to the power of another. He would not be said only to have immortality as he is (I Tim. 6:16), if he had it dependent upon another; nor could he have a beginning from himself; if he had given beginning to himself, then he was once nothing; there was a time when he was not; if he was not, how could he be the Cause of himself? It is impossible for any to give a beginning and being to itself: if it acts it must exist, and so exist before it existed. A thing would exist as a cause before it existed as an effect. He that is not, cannot be the cause that he is; if, therefore, God doth exist, and hath not his being from another, he must exist from eternity. Therefore, when we say God is of and from himself, we mean not that God gave being to himself; but it is negatively

---

15. Coccei Sum. p. 48. Theol. Gerhard Exeges. c. 86. 4. p. 266.

to be understood that he hath no cause of existence without himself. Whatsoever number of millions of millions of years we can imagine before the creation of the world, yet God was infinitely before those; he is therefore called the "Ancient of Days" (Dan. 7:9), as being before all days and time, and eminently containing in himself all times and ages. Though, indeed, God cannot properly be called ancient, that will testify that he is decaying, and shortly will not be; no more than he can be called young, which would signify that he was not long before. All created things are new and fresh; but no creature can find out any beginning of God: it is impossible there should be any beginning of him.

2. God is without end. He always was, always is, and always will be what he is. He remains always the same in being; so far from any change, that no shadow of it can touch him (James 1:17). He will continue in being as long as he hath already enjoyed it; and if we could add never so many millions of years together, we are still as far from an end as from a beginning; for "the Lord shall endure forever" (Ps. 9:7). As it is impossible he should not be, being from all eternity, so it is impossible that he should not be to all eternity. The Scripture is most plentiful in testimonies of this eternity of God, *à parte post,* or after the creation of the world: he is said to "live forever" (Rev. 4:9, 10). The earth shall perish, but God shall "endure forever," and his "years shall have no end" (Ps. 102:27). Plants and animals grow up from small beginnings, arrive to their full growth, and decline again, and have always remarkable alterations in their nature; but there is no declination in God by all the revolutions of time. Hence some think the incorruptibility of the Deity was signified by the shittim, or cedar wood, whereof the ark was made, it being of an incorruptible nature (Exod. 25:10). That which had no beginning of duration can never have an end, or any interruptions in it. Since God never depended upon any, what should make him cease to be what eternally he hath been, or put a stop to the continuance of his perfections? He cannot will his own destruction; that is against universal nature in all things to cease from being, if they can preserve themselves. He cannot desert his own being, because he cannot but love himself as the best and chiefest good. The reason that anything decays is either its own native weakness, or a superior power of something contrary to it. There is no weakness in the nature of God that can introduce any corruption, because he is infinitely simple without any mixture; nor can he be overpowered by anything else; a weaker cannot hurt him, and a stronger than he there cannot be; nor can he be outwitted or

circumvented, because of his infinite wisdom.[16] As he received his being from none, so he cannot be deprived of it by any: as he doth necessarily exist, so he doth necessarily always exist. This, indeed, is the property of God; nothing so proper to him as always to be. Whatsoever perfections any being hath, if it be not eternal, it is not divine. God only is immortal;[17] he only is so by a necessity of nature. Angels, souls, and bodies too, after the resurrection, shall be immortal, not by nature, but grant; they are subject to return to nothing, if that word that raised them from nothing should speak them into nothing again. It is as easy with God to strip them of it, as to invest them with it; nay, it is impossible but that they should perish, if God should withdraw his power from preserving them, which he exerted in creating them; but God is immovably fixed in his own being; that as none gave him his life, so none can deprive him of his life, or the least particle of it. Not a jot of the happiness and life which God infinitely possesses can be lost; it will be as durable to everlasting, as it hath been possessed from everlasting.

3. There is no succession in God. God is without succession or change. It is a part of eternity; "from everlasting to everlasting he is God," *i.e.* the same. God doth not only always remain in being, but he always remains the same in that being: "thou art the same" (Ps. 102:27). The being of creatures is successive; the being of God is permanent, and remains entire with all its perfectons unchanged in an infinite duration. Indeed, the first notion of eternity is to be without beginning and end, which notes to us the duration of a being in regard of its existence; but to have no succession, nothing first or last, notes rather the perfection of a being in regard of its essence. The creatures are in a perpetual flux; something is acquired or something lost every day. A man is the same in regard of existence when he is a man, as he was when he was a child; but there is a new succession of quantities and qualities in him. Every day he acquires something till he comes to his maturity; every day he loseth something till he comes to his period. A man is not the same at night that he was in the morning; something is expired, and something is added; every day there is a change in his age, a change in his substance, a change in his accidents. But God hath his whole being in one and the same point, or moment of eternity. He receives nothing as an addition to what he was before; he loseth nothing of what he was before; he is always the same excellency and perfec-

---

16. Crellius de Deo, c. 18, p. 41.
17. I Tim. 6:16. Daille, *in loc.*

tion in the same infiniteness as ever. His years do not fail (Heb. 1:12), his years do not come and go as others do; there is not this day, to-morrow, or yesterday, with him. As nothing is past or future with him in regard of knowledge, but all things are present, so nothing is past or future in regard of his essence. He is not in his essence this day what he was not before, or will be the next day and year what he is not now. All his perfections are most perfect in him every moment; before all ages, after all ages.[18] As he hath his whole essence undivided in every place, as well as in an immense space, so he hath all his being in one moment of time, as well as in infinite intervals of time. Some illustrate the difference between eternity and time by the similitude of a tree, or a rock standing upon the side of a river, or shore of the sea; the tree stands always the same and unmoved, while the waters of the river glide along at the foot. The flux is in the river, but the tree acquires nothing but a diverse respect and relation of presence to the various parts of the river as they flow. The waters of the river press on, and push forward one another, and what the river had this minute, it hath not the same the next.[19] So are all sublunary things in a continual flux. And though the angels have no substantial change, yet they have an accidental; for the actions of the angels this day are not the same individual actions which they performed yesterday: but in God there is no change; he always remains the same. Of a creature, it may be said he was, or he is, or he shall be; of God it cannot be said but only he is.[20] He is what he always was, and he is what he always will be; whereas a creature is what he was not, and will be what he is not now. As it may be said of the flame of a candle, it is a flame: but it is not the same individual flame as was before, nor is it the same that will be presently after; there is a continual dissolution of it into air, and a continual supply for the generation of more. While it continues it may be said there is a flame; yet not entirely one, but in a succession of parts. So of a man it may be said, he is in a succession of parts; but he is not the same that he was, and will not be the same that he is. But God is the same, without any succession of parts and of time; of him it may be said, "He is." He is no more now than he was, and he shall be no more hereafter than he is. God possesses a firm and absolute being, always constant to himself.[21] He sees all things

18. Lessius de Perfect. Divin. lib. iv. c. 1.

19. Gamacheus in Aquin. Part I. Qu. 10. c. 1.

20. Gassend. Tom. I. Physic. §1. lib. ii. c. 7. p. 223.

21. Daille, Melange de Sermon, p. 252.

sliding under him in a continual variation; he beholds the revolutions in the world without any change of his most glorious and immovable nature. All other things pass from one state to another; from their original, to their eclipse and destruction; but God possesses his being in one indivisible point, having neither beginning, end, nor middle.

(1.) There is no succession in the knowledge of God. The variety of successions and changes in the world make not succession, or new objects in the Divine mind; for all things are present to him from eternity in regard of his knowledge, though they are not actually present in the world, in regard of their existence. He doth not know one thing now, and another anon; he sees all things at once; "Known unto God are all things from the beginning of the world" (Acts 15:18); but in their true order of succession, as they lie in the eternal council of God, to be brought forth in time. Though there be a succession and order of things as they are wrought, there is yet no succession in God in regard of his knowledge of them. God knows the things that shall be wrought, and the order of them in their being brought upon the stage of the world; yet both the things and the order he knows by one act. Though all things be present with God, yet they are present to him in the order of their appearance in the world, and not so present with him as if they should be wrought at once. The death of Christ was to precede his resurrection in order of time; there is a succession in this; both at once are known by God; yet the act of his knowledge is not exercised about Christ as dying and rising at the same time; so that there is succession in things when there is no succession in God's knowledge of them. Since God knows time, he knows all things as they are in time; he doth not know all things to be at once, though he knows at once what is, has been, and will be. All things are past, present, and to come, in regard of their existence; but there is not past, present, and to come, in regard of God's knowledge of them,[22] because he sees and knows not by any other, but by himself; he is his own light by which he sees, his own glass wherein he sees; beholding himself, he beholds all things.

(2.) There is no succession in the decrees of God. He doth not decree this now, which he decreed not before; for as his works were known from the beginning of the world, so his works were decreed from the beginning of the world; as they are known at once, so they are decreed at once; there is a succession in the execution of them; first grace, then glory; but the purpose of God for the bestowing of

---

22. Parsiensis.

both, was in one and the same moment of eternity. "He chose us in him before the foundation of the world, that we should be holy" (Eph. 1:4): The choice of Christ, and the choice of some in him to be holy and to be happy, were before the foundation of the world. It is by the eternal counsel of God all things appear in time; they appear in their order according to the counsel and will of God from eternity. The redemption of the world is after the creation of the world; but the decree whereby the world was created, and whereby it was redeemed, was from eternity.

(3.) God is his own eternity. He is not eternal by grant, and the disposal of any other, but by nature and essence.[23] The eternity of God is nothing else but the duration of God; and the duration of God is nothing else but his existence enduring.[24] If eternity were anything distinct from God, and not of the essence of God, then there would be something which was not God, necessary to perfect God. As immortality is the great perfection of a rational creature, so eternity is the choice perfection of God, yea, the gloss and lustre of all others. Every perfection would be imperfect, if it were not always a perfection. God is essentially whatsoever he is, and there is nothing in God but his essence. Duration or continuance in being in creatures, differs from their being; for they might exist but for one instant, in which case they may be said to have being, but not duration, because all duration includes *prius et posterius*. All creatures may cease from being if it be the pleasure of God; they are not, therefore, durable by their essence, and therefore are not their own duration, no more than they are their own existence. And though some creatures, as angels, and souls, may be called everlasting, as a perpetual life is communicated to them by God; yet they can never be called their own eternity, because such a duration is not simply necessary, nor essential to them, but accidental, depending upon the pleasure of another; there is nothing in their nature that can hinder them from losing it, if God, from whom they received it, should design to take it away; but as God is his own necessity of existing, so he is his own duration in existing; as he doth necessarily exist by himself, so he will always necessarily exist by himself.[25]

(4.) Hence all the perfections of God are eternal. In regard of the Divine eternity, all things in God are eternal; his power, mercy, wisdom, justice, knowledge. God himself were not eternal if any

---

23. Calov. Socinian.
24. Existentia durans.
25. Gassend.

of his perfections, which are essential to him, were not eternal also; he had not else been a perfect God from all eternity, and so his whole self had not been eternal. If anything belonging to the nature of a thing be wanting, it cannot be said to be that thing which it ought to be. If anything requisite to the nature of God had been wanting one moment, he could not have been said to be an eternal God.

The Essence of God's Eternity

II. God is eternal. The Spirit of God in Scripture condescends to our capacities in signifying the eternity of God by days and years, which are terms belonging to time, whereby we measure it (Ps. 102:27). But we must no more conceive that God is bounded or measured by time, and hath succession of days, because of those expressions, than we can conclude him to have a body, because members are ascribed to him in Scripture, to help our conceptions of his glorious nature and operations. Though years are ascribed to him, yet they are such as cannot be numbered, cannot be finished, since there is no proportion between the duration of God, and the years of men. "The number of his years cannot be searched out, for he makes small the drops of water; they pour down rain according to the vapor thereof (Job 36:26, 27). The numbers of the drops of rain which have fallen in all parts of the earth since the creation of the world, if subtracted from the number of the years of God, would be found a small quantity, a mere nothing, to the years of God. As all the nations in the world compared with God, are but as the "drop of a bucket, worse than nothing, than vanity" (Isa. 40:15); so all the ages of the world, if compared with God, amount not to so much as the one hundred thousandth part of a minute; the minutes from the creation may be numbered, but the years of the duration of God being infinite, are without measure. As one day is to the life of man, so are a thousand years to the life of God. The Holy Ghost expresseth himself to the capacity of man, to give us some notion of an infinite duration, by a resemblance suited to the capacity of man.[26] If a thousand years be but as a day to the life of God, then as a year is to the life of man, so are three hundred and sixty-five thousand years to the life of God; and as seventy years are to the life of man, so are twenty-five millions four hundred and fifty thousand years to the life of God. Yet still, since there is no proportion between time and eternity, we must dart our thoughts beyond all those; for years and days measure only the duration of created things,

26. Ps. 90:4. Amyrald, Trin. p. 44.

and of those only that are material and corporeal, subject to the motion of the heavens, which makes days and years.[27] Sometimes this eternity is expressed by parts, as looking backward and forward; by the differences of time, "past, present, and to come" (Rev. 1:8), "which was, and is, and is to come" (Rev. 4:8).[28] Though this might be spoken of anything in being, though but for an hour, it was the last minute, it is now, and it will be the next minute; yet the Holy Ghost would declare something proper to God, as including all parts of time; he always was, is now, and always shall be. It might always be said of him, he was, and it may always be said of him, he will be; there is no time when he began, no time when he shall cease. It cannot be said of a creature he always was, he always is what he was, and he always will be what he is; but God always is what he was, and always will be what he is; so that it is a very significant expression of the eternity of God, as can be suited to our capacities.

1. His eternity is evident, by the name God gives himself (Exod. 3:4): "And God said unto Moses, I am that I am; thus shalt thou say to the children of Israel, 'I Am hath sent me unto you.'" This is the name whereby he is distinguished from all creatures; I Am, is his proper name. This description being in the present tense, shows that his essence knows no past, nor future; if it were *he was*, it would intimate he were not now what he once was; if it were *he will be*, it would intimate he were not yet what he will be; but *I Am;* I am the only being, the root of all beings; he is therefore, at the greatest distance from not being, and that is eternal. So that *is* signifies his eternity, as well as his perfection and immutability. As *I Am* speaks the want of no blessedness, so it speaks the want of no duration; and therefore the French, wherever they find this word Jehovah, in the Scripture, which we translate Lord, and Lord eternal, render it the Eternal,—I am always and immutably the same. The eternity of God is opposed to the volubility of time, which is extended into past, present and to come. Our time is but a small drop, as a sand to all the atoms and small particles of which the world is made; but God is an unbounded sea of being. "I Am that I Am"; *i.e.* an infinite life; I have not that now, which I had not formerly; I shall not afterwards have that which I have not now; I am that in every moment which I was, and will be in all moments of time; nothing can be added to me, nothing can be detracted from me; there is nothing superior to him, which can detract from him; nothing de-

---

27. Daille, Vent. Sermons, Serm. I. sur 102 Ps. 27, p. 21.
28. Crellius weakens this argument, De Deo, c. 18, p. 42.

sirable that can be added to him. Now if there were any beginning and end of God, any succession in him, he could not be "I Am";[29] for in regard of what was past, he would not be; in regard of what was to come, he is not yet; and upon this account a heathen argues well;[30] of all creatures it may be said they were, or they will be; but of God it cannot be said anything else but *est,* God is, because he fills an eternal duration. A creature cannot be said to be, if it be not yet, nor if it be not now, but hath been.[31] God only can be called "I Am"; all creatures have more of not being, than being; for every creature was nothing from eternity, before it was made something in time; and if it be incorruptible in its whole nature, it will be nothing to eternity after it hath been something in time; and if it be not corruptible in its nature, as the angels, or in every part of its nature, as man in regard of his soul; yet it hath not properly a being, because it is dependent upon the pleasure of God to continue it, or deprive it of it; and while it is, it is mutable, and all mutability is a mixture of not being. If God therefore be properly "I Am," *i.e.* being, it follows that he always was; for if he were not always, he must, as was argued before, be produced by some other, or by himself; by another he could not; then he had not been God, but a creature; nor by himself, for then as producing, he must be before himself, as produced; he had been before he was. And he always will be; for being "I Am," having all being in himself, and the fountain of all being to everything else, how can he ever have his name changed to I am not.

2. God hath life in himself (John 5:26): "The Father hath life in himself"; he is the "living God"; therefore "steadfast forever" (Dan. 6:26). He hath life by his essence, not by participation. He is a sun to give light and life to all creatures, but receives not light or life from anything; and therefore he hath an unlimited life, not a drop of life, but a fountain; not a spark of a limited life, but a life transcending all bounds. He hath life in himself; all creatures have their life in him and from him. He that hath life in himself doth necessarily exist, and could never be made to exist; for then he had not life in himself, but in that which made him to exist, and gave him life. What doth necessarily exist therefore, exists from eternity; what hath being of itself could never be produced in time, could not want being one moment, because it hath being from its

---

29. Thes. Salmur. p. 1. p. 145, Thes. 14.

30. Plutarch de *El,* I. p. 392.

31. Perrer. in Exo. 3. Disput. 13.

essence, without influence of any efficient cause. When God pronounced his name, "I Am that I Am," angels and men were in being; the world had been created above two thousand four hundred years; Moses, to whom he then speaks, was in being; yet God only is, because he only hath the fountain of being in himself; but all that they were was a rivulet from him. He hath from nothing else, that he doth subsist; everything else hath its subsistence from him as their root, as the beam from the sun, as the rivers and fountains from the sea.[32] All life is seated in God, as in its proper throne, in its most perfect purity. God is life; it is in him originally, radically, therefore eternally. He is a pure act, nothing but vigor and act; he hath by his nature that life which others have by his grant; whence the Apostle saith (I Tim. 6:16) not only that he is immortal, but he hath immortality in a full possession; fee simple, not depending upon the will of another, but containing all things within himself. He that hath life in himself, and is from himself, cannot but be. He always was, because he received his being from no other, and none can take away that being which was not given by another. If there were any space before he did exist, then there was something which made him to exist; life would not then be in him, but in that which produced him into being; he could not then be God, but that other which gave him being would be God.[33] And to say God sprung into being by chance, when we see nothing in the world that is brought forth by chance, but hath some cause of its existence, would be vain; for since God is a being, chance, which is nothing, could not bring forth something; and by the same reason, that he sprung up by chance, he might totally vanish by chance. What a strange notion of a God would this be! such a God that had no life in himself but from chance! Since he hath life in himself, and that there was no cause of his existence, he can have no cause of his limitation, and can no more be determined to a time, than he can to a place. What hath life in itself, hath life without bounds, and can never desert it, nor be deprived of it; so that he lives necessarily, and it is absolutely impossible that he should not live; whereas all other things "live, and move, and have their being in him" (Acts 17:28); and as they live by his will, so they can return to nothing at his word.

3. If God were not eternal, he were not immutable in his nature. It is contrary to the nature of immutability to be without eternity; for whatsoever begins, is changed in its passing from not

---

32. Petav. Theol. Dogm. Tom. I. lib. i. c. 6, §6, 7.

33. Amyrald de Trinit. p. 48.

being to being. It began to be what it was not; and if it ends, it ceaseth to be what it was; it cannot therefore be said to be God, if there were neither beginning or ending, or succession in it (Mal. 3:6): "I am the Lord, I change not"; (Job 37:23): "Touching the Almighty, we cannot find him out." God argues here, saith Calvin, from his unchangeable nature as Jehovah, to his immutability in his purpose. Had he not been eternal, there had been the greatest change from nothing to something. A change of essence is greater than a change of purpose. God is a sun glittering always in the same glory; no growing up in youth; no passing on to age. If he were not without succession, standing in one point of eternity, there would be a change from past to present, from present to future. The eternity of God is a shield against all kind of mutability. If anything sprang up in the essence of God that was not there before, he could not be said to be either an eternal, or an unchanged substance.

4. God could not be an infinitely perfect Being, if he were not eternal. A finite duration is inconsistent with infinite perfection. Whatsoever is contracted within the limits of time, cannot swallow up all perfections in itself. God hath an unsearchable perfection. "Canst thou by searching find out God? canst thou find out the Almighty unto perfection?" (Job 11:7) He cannot be found out: he is infinite, because he is incomprehensible. Incomprehensibility ariseth from an infinite perfection, which cannot be fathomed by the short line of man's understanding. His essence in regard of its diffusion, and in regard of its duration, is incomprehensible, as well as his action: if God, therefore, had beginning, he could not be infinite; if not infinite, he did not possess the highest perfection; because a perfection might be conceived beyond it. If his being could fail, he were not perfect; can that deserve the name of the highest perfection, which is capable of corruption and dissolution? To be finite and limited, is the greatest imperfection, for it consists in a denial of being. He could not be the most blessed Being if he were not always so, and should not forever remain so; and whatsoever perfections he had, would be soured by the thoughts, that in time they would cease, and so could not be pure affections, because not permanent; but "He is blessed from everlasting to everlasting" (Ps. 41:13). Had he a beginning, he could not have all perfection without limitation; he would have been limited by that which gave him beginning; that which gave him being would be God, and not himself, and so more perfect than he: but since God is the most sovereign perfection, than which nothing can be imagined perfecter by the most capacious un-

derstanding, He is certainly "eternal"; being infinite, nothing can be added to him, nothing detracted from him.

5. God could not be omnipotent, almighty, if he were not eternal. The title of almighty agrees not with a nature that had a beginning; whatsoever hath a beginning was once nothing; and when it was nothing, could act nothing: where there is no being there is no power. Neither doth the title of almighty agree with a perishing nature: he can do nothing to purpose, that cannot preserve himself against the outward force and violence of enemies, or against the inward causes of corruption and dissolution. No account is to be made of man, because "his breath is in his nostrils" (Isa. 2:22); could a better account be made of God, if he were of the like condition? He could not properly be almighty, that were not always mighty; if he be omnipotent, nothing can impair him; he that hath all power, can have no hurt. If he doth whatsoever he pleaseth, nothing can make him miserable, since misery consists in those things which happen against our will.[34] The almightiness and eternity of God are linked together: "I am Alpha and Omega, the beginning and ending, saith the Lord, which was, and which is, and which is to come, the Almighty" (Rev. 1:8): almighty because eternal, and eternal because almighty.

6. God would not be the first cause of all if he were not eternal; but he is the first and the last; the first cause of all things, the last end of all things:[35] that which is the first cannot begin to be; it were not then the first; it cannot cease to be: whatsoever is dissolved, is dissolved into that whereof it doth consist, which was before it, and then it was not the first. The world might not have been; it was once nothing; it must have some cause to call it out of nothing: nothing hath no power to make itself something; there is a superior cause, by whose will and power it comes into being, and so gives all the creatures their distinct forms.[36] This power cannot but be eternal; it must be before the world; the founder must be before the foundation; and his existence must be from eternity; or we must say nothing did exist from eternity:[37] and if there were no being from eternity, there could not now be any being in time. What we see, and what we are, must arise from itself or some other; it cannot from itself: if anything made itself, it had a power to make itself;

---

34. Voet. Natural. Theol. p. 310.
35. Rev. 1:8. Ficin. de Immort. lib. ii. c. 5.
36. Coccei Sum. Theol. c. 8.
37. Crellius de Deo, c. 18. p. 43.

it then had an active power before it had a being; it was something in regard of power, and was nothing in regard of existence at the same time. Suppose it had a power to produce itself, this power must be conferred upon it by another; and so the power of producing itself, was not from itself, but from another; but if the power of being was from itself, why did it not produce itself before? why was it one moment out of being?[38] If there be any existence of things, it is necessary that that which was the "first cause," should "exist from eternity." Whatsoever was the immediate cause of the world, yet the first and chief cause wherein we must rest, must have nothing before it; if it had anything before it, it were not the first; he therefore that is the first cause, must be without beginning; nothing must be before him; if he had a beginning from some other, he could not be the first principle and author of all things; if he be the first cause of all things, he must give himself a beginning, or be from eternity: he could not give himself a beginning; whatsoever begins in time was nothing before, and when it was nothing, it could do nothing; it could not give itself anything, for then it gave what it had not, and did what it could not. If he made himself in time, why did he not make himself before? what hindered him? It was either because he could not, or because he would not; if he could not, he always wanted power, and always would, unless it were bestowed upon him, and then he could not be said to be from himself. If he would not make himself before, then he might have made himself when he would: how had he the power of willing and nilling without a being? Nothing cannot will or nill; nothing hath no faculties; so that it is necessary to grant some eternal being, or run into inextricable labyrinths and mazes. If we deny some eternal being, we must deny all being; our own being, the being of everything about us; unconceivable absurdities will arise. So, then, if God were the cause of all things, he did exist before all things, and that from eternity.

The Uniqueness of God's Eternity

III. Eternity is only proper to God, and not communicable. It is as great a madness to ascribe eternity to the creature, as to deprive the Lord of the creature of eternity.[39] It is so proper to God, that when the apostle would prove the deity of Christ, he proves it by his immutability and eternity, as well as his creating power: "Thou art

---

38. Petav. Theol. Dogmat. Tom. I. lib. i. c. 10, 11.
39. Bapt.

the same, and thy years shall not fail" (Heb. 1:10-12). The argument had not strength, if eternity belonged essentially to any but God; and therefore he is said only to have "immortality" (I Tim. 6:16): all other things receive their being from him, and can be deprived of their being by him: all things depend on him; he of none: all other things are like clothes, which would consume if God preserved them not. Immortality is appropriated to God, *i.e.* an independent immortality. Angels and souls have an immortality, but by donation from God, not by their own essence; dependent upon their Creator, not necessary in their own nature: God might have annihilated them after he had created them; so that their duration cannot properly be called an eternity, it being extrinsical to them, and dependent upon the will of their Creator, by whom they may be extinguished; it is not an absolute and necessary, but a precarious immortality. Whatsoever is not God, is temporary; whatsoever is eternal, is God. It is a contradiction to say a creature can be eternal; as nothing eternal is created, so nothing created is eternal. What is distinct from the nature of God cannot be eternal, eternity being the essence of God. Every creature, in the notion of a creature, speaks a dependence on some cause, and therefore cannot be eternal. As it is repugnant to the nature of God not to be eternal, so it is repugnant to the nature of a creature to be eternal; for then a creature would be equal to the Creator, and the Creator, or the Cause, would not be before the creature, or effect.[40] It would be all one to admit many gods, as many eternals; and all one to say, God can be created, as to say a creature can be uncreated, which is to be eternal.

1. Creation is a producing something from nothing. What was once nothing, cannot therefore be eternal; not being was eternal; therefore its being could not be eternal, for it should be then before it was, and would be something when it was nothing. It is the nature of a creature to be nothing before it was created; what was nothing before it was, cannot be equal with God in an eternity of duration.

2. There is no creature but is mutable, therefore not eternal. As it had a change from nothing to something, so it may be changed from being to not being. If the creature were not mutable, it would be most perfect, and so would not be a creature, but God; for God only is most perfect. It is as much the essence of a creature to be mutable, as it is the essence of God to be immutable. Mutability and eternity are utterly inconsistent.

3. No creature is infinite, therefore not eternal: to be infinite

---

40. Lessius de Perfect. lib. iv. c. 2.

in duration is all one as to be infinite in essence. It is as reasonable to conceive a creature immense, filling all places at once, as eternal, extended to all ages; because neither can be without infiniteness, which is the property of the Deity.[41] A creature may as well be without bounds of places, as limitations of time.

4. No effect of an intellectual free agent can be equal in duration to its cause. The productions of natural agents are as ancient often as themselves; the sun produceth a beam as old in time as itself; but who ever heard of a piece of wise workmanship as old as the wise artificer? God produced a creature, not necessarily and naturally, as the sun doth a beam, but freely, as an intelligent agent. The sun was not necessary; it might be or not be, according to the pleasure of God. A free act of the will is necessary to precede in order of time, as the cause of such effects as are purely voluntary.[42] Those causes that act as soon as they exist act naturally, necessarily, not freely, and cannot cease from acting. But suppose a creature might have existed by the will of God from eternity; yet, as some think, it could not be said absolutely, and in its own nature to be eternal, because eternity was not of the essence of it. The creature could not be its own duration; for though it were from eternity, it might not have been from eternity, because its existence depended upon the free will of God, who might have chose whether he would have created it or no. God only is eternal; "the first and the last, the beginning and the end"; who, as he subsisted before any creature had a being, so he will eternally subsist if all creatures were reduced to nothing. . . .

---

41. Ibid.
42. Crellius de Deo, c. 18, p. 43.

Thomas Manton
1620-1677

5

Man and Sin

One of the most eminent Puritan theologians, Thomas Manton was born at Somerset and educated at Tiverton and at Wadham College, Oxford. He was ordained a deacon at nineteen, and believing this authorized him to preach, he continually refused priest's orders. After three years at Culliton in Devon, he spent seven years ministering at Stoke-Newington, near London. While there he prepared his expositions of James and Jude. During the Revolution, Manton was frequently called to preach before Parliament. In 1653 he succeeded Obadiah Sedgwick as rector of St. Paul's Covent Garden, remaining at this prominent Puritan church until 1662.

Manton became one of Oliver Cromwell's chaplains during the Rebellion, but he promoted the Restoration in 1660 and was chosen as one of the king's chaplains. At the same time he was awarded a D.D. by Oxford at the request of Charles II. In 1662, however, he was ejected with the other nonconformists by the Act of Uniformity. He led the Presbyterians in an attempt to be reinstated, but their request was denied. Manton then opened his rooms in Covent Gardens and preached to a congregation there. When he refused to take the Oxford oath, he was imprisoned for six months, after which he preached wherever he was given opportunity by Puritan congregations.

An outstanding preacher and expositor, like most of the Puritans, Manton was called by James Ussher "one of the greatest preachers in England." Some of his writings were collected and published in five volumes from 1681 to 1701, and *The Works of Thomas Manton, D.D.*, a complete collection, was published in twenty-two volumes from 1870 to 1875. During his lifetime Manton published *Exposition of the Epistle of James* (1651) and *Exposition of the Epistle of Jude* (1658).

In this treatise on the nature of man and sin, Manton shows the complete inability of man to save himself, relating man's condition to both the law and grace. He also presents the Puritan concept of "seeking" God by various means, showing that the Puritans dealt patiently with the unconverted rather than giving up on them prematurely. This selection is one of the finest in this symposium.

Romans 5:6—*For when we were yet without strength, in due time Christ died for the ungodly.*

In this chapter there are two parts: in the first, the apostle lays down the comfortable fruits and privileges of a justified estate; in the second, he argues the firmness of these comforts, because they are so rich that they are scarce credible, and hardly received. The firmness and soundness of these comforts the apostle representeth by a double comparison:—(1.) By comparing Christ with Christ; and (2.) Christ with Adam. Christ with Christ, or one benefit that we have by him with another, from the text to ver. 12; then Christ with Adam, the second Adam with the first, to the end of the chapter.

1. In comparing Christ with Christ, three considerations do occur:—

[1.] The efficacy of his love toward us before justification, with the efficacy of his love toward us after justification. The argument standeth thus: If Christ had a love to us when sinners, and his love prevailed with him to die for us, much more may we expect his love when made friends: if when we were in sin and misery, shiftless and helpless, Christ had the heart to die for us, and to take us with all our faults, will he cast us off after we are justified and accepted with God in him? This love of Christ is asserted in ver. 6, amplified in ver. 7 and 8, and the conclusion is inferred in ver. 9: "Much more then, being now justified by his blood, we shall be saved from wrath through him."

[2.] The second comparison is of the efficacy of the death of Christ, and the efficacy of the life of Christ. It is absurd to think that Christ rising from the dead, and living in heaven, should not be as powerful to save, and bring us to God, as Christ dying was to reconcile us to him.

[3.] The third comparison is the privative mercy, or being saved from hell, with the positive mercy, or obtaining a title to heaven: "And not only so, but we also joy in God through our Lord Jesus Christ, by whom we have now received the atonement," ver. 11.

2. For the comparison between Christ and Adam, the sum of it is, that Christ is more able to save than Adam to destroy, and therefore justified persons need to fear nothing. As Adam was a public person, and root of mankind, so is Christ a public person; for Adam was τύπος τοῦ μέλλοντος, "the figure of him that was to come," ver. 14. Adam was a public person, but a finite person, having no intrinsic value in himself, and only was all us by divine institution; but Christ, beside the institution of God, was an infinite person, and therefore there is a πολλῷ μᾶλλον, a "much more," upon Christ. His sacred virtue exceedeth that cursed influence of Adam in many particulars, amply set down in the latter end of the chapter by the apostle.

The words begin the first comparison. In them,—

1. The condition wherein we are by nature is set forth by two notions—*ungodly*, and *without strength*: the one noteth that we have no worth to move God to help us, for we were "ungodly"; the other, that we have no power to help ourselves, for "we were without strength": we were "without strength," and so need help; "ungodly," and so refused help.

2. The means of our recovery, *Christ died for us.*

3. The seasonableness of our redemption, *in due time.*

For the first notion, whereby our natural estate is expressed, "ungodly," I shall pass it by; the next notion, "without strength," will yield us this point:—

Doct. That man, fallen, is destitute of all power and means of rising again, or helping himself out of that misery into which he hath plunged himself by sin.

This will appear, if you consider his condition with respect to the law, or with respect to the gospel, and those terms of grace which God offers in Christ. The former more properly falls under the consideration of this place; but, because of the method of this exercise, you expect the discussion of the latter also, I shall take occasion from hence to speak of that.

Man's Condition
with Respect to the Law

First, With respect to the law. That will be understood by a view of that scripture that expresseth the tenor of the law: "Cursed is every one that continueth not in all the words of this law to do them," Gal. 3:10; where is considerable,—

1. The duty it exacts.
2. The penalty it inflicts.
3. The operation that both these have upon the fallen creature.

1. The duty it exacts. An innocent nature, that is presupposed; for the person must "continue." It doth not say, "now begin"; the sentence of the law doth not suppose man as lapsed and fallen, or as having already broken with God; but as in a good and sound estate. And then universal, perpetual, perfect obedience is indispensably required: he must "continue in all things" with all his heart, and that continually; if he fails in one point, he is gone. This is personally exacted of all men, as long as they abide under Adam's covenant: "He that doeth them shall live in them"; and "the soul that sinneth, it shall die," Ezek. 18:4; 20:11. Now if God should call us to an account for the most inoffensive day that ever we passed over, what would become of us? "If thou shouldest mark iniquities, O Lord, who could stand?"[1] Ps. 130:3. Better never born, than to be liable to that judgment, when the law shall take the sinner "by the throat," and say, "Pay me that thou owest," Matt. 18:28. What shall the poor wretch do? So that here we are "without strength," altogether unable to come up to the obedience of the law of works. The law can make nothing perfect, because it is become "weak through our flesh," Rom. 8:3. To fallen man it establisheth a course of punishing sin, not of taking away sin: we may increase the debt, but we cannot lessen it. If our obedience were exact for the future (let us suppose it), yet the paying of new debts doth not quit old scores. They that could not keep themselves when entire and innocent, cannot recover themselves when lost and fallen.

2. The penalty it inflicts: "Cursed is every one." How cursed? Cursed in all that he hath, Deut. 28:15-18. All his enjoyments become a snare, and temporal comforts do but harden him, and prepare him for a greater misery. Cursed in all that he doeth: his prayer is turned into sin; his hearing, the "savour of death unto death"; all his toil and labour in outward service is to no purpose: "The sacri-

---

1. That is, *rectus in curiâ*—be able to make a bold defence.

fice of the wicked is abomination: how much more when he bringeth
it with a wicked mind?" Prov. 21:27. At the best it is but an "abomination." God will not accept an offering at his hands; much more
when it is polluted with sinful and evil aims. But this is not all;
he is cursed for evermore: the law bindeth him over, body and soul,
to everlasting torments; and in time he shall hear that dreadful
sentence, "Depart from me, ye cursed, into everlasting fire, prepared
for the devil and his angels," Matt. 25:41. There is but the slender
thread of a frail life that hinders the execution of this sentence upon
him: a sinner stands upon the very brink of hell, and ever and
anon is ready to be cast in; where he shall eternally lie under the
wrath of God. So that here we are "without strength," because we
cannot satisfy the justice of God for one sin, but are always satisfying, and can never be said to have satisfied; like a poor man that
pays a debt of a thousand pounds by a farthing a week.

3. Consider how this works with him. An exaction of duty under
so severe a penalty doth either terrify or stupefy the conscience; he
that escapeth the one suffereth the other; or else, thirdly, doth irritate
corruption; or, fourthly, obtrude us upon a sottish despair, so as to
give over all endeavours and hope of salvation.

First, Sometimes it terrifieth. That is easily done; the conscience
of a sinner is a sore place; they are "all their lifetime subject to bondage," Heb. 2:15. There is a hidden fear in the heart of a wicked
man, not always felt, but soon awakened, either by a sound conviction from the word, or some sore judgment, or by the agonies of
death, or serious thoughts of the world to come. Felix trembled when
Paul did but mention God's "judgment," Acts 24:25; the prisoner
makes the judge tremble. A sinner is afraid to think of his condition, if God do but a little break in upon his heart: do what he can,
he lies under the bondage of a wounded spirit, and wherever he
goes, like the devils, he carrieth his own hell about with him.

Secondly, If it terrifieth not the conscience, it stupefieth the conscience, that they grow senseless of their misery, "past feeling," Eph.
4:19. And that is a dangerous crisis and estate of soul, when once a
man comes to that, and goeth like a fool to the correction of the stocks.

Thirdly, It irritateth their inbred corruption: "The commandment
came," that is, in full conviction and power, and "sin revived, and
I died," Rom. 7:9. The more we understand of the necessity of our
subjection to God, the more opposite is the soul to him; as a dam
makes a river or strong stream the more violent, or as a bullock at
the first yoking becometh the more unruly. Or,

Fourthly, It breedeth a sottish despair: "There is no hope; therefore we will walk after our own devices, and do every one according to the evil imaginations of our own heart," Jer. 18:12. It is to no purpose to speak to us, or strive further about us; as if they had said, There is no hope; and therefore we will live as we list, without any further care of turning to God. This is the worst kind of despair, when a man is given up to his "own heart's lust," Ps. 81:12, and runneth headlong in the way of destruction, without hope of returning. There is more hope of them that are under despairing fears or a terrified conscience than there is of those who are under despairing resolutions or a stupid and sottish obstinacy. Thus as to the law, man is helpless.

Man's Condition with Respect to the Gospel

Secondly, Consider man as to terms of grace offered in the gospel. He is still "without strength"; not only in a damnable condition by the law, but, without grace, unable to accept the gospel. This will appear by two considerations:—

1. By those emphatical terms of scripture by which the case and cure of man are set forth.

2. By those positive assertions whereby all power is denied to man to convert himself to God, or to do anything that is spiritually good.

1. Those emphatical expressions which represent his case and his cure.

[1.] His case. The scripture sets forth man's condition thus: that he is born in sin, Ps. 51:5; and things natural are not easily altered. Greedy of sin: "He drinketh in iniquity like water," Job. 15:16; it noteth a vehement propension, as greedy to sin as a thirsty man to drink. Thirst is the most implacable appetite; hunger is far better borne. But this, you will say, is but now and then, in a great temptation or vehement passion. No; "Every imagination of the thoughts of his heart is" evil, "only evil," and that "continually," Gen. 6:5. By how many aggravating and increasing circumstances is man's sin there set forth! There is in him a mint always at work: his mind coining evil thoughts, his heart evil desires, and carnal motions; and his memory is the closet and storehouse wherein they are kept. But may not a man be reclaimed? is not this his bondage and trouble? No; his heart is a heart of stone, Ezek. 36:26; that is, inflexible, insensible. When God useth the word, some common motions of his Spirit, some rousing providences, yet all is in vain; for man's "heart is deceitful above all things, and desperately wicked," Jer. 17:9;

inventing shifts and excuses to avoid God, and to cheat itself of its own happiness. But is not the New Testament more favourable than the Old? or is not man grown better, since there was so much grace discovered? I answer—No; there is a perfect harmony between the Testaments; there you will find man represented as a "child of wrath by nature," Eph. 2:3, even the elect as well as others to be a "servant of sin," Rom. 6:17. Never such an imperious master, never such a willing servant: sin never leaveth commanding, and we love the work. You will find him again expressed as one averse from God, "alienated from his life," Eph. 4:18. It is a melancholy thought to a carnal heart to think of the life of God. As an enemy to the law, Rom. 8:7; one that neither can nor will please God. As "blind," and knoweth not what to do, II Peter 1:9; and this blindness spiritual is worse than bodily. A man that is blind in body seeketh for a fit guide; as Elymas, when he was stricken blind, "sought about for one to lead him by the hand," Acts 13:11. As weak and "without strength," here in the text; yea, stark "dead in trespasses and sins," Eph. 2:1-5; yea, worse than dead: a dead man doeth no more hurt, his evil dieth with him; but there is a life of resistance and rebellion against God that goeth along with this death in sin. Now, put all this together, and you may spell out man's misery, what a wretched, impotent creature he is in his natural estate. The scripture does not speak this by glances or short touches; neither is it a hyperbole used once or twice, but everywhere, where it professedly speaks of this matter. Certainly man contributeth little to his own conversion: he cannot "hunger and thirst" after Christ that "drinks in iniquity like water"; there is nothing in nature to carry him to grace who is altogether sinful. If the scripture had only said that man had accustomed himself to sin, and was not "born in sin"; that man was somewhat prone to iniquity, and not "greedy" of it; and did often think evil, and not "continually"; that man was somewhat obstinate, and not a "stone," an "adamant"; if the scripture had only said that man was indifferent to God, and not a professed "enemy"; if a captive of sin, and not a "servant"; if only weak, and not "dead"; if only a neuter, and not a "rebel";—then there might be something in man, and the work of conversion not so difficult. But the scripture saith the quite contrary.

[2.] The cure. Certainly to remedy so great an evil requires an almighty power, and the all-sufficiency of grace; therefore it is good to see how conversion is described in scripture. Sometimes by enlightening the mind: "And the eyes of your understandings being enlightened," &c., Eph. 1:18. Man, the wisest creature on this side

heaven, is stark blind in the things of God. Though he hath the
light of nature, and can put on the spectacles of art, and dress his
notions of divine things by the glass of the word, yet ere the cure is
wrought, something must be done upon the faculty: the eyes of our
understandings must be enlightened, as well as the object revealed.
Ay! but this infusion of light is not all; the scripture speaks of opening the heart: "He opened the heart of Lydia," Acts 16:14. God
doth not only knock at the heart, but open it. He knocks many
times by the outward means, but finds no entrance. Yea, as one that
would open a door,—he tries key after key, till he hath tried all the
keys in the bunch; so does God use means after means; but till he
putteth his fingers upon the handles of the lock, Song of Sol. 5:4, 5,
the door is not opened to him. Well, then, the mind must be enlightened, and the heart opened. If these words are not emphatical
enough, you will find conversion expressed by regeneration: "Except
a man be born again, he cannot see the kingdom of God," John 3:3.
Mark, we must not only be reformed, but regenerated. Now because
generation is an ordinary work of nature, and often falls out in the
course of second causes, therefore it is expressed by the metaphor
of resurrection, Eph. 2:5. But that which hath been may be again;
therefore it is called a creation: "We are" ποίημα αὐτοῦ, "his workmanship," Eph. 2:10; II Cor. 4:6; 5:17; Ps. 51:10. Yea, further it is
expressed by victory, I John 4:4; or the beating and binding of the
"strong man," by one that is "stronger than he," Luke 11:21, 22;
by "bringing into captivity every proud thought," II Cor. 10:5. All
these expressions doth the scripture use to set out the mystery of
grace. One expression may not enough be heeded, and therefore are
many types and figures of it used, that what is wanting in one notion
may be supplied by another. As let us gather them up a little. There
must be not only light in the mind, but the heart must be moved;
and that not a little stirred, but changed, fashioned anew, born again.
And because generation supposeth a previous disposition in the matter, not only is it called "regeneration," but the term "resurrection"
is used, in which the matter is wholly unprepared. But yet because
still here is matter to work upon, therefore it is called creation, which
was a making all things out of nothing. God works faith where there
is no faith, and repentance where was no repentance; "and calleth
the things that are not as though they were." But now because sin
makes us worse than nothing, and as in creation, as there was nothing
to help, so there was nothing to resist and hinder, therefore it is
expressed by victory; implying the opposition of God's work, and

the resistance that there is in the heart of man till it be overpowered by grace.

2. The next proof is from those assertions whereby all power is denied to man to convert himself to God, or to do anything that is spiritually good. As when it is said he cannot know, I Cor. 2:14; he cannot believe, John 6:44; he cannot obey, Rom. 8:7. Nay, to instance in single acts: he cannot think a good thought of himself, II Cor. 3:5; he cannot speak a good word: "How can ye, being evil, speak good things?" Matt. 12:34. He cannot do anything, John 15:5. He doth not say, *nihil magnum,* but *nihil;* not "no great thing," but "Without me ye can do *nothing.*" Well, then, when man can neither know, nor believe, nor obey, nor think, nor speak, nor do anything without grace, surely man is "without strength," wholly impotent and unable to turn himself to God.

Obj. 1. But here is an objection: If it be so, how can these things stand with the mercy of God, as the Creator of mankind, to require the debt of him that is not able to pay? with the justice of God, as the judge of the world, to punish him with eternal death for the neglect of that which he could not perform? or with the wisdom of the supreme lawgiver, to exhort him by promises who hath no power to do what he is exhorted unto?

Ans. 1. I answer to the first—God doth not lose his right, though man hath lost his power; their impotency doth not dissolve their obligation; a drunken servant is a servant, and it is against all reason that the master should lose his right to command by the servant's default. A prodigal debtor, that hath nothing to pay, yet is liable to be sued for the debt without any injustice. God contracted with us in Adam; and that obedience which he requireth is not only due by covenant, but by law; not only by positive law and contract, but by immutable right. It is harsh, men think, to suffer for Adam's fault, to which they were not conscious and actually consenting; but every man will find an Adam in his own heart: the old man is there, wasting away the few remains of natural light and strength. And shall not God challenge the debt of obedience from a debtor that is both proud and prodigal? We are proud; for when we are miserable, we think ourselves happy; and when we are poor, we think ourselves rich; and when we are blind, we conceit ourselves very seeing; and when we are naked, we think ourselves well clad, Rev. 3:17. And therefore God may admonish us of our duty, and demand his right; if for no other reason but to show us our impotency, and that we may not pretend that we were not called upon for what we owe. And as man is proud, so he is prodigal. We spend what is left, and throw away those relics of conscience and moral inclinations which escaped out of the ruins of the fall.

Ans. 2. As to the second, how God can with justice punish him for the neglect of what he could not do, I answer—Our natural impotency is voluntary. We must not consider man only as impotent to good, but as delighting in evil, and loving it with all his heart. As man cannot, so he will not, come to God, John 5:40. Our impotency lies in our obstinacy, and so man is left without excuse. We refuse the grace that is offered to us, and by continuing in sin, increase our bondage, our inveterate customs turning to another nature.

Ans. 3. As to the last, how God can exhort and persuade us, for answer, suppose we should say—This is only for the elect's sake, who certainly "are the called according to purpose," Rom. 8:28; whereas others are called *obiter*, "by the by," and as they live intermingled with them. If the elect did dwell alone, and were a distinct community by themselves, the objection were plausible; but they are hidden amongst others, and therefore the reprobate have the like favour in the external means with them. The world standeth for the elect's sake, yet the sun doth not shine upon them alone, nor the showers fall upon their fields alone. Or let me illustrate it thus: The sun shineth, though blind men see it not; the rain falls upon the rocks and mountains, as well as the fruitful valleys: so are exhortations of duty promiscuously tendered to good and bad. This might be answer enough; but that which I rather say is, that these exhortations have their use; for they carry their own blessing with them, to them to whom God means them for good. The word has a ministerial subserviency to the power of God; as when Christ said, "Lazarus, come forth," it raised him out of his grave. As for others that are not converted by them, it is for their conviction, and to bridle their fierceness, and a means to civilise them, and keep them from growing worse, whereby many temporal blessings do accrue to them; as Pagan Rome flourished in all manner of virtue and success as long as moral precepts were in force. But of this more in the next objection.

Obj. 2. If man be so altogether without strength, why do ye press him to the use of means?

Ans. I answer—Though man cannot change himself, yet he is to use the means; and that for several reasons:—

1. That we may practically see our own weakness. Men think the work of grace is easy, till they put themselves upon a trial: the lameness of the arm is found in exercise: "Apply thy heart to understanding," then "cry for knowledge," Prov. 2:2, 3. Whosoever sets

himself in good earnest to get any grace, will be forced to cry for it before he hath done. We never seek strength at God's hands in so feeling a manner, till our experience convince us of our weakness. When a man goes to lift up a piece of timber heavy above his strength, he is forced to call in help.

2. The use of the means we owe to God, as well as the change of the heart. We lie under a moral obligation to use them. God, that hath required faith and conversion, hath required prayer, hearing, reading, meditating; and we are bound to obey, though we know not what good will come of it: as Abraham obeyed God, "not knowing whither he went," Heb. 11:8; and Peter, when there was little hope, saith, "Howbeit, at thy command," &c., Luke 5:5. Our great rule is, we are to do what he commandeth, and let God do what he will.

3. To lessen our guilt. For when men do not use the means, they have no excuse: it is plain laziness and want of will, not want of power, when we will not so much as try to come out of our condition; we love our bondage, and shut the door upon ourselves; or, as that phrase, "judge ourselves unworthy of eternal life," Acts 13:46; pass sentence upon our own souls. It is a sign we care not whether God show us mercy, yea, or no; for you will not so much as bestow a thought upon it; you come under the censure of wicked and slothful servants, Matt. 25:26.

4. There is encouragement in the use of means many ways.

[1.] If we do not something, we shall grow worse. Standing pools are apt to putrefy. Man is of an active nature, either growing better or worse: when we do not improve nature, we deprave it: "They corrupt themselves in what they know naturally," Jude 10. Voluntary neglects draw on penal hardness; and so your impotency is increased. There is this benefit of using means—it prevents much sin and hardness of heart: it is like the embalming of a dead body; it keeps it from stinking, though it does not restore life.

[2.] Without the use of means they can never hope for anything: "How shall they believe without a preacher?" Rom. 10:14. If ever I meet with God, with Christ, it must be in this way; it is good to lie at the pool, as the poor man did who was unable to get in when the angel stirred the waters, John 5:3-5. Marriage is instituted for the propagation of mankind, yet the soul is of God only. No man abstaineth from marriage because he cannot beget a reasonable soul. So grace is of God; but hearing, reading, praying, are the instituted means; and we must not abstain from these means because grace is not of ourselves, but God.

[3.] It may be God will meet with us. It is the ordinary practice of his free grace so to do; and it is good to make trial upon a common hope: "Pray God, if perhaps the thought of thine heart may be forgiven thee," Acts 8:22. There is a great uncertainty, yet pray; it is God's usual way to meet with them that seek him: "I say unto you, Though he will not rise and give him because he is his friend, yet because of his importunity he will rise and give him as many as he needeth," Luke 11:8: "for his importunity's sake," διὰ τὴν ἀναίδειαν, "for his impudence."[2] God is not engaged; but who knows what importunity may do? He may, and he may not, give grace; but usually he doth. It is God's usual way to bless man's industry; and yet all they that labour have not an absolute certainty of success. Who would forbear ploughing, because in one year of ten there may happen a dearth or a lean harvest? Act; God may come in (for usually he doth) with his influence and blessing.

Let me now give you some reasons why God permits this weakness and want of strength to lie upon the fallen creature.

1. To exalt the freeness and power of his grace. First, The freeness of his grace; for God hath shut up all under the curse, that there may be no way of escape but by his mercy; their eternal ruin and damnation is else certain and inevitable: "God hath concluded them all under unbelief, that he might have mercy upon all," Rom. 11:32. Συνέκλεισε, that is the word: the state of unbelief is there compared to a prison, made sure and fast with iron bars and bolts; and by God's permission man hath "shut up" himself in such a prison that mercy alone might open the door to him. Jew and Gentile lie fast bound with a chain that can be loosened by no hand but God's. So, Gal. 3:22: "The scripture hath concluded all under sin, that the promise by faith of Jesus Christ might be given to them that believe": it is the same word and notion: we may mourn and sigh through the grates of the flaming prison, but can never get out till God look upon us in mercy through Christ. And so also the power of his grace in rescuing us out of this misery: it is a mighty power that works in them that believe, Eph. 1:19. When we consider it, we may wonder at it that ever such a change should be wrought in us that are so carnal, so obstinate: "Who hath called us out of darkness into his marvellous light," I Peter 2:9. It is indeed marvellous that ever we should get out of the prison of sin; more miraculous than Peter's getting out of prison, having so many chains, and doors, and keepers upon him, Acts 12.

---

2. And so fitly expressing our restlessness in the use of means.

2. To humble the creature thoroughly by a sense of his own guilt, unworthiness, and nothingness. In our natural state we are "ungodly" and "without strength." Why has God permitted it? "That every mouth may be stopped, and all the world may become guilty before God, ὑπόδικος τῷ θεῷ, Rom. 3:19, liable to the process of his revenging justice; and so to humble us for our inability and obstinacy, that we may go complainingly to God, saying, "Lord, I am as a bullock unaccustomed to the yoke," Jer. 31:18. Whosoever hath passed this trial, doth sensibly find it.

Use of all.

1. To the unconverted,—to be sensible of their condition, and mourn over it to God. Acknowledge the debt; confess your impotency; beg pardon and grace; and, in a humble sense of your misery, endeavour earnestly to come out of it. By such doctrines as these men are either "cut at heart," Acts 7:54, or "pricked at heart," Acts 2:37, which is the far more kindly work. Some men's hearts and lusts are exasperated; and they rage and storm when they are warned of their danger by a closer application. Oh! it is better to bemoan yourselves, than fret against the Lord, and yield to a sottish despair. There is some hope when conviction ends in groaning rather than murmuring; and you do not fret against the Lord's sovereignty, but complain to him of the naughtiness of your hearts, begging his grace for Christ's sake. Therefore go and lie at his feet, and say, Lord, I have a blind mind, a froward heart; none more. I shall never of myself fly the evil forbidden, perform the good commanded, renounce these bewitching lusts, take up such a course of service to thy blessed majesty. Oh! take away this stony, untractable heart! &c. You are in prison, but you are "prisoners of hope," if you do so.

2. To press the converted to thankfulness. We were once in such a pitiful case, till God plucked us as brands out of the burning; we were utterly miserable and destitute of all good. Oh! blessed be God, that opened the prison-door, and proclaimed deliverance by Christ to poor captives; and not only proclaimed it, but wrought it for us: none but an Almighty arm could loosen the bolts, and shoot back the many locks that were upon us. Peter, when the angel made his chains fall off, "considered" the matter, Acts 12:12, and went to give thanks among the saints. Oh! when there were so many doors and bolts upon you, such difficulties and disadvantages in the way of your conversion, consider it, and bless God for your escape: "Blessed be the Lord, that gave me counsel in my reins," Ps. 16:7.

3. Let us compassionate others that are in this estate. Poor souls!

in what a sad condition are they! We have not usually such a deep sense of their misery as we should have. Israel was to pity strangers, because they were once strangers in the land of Egypt: we ourselves have been in the house of bondage. Oh! pity poor captive souls. Especially doth this concern the ministry; they that do *induere personam Christi,* that "stand in the stead of Christ," should *induere viscera Christi,* "put on the bowels of Christ": "God is my record how greatly I long after you all in the bowels of Christ Jesus," Phil. 1:8. When we were "ungodly," and "without strength, Christ died for" sinners; and wilt not thou labour for them, and employ thy talent to edification? Oh! if we had more weighty thoughts about the worth and danger of souls, we would not do the Lord's work so sleepily as usually we do; but as "co-workers with God," we would beseech you with all earnestness "not to receive the grace of God in vain," II Cor. 6:1. Every advantage should be taken hold of: as a sinking, perishing man, if it be but a bough in the waters, catcheth at it, so should we press you to improve all closer applications and ministerial helps, and that with compassion and tenderness, as having ourselves been acquainted with the heart of a poor, impotent, captive sinner.

James Ussher
1581-1656

6

Christ

Though not a Puritan as such, James Ussher was a Calvinist and the Puritans esteemed him highly. He was born in Dublin, Ireland, and educated at Trinity College, being one of its first students. Ordained in 1601, he became chancellor of St. Patrick's in 1603. In 1607 he was appointed professor of divinity at Trinity College, and eight years later he became vice chancellor of the University of Dublin. He continued to rise, becoming bishop of Meath (1620), then privy councilor for Ireland (1623), and finally archbishop and primate of Armagh (1625).

Conflicts stemming from the war between Charles I and Parliament forced Ussher to leave Ireland in 1640, and he became a preacher at Lincoln's Inn. This unusual man retained the favor of both the High Church advocates (because he supported the episcopacy and the king) and the Puritans (Cromwell admired him for his learning and Calvinism). He declined a professorship at the University of Leyden, Holland, and spent his last years with the family of Lady Peterborough at Reigate, where he died on 21 March 1656.

His *Annales Vetes et Novi Testamentae* (1650-1654) established him as a Biblical scholar and chronologist. Though outdated now, his chronology was adopted by the King James Version of the Bible.

He also produced *Britannicarum Ecclesiarum Antiquitates* (1639), *De Graeca LXX Versione Syntagma* (1652), *An Answer to a Jesuit in Ireland* (1624), and many other historical and theological works. C. R. Elrington and J. H. Todd edited *The Whole Works of the Most Rev. James Ussher, D.D.*, a seventeen-volume work published 1847-1864.

This selection by Ussher, a study of the incarnation of Christ, discusses the distinction between the person of Christ and His human nature. Ussher clearly regards the virgin birth as the incarnation of deity ("Immanuel"). In the second portion of the essay, he deals with the mediation of Christ, His gathering of God's elect children. His discussion is fluent and well organized, and it includes extensive Scriptural references by way of support. Ussher's work on the incarnation of Christ is one of the finest ever written on this subject.

The holy Prophet, in the Book of the *Proverbs*,[1] poseth all such as have not *learned wisedome, nor knowne the knowledge of the holy*, with this Question. *Who hath ascended up into heaven, or descended? who hath gathered the winde in his fists? who hath bound the waters in a garment? who hath established all the ends of the earth? What is his name, and what is his* SONS *name, if thou canst tell?* To help us herein, the SON Himselfe did tell us, when he was here upon earth, that *None*[2] *hath ascended up to heaven, but he that descended from heaven, even the Son of man which is in heaven.* And that we might not be ignorant of his *name*, the Prophet *Esay* did long before foretell, that *Vnto*[3] *us a Childe is borne, and unto us a Son is given; whose name shall be called Wonderfull, Counseller, The Mighty God, The Everlasting Father, The Prince of Peace.*

Where, if it be demanded, how these things can stand together? that the *Son of man* speaking upon *earth*, should yet at the same instant be *in heaven*? that the *Father of Eternity* should be *borne in time*? and that the *Mighty God* should become a *Childe*; which is the weakest state of Man himselfe? we must call to minde, that the first letter of this great Name, is WONDERFULL. When he appeared of old to *Manoah*, his *name* was *Wonderfull*, and he did wonderously. Iudg. 13:18, 19. But that, and all the wonders that ever were, must

---

1. Prov. 30:3, 4.
2. John 3:13.
3. Isa. 9:6.

give place to the great mystery of his Incarnation, and in respect thereof cease to be wonderfull. for of this worke that may be verified, which is spoken of those wonderfull judgments, that God brought upon Egypt; when he would shew[4] his power, and have his name declared throughout all the earth. *Before[5] them were no such; neither after them shall be the like.*

Neither the creation of all things out of nothing, which was the beginning of the works of God (those six working dayes putting as it were an end to that long Sabbath that never had beginning; wherein the Father, Son, and holy Ghost did infinitely glorifie[6] themselves and rejoyce[7] in the fruition one of another, without communicating the notice thereof unto any creature) nor the Resurrection from the dead and the restauration of all things, the last works that shal go before that everlasting Sabbath (which shall have a beginning, but never shall have end:) neither that first, I say, nor these last, though most admirable peeces of work, may be compared with this; wherein the Lord was pleased to shew the highest pitch (if any thing may be said to be highest in that which is infinite and exempt from all measure and dimensions) of his Wisedome, Goodnesse, Power and Glory.

The Heathen Chaldeans, to a question propounded by the King of *Babel,* make answer; that[8] it was a *rare thing* which he required, and that none other could shew it, *except the Gods, whose dwelling is not with flesh.* But the rarity of this lyeth in the contrary to that which they imagined to be so plain: that he *who[9] is over all, God blessed for ever,* should take our flesh and dwell, or pitch[10] his *tabernacle* with us. That as the glory of God[11] filled the *Tabernacle* (which was a figure[12] of the humane nature of our Lord) with such a kinde of fulnesse, that Moses himselfe was not able to approach unto it; (therein comming short, as in all things,[13] of the Lord of the house)

---

4. Exod. 9:16.
5. Exod. 10:14; 11:6.
6. John 17:5.
7. Prov. 8:30.
8. Dan. 2:11.
9. Rom. 9:5.
10. John 1:14.
11. Exod. 40:34, 35.
12. Heb. 9:9, 11.
13. Heb. 3:3, 6.

and filled the Temple of *Solomon* (a type likewise of the body[14] of our *Prince of Peace*) in such sort[15] that the Priests could not enter therein: so[16] *in him all the fulnesse of the Godhead should dwell bodily.*

And therefore, if of that Temple, built with hands, *Solomon* could say with admiration: *But*[17] *will God in very deed dwell with men on the earth? Behold, heaven and the heaven of heavens can not contain thee; how much lesse this house, which I have built?* of the true Temple, that is not of this building, we may with greater wonderment say with the Apostle, *Without*[18] *controversie, great is the mystery of religion: God was manifested in the flesh.* yea, was made of a Woman, and born of a Virgin. a thing so wonderfull,[19] that it was given for a signe unto unbeleevers seven hundred and forty years before it was accomplished; even a signe of Gods owne choosing, among all the wonders in the depth, or in the heighth above. *Therefore the Lord himselfe shall give you a signe. Behold, a Virgin shall conceive and beare a Son, and shall call his name Immanuel.* Isa. 7:14.

The Person and Natures of Christ

A notable wonder indeed, and great beyond all comparison. That the Son of God should be *made*[20] *of a Woman;* even made of that Woman, which was made[21] by himselfe. That her *wombe* then, and the *heavens*[22] now, should *containe* him, whom *the*[23] *Heaven of Heavens can not containe.* That he who had both Father and Mother, whose pedigree is upon record even up unto *Adam,* who in the fulnesse of time was brought forth in *Bethlehem,* and when hee had finished his course was *cut off out of the land of the living at Ierusalem;* should yet notwithstanding bee in truth, that which his shadow *Melchisedeck* was onely in the conceit of the men of his time, *without*[24] *Father, without Mother, without Pedegree, having neither be-*

---

14. John 2:19, 21.
15. II Chron. 7:1, 2.
16. Col. 2:9.
17. II Chron. 6:18.
18. I Tim. 3:16.
19. Isa. 7:11, 14.
20. Gal. 4:4.
21. John 1:3; Col. 1:16.
22. Acts 3:21.
23. I Kings 8:27.
24. Heb. 7:3 *with* Isa. 53:8 and Mic. 5:2.

ginning of dayes nor end of life. That his Father should bee *greater*[25] than hee; and yet hee his Fathers *equall.*[26] That he *is*,[27] before *Abraham was;* and yet Abrahams birth preceded his, wel-nigh the space of 2000 years. And finally, that hee who was *Davids Son,* should yet be *Davids* Lord: a case[28] which plunged the greatest Rabbies among the Pharisees; who had not yet *learned this wisdom, nor known this knowledge of the holy.*

The untying of this knot dependeth upon the right understanding of the wonderfull conjunction of the divine and humane Nature in the unity of the Person of our Redeemer. For by reason of the strictnesse of this personall union, whatsoever may be verified of either of those Natures, the same may bee truly spoken of the whole Person, from whethersoever of the Natures it be denominated. For the clearer conceiving whereof, we may call to mind that which the Apostle hath taught us touching our Saviour. *In*[29] *him dwelleth all the fulnesse of the Godhead bodily,* that is to say by such a personall and reall union, as doth inseparably and everlastingly conjoyne that infinite Godhead with his finite Manhood in the unity of the selfe-same individuall Person.

Hee in whom that fulnesse dwelleth, is the PERSON: *that* fulnesse which so doth dwell in him, is the NATVRE. Now there dwelleth in him not onely the fulnesse of the *Godhead,* but the *fulnesse* of the *Manhood* also. For we believe him to be both perfect God, begotten of the substance of his Father before all worlds; and perfect Man, made of the substance of his Mother in the fulnes of time. And therefore we must hold, that there are two distinct *Natures* in him: and two so distinct, that they doe not make one compounded nature: but still remaine uncompounded and unconfounded together. But *Hee* in whom the fulnesse of the Manhood dwelleth is not one, and hee in whom the fulnesse of the Godhead, another: but he in whom the fulnesse of both those natures dwelleth, is one and the same *Immanuel,* and consequently it must be believed as firmly, that he is but one *Person.*

And here we must consider, that the divine Nature did not assume an humane Person, but the divine Person did assume an humane Nature: and that of the three divine Persons, it was neither the first

---

25. John 14:28.
26. John 5:18; Phil. 2:6.
27. John 8:58.
28. Matt. 22:42, 43, &c.
29. Col. 2:9.

nor the third that did assume this Nature; but it was the middle Person, who was to be the middle one, that must undertake this mediation betwixt God and us. which was otherwise also most requisite, as well for the better preservation of the integrity of the blessed Trinity in the Godhead, as for the higher advancement of Mankinde by meanes of that relation which the second Person the Mediator did beare unto his Father. For if the fulnesse of the Godhead should have thus dwelt in any humane Person, there should then a fourth Person necessarily have been added unto the Godhead: and if any of the three Persons, beside the second, had been borne of a woman; there should have been two Sons in the Trinity. Whereas now the Son of God and the Son of the blessed Virgin, being but one Person, is consequently but one Sonne; and so no alteration at all made in the relations of the Persons of the Trinity.

Againe, in respect of us, the Apostle sheweth, that for this very end *God*[30] *sent his own* SON, *made of a Woman; that* WE *might receive the adoption of* SONS: and thereupon maketh this inference; *Wherefore thou art no more a Servant but a* SON, *and if a* SON, *then an* HEIRE *of God through Christ.* intimating thereby, that what relation Christ hath unto God by Nature, we being found in him have the same by Grace. By nature he is *the*[31] *onely begotten Son of the Father*: but this is the high grace he hath purchased for us; that *as*[32] *many as received him, to them he gave power*, or priviledge, *to become the Sons of God*, even *to them that believe on his Name*. For although he reserve to himselfe the preheminence, which is due unto him in a peculiar[33] manner, of being *the*[34] *first borne among many brethren*: yet in him, and for him, the rest likewise by the grace of adoption are all of them accounted as *first-borns*.

So God biddeth *Moses* to say unto *Pharaoh: Israel*[35] *is my Son, even my first borne. And I say unto thee; Let my son goe, that he may serve me: and if thou refuse to let him goe; behold I will slay thy sonne,* even *thy first borne*. And the whole *Israel* of God, consisting of Jew and Gentile, is in the same sort described by the Apostle to be *the*[36] *generall assembly and Church of the first borne inrolled*

---

30. Gal. 4:4, 5, 7.
31. John 1:14; 3:16.
32. John 1:12.
33. *Propter quod unumquodq; est tale, illud ipsum est magis tale.*
34. Rom. 8:29.
35. Exod. 4:22, 23.
36. Heb. 12:23.

in heaven. For the same reason that maketh them to be *Sons,* to wit, their incorporation into Christ, the self-same also maketh them to be *first-bornes:* so as (however it fall out by the grounds of our Common Law) by the rule of the Gospel this consequence will still hold true; *if[37] children, then heirs, heires of God and joynt-heires with Christ.* And so much for the SON, the *Person* assuming.

The *Nature* assumed, is *the seed of Abraham,* Heb. 2:16. *the seed of David,* Rom. 1:3. *the seed of the Woman,* Gen. 3:15. the WORD,[38] the second person of the Trinity, being made[39] FLESH, that is to say, *Gods[40] owne Son* being *made of a Woman,* and so becomming truely and really *the[41] fruit of her wombe.* Neither did hee take the substance of our nature onely, but all the properties also and the qualities thereof: so as it might be said of him, as it was of *Elias[42]* and the Apostles;[43] that hee was *a man subject to like passions as wee are.* Yea he subjected himself *in[44] the dayes of his flesh* to the same *weaknesse[45]* which we find in our owne fraile nature, and was compassed with like *infirmities;* and in a word, *in all things was made like unto his brethren,* sin[46] onely excepted. Wherein yet we must consider, that as he took upon him, not an humane *Person,* but an humane *Nature:* so it was not requisite he should take upon him any *Personall* infirmities, such as are, madnesse, blindnesse, lamenesse, and particular kindes of diseases, which are incident to some onely and not to all men in generall; but those alone which doe accompany the whole nature of mankinde, such as are hungring, thirsting, wearinesse, griefe, paine, and mortality.

We are further here also to observe in this our *Melchisedek,[47]* that as he had no *Mother* in regard of one of his natures, so hee was to have no *Father* in regard of the other; but must be borne of a pure and immaculate Virgin, without the helpe of any man.

---

37. Rom. 8:17.

38. I John 5:7.

39. John 1:14.

40. Gal. 4:4.

41. Luke 1:42.

42. James 5:17.

43. Acts 14:15.

44. Heb. 5:7.

45. II Cor. 13:4; Heb. 2:17, 18; 4:15.

46. *Inter Trinitatem, et hominum infirmitatem, et iniquitatem, Mediator factus est homo, non iniquus, sed tamen infirmus: ut ex eo quod non iniquus, jungeretur Deo; ex eo quod infirmus, propinquaret tibi.* Aug. praef. in enarrat. 2. Ps. 29.

47. Heb. 7:3.

And this also was most requisite, as for other respects, so for the exemption of the assumed nature from the imputation and pollution of *Adams* sin. For sin[48] having by that one man entred into the world; every Father becommeth an *Adam* unto his childe, and conveyeth the corruption of his nature unto all those whom he doth beget. Therefore our Saviour assuming the substance of our nature, but not by the ordinary way of natural generation, is thereby freed from all the touch and taint of the corruption of our flesh; which by that means only is propagated from the first man unto his posterity. Whereupon, hee being made *of* man but not *by* man, and so becomming the immediate fruit of the *womb,* and not of the *loyns,* must of necessity be acknowledged to be that[49] HOLY THING, which so was born of so blessed a Mother. Who although she were but the passive and materiall principle of which that precious flesh was made, and the holy Ghost the agent and efficient; yet cannot the man Christ Jesus thereby be made the *Son* of his owne[50] Spirit. because Fathers doe beget their children out of their owne substance: the holy Ghost did not so, but framed the flesh of him, from whom himselfe proceeded, out of the creature of them both, *the*[51] *handmaid of our Lord;* whom from thence *all generations shall call blessed.*

That blessed wombe of hers was the Bride-chamber, wherein the holy Ghost did knit that indissoluble knot betwixt our humane nature and his Deity: the Son of God assuming into the unity of his person that which before hee was not; and yet without change (for so must God still bee) remaining that which he was. whereby it came to passe, that this *holy*[52] *thing which was borne of her,* was indeed and in truth to be *called the* SON OF GOD. Which wonderfull connexion of two so infinitely differing natures in the unity of one person, how it was there effected; is an inquisition fitter for an Angelicall intelligence, than for our shallow capacity to looke after. to which purpose also wee may observe, that in the fabrick of the *Ark* of the Covenant, the posture[53] of the faces of the *Cerubims* toward the *Mercy-seat* (the type of our Savior) was such, as would point unto us, that these are the things which *the Angels desire to stoop*[54] *and look into.*

---

48. Rom. 5:12.

49. Luke 1:35.

50. Gal. 4:6; Rom. 8:9.

51. Luke 1:38, 48.

52. Luke 1:35.

53. Exod. 37:9.

54. I Peter 1:12.

And therefore let that satisfaction, which the Angel gave unto the Mother Virgin (whom it did more especially concerne to move the question, *How[55] may this be?*) content us, *The[56] power of the Highest shall over-shadow thee.* For as the former part of that speech may informe us, that *with[57] God nothing is impossible:* so the latter may put us in minde, that the same God having *over-shadowed* this mystery with his owne vaile, we should not presume with the men of *Bethshemesh[58]* to look into this *Ark* of his; lest for our curiosity wee bee smitten as they were. Onely this wee may safely say, and must firmly hold: that as the distinction of the Persons in the holy Trinity hindreth not the unity of the Nature of the Godhead, although every Person intirely holdeth his owne incommunicable property; so neither doth the distinction of the two Natures in our Mediator any way crosse the unity of his Person, although each nature remaineth intire in it self, and retaineth the properties agreeing thereunto, without[59] any conversion, composition, commixion, or confusion.

When *Moses[60]* beheld the bush burning with fire, and yet no whit consumed, he wondred at the sight, and said; *I will now turne aside, and see this great sight, why the bush is not burnt.* But when God thereupon called unto him out of the midst of the bush, and said, *Draw not nigh hither,* and told him who he was; *Moses* trembled, hid his face, and durst not behold God. Yet although, being thus warned, we dare not draw so nigh; what doth hinder but we may stand aloofe off, and wonder at this great sight? *Our[61] God is a consuming fire;* saith the Apostle: and a question we finde propounded in the Prophet. *Who[62] among us shall dwell with the devouring fire? who amongst us shall dwell with the everlasting burnings?* *Moses* was not like other Prophets, but God[63] spake unto him face to face, as a man speaketh unto his friend: and yet for all that, when he besought the Lord that hee would shew him his glory; he received

---

55. Luke 1:34.

56. Luke 1:35.

57. Luke 1:37.

58. I Sam. 6:19.

59. *Concil. Chalcedonen.* Act. 5. et *apud Evag. lib.* 2. *hist. Eccl.* cap. 4. inconfusè, incomutabilitèr, indivisè, inseparabilitèr. *Jo. Maxentius in Catholicae suae Professionismitio. Concil. Roman. sub Martino I.*

60. Exod. 3:2, 3, 5, 6; Acts 7:31, 32.

61. Heb. 12:29.

62. Isa. 33:14.

63. Num. 12:6, 7, 8; Exod. 33:11.

this answer, *Thou*[64] *canst not see my face: for there shall no man see me, and live.* *Abraham* before him, though a speciall *friend*[65] of God, and the *father*[66] of the faithfull, the children of God; yet held it a great matter that hee should take upon him so much as to speak[67] unto God, being *but dust and ashes.* Yea, the very Angels themselves (*which*[68] *are greater in power and might*) are faine to cover[69] their faces, when they stand before him; as not being able to behold the brightnesse of his glory.

With what astonishment then may we behold our dust and ashes assumed into the undivided unity of Gods owne Person; and admitted to dwell here, as an inmate, under the same roofe? and yet in the midst of those everlasting burnings, the bush to remaine unconsumed, and to continue fresh and green for evermore. Yea, how should not wee with *Abraham* rejoyce to see this day, wherein not onely our nature in the person of our Lord Jesus is found to dwell for ever in those everlasting burnings; but, in and by him, our owne persons also are brought so nigh thereunto, that God[70] doth set his Sanctuary and Tabernacle among us, and dwell with us; and (which is much more) maketh us our selves to be the *house*[71] and the *habitation,*[72] wherein hee is pleased to dwell by his Spirit. according to that of the Apostle: *Ye*[73] *are the temple of the living God, as God hath said; I will dwell in them and walk in them, and I will be their God, and they shall be my people.* and that most admirable prayer, which our Saviour himselfe made unto his Father in our behalfe. *I*[74] *pray not for these alone, but for them also which shall believe on me through their word: that they all may be one, as thou Father art in me, & I in thee, that they also may be one in us; that the world may beleeve that thou hast sent me. I in them, and thou in me, that they may bee made perfect in one; and that the world may know that thou hast sent me, and hast loved them as thou hast loved me.*

---

64. Exod. 33:18, 20.

65. Isa. 41:8; II Chron. 20:7; James 2:23.

66. Rom. 4:11, 16; Gal. 3:7.

67. Gen. 18:27.

68. II Peter 2:11.

69. Isa. 6:2.

70. Lev. 26:11, 12; Ezek. 37:26, 27; Rev. 21:3.

71. Heb. 3:6.

72. Eph. 2:22.

73. II Cor. 6:16.

74. John 17:20, 21, 22, 23.

The Mediatorial Office of Christ

To compasse this conjunction betwixt God and us, he that was to be our JESUS[75] or *Saviour,* must of necessity also be IMMANUEL; which being interpreted is, *God with us.* and therefore in his *Person* to be Immanuel, that is, God dwelling with our flesh; because he was by his *Office* too to be Immanuel, that is, he who must make God to be at one with us. For this being his proper office, to be *Mediator*[76] *between God and men,* he must partake with both: and being from all eternity consubstantiall with his Father, hee must at the appointed time become likewise consubstantiall with his children. *Forasmuch*[77] *then as the children are partakers of flesh and bloud; he also himself likewise took part of the same,* saith the Apostle. We read in the Roman History, that the Sabines and the Romans joyning battell together, upon such an occasion as is mentioned in the last Chapter of the book of *Iudges;* of the children of *Benjamin,* catching every man a wife of the daughters of *Shiloh:* the women being daughters to the one side, and wives to the other, interposed themselves, and took up the quarrell, so that by the mediation of these, who had a peculiar interest in either side, and by whose meanes this new allyance was contracted betwixt the two adverse parties; they who before stood upon highest tearmes of hostility, did[78] not onely entertaine peace, but also joyned themselves together into one body and one state.

God and we were *enemies;*[79] before we were *reconciled to him by his Son.* He that *is to be our*[80] *peace,* and to *reconcile us unto God,* and to *slay this enmity,* must have an interest in both the parties that are at variance, and have such a reference unto either of them, that he may bee able to send this comfortable message unto the sons of men. *Go*[81] *to my brethren, and say unto them: I ascend unto my Father, and your Father; and to my God, and your God.* For as long as he[82]

---

75. Matt. 1:21, 23. See Anselmes *Cur Deus homo.*

76. I Tim. 2:5.

77. Heb. 2:14.

78. *Sic pax facta, foedusque persussun: secutaq; res mira dictu, ut relictis sedibus suis novam in Vrben hostes demigrarent, et cum generis suis avitas opes pro dote sociarent.* L. Flor. histor. Rom. li. 61. c. 1.

79. Rom. 5:10.

80. Eph. 2:14, 16.

81. John 20:17.

82. Heb. 2:11.

is not ashamed to call us brethren; God[83] *is not ashamed to be called our God.* and his entring of our appearance, in his owne name and ours, after this manner; *Behold,*[84] *I, and the children which God hath given me;* is a motive strong enough to appease his Father, and to turne his favourable countenance toward us: as on the other side, when we become unruly and prove rebellious children; no reproofe can be more forcible, nor inducement so prevalent (if there remaine any sparke of grace in us) to make us cast downe our weapons and yeeld, then this. *Doe*[85] *yee thus requite the Lord, O foolish people and unwise? Is not he thy Father that hath bought thee?* and bought thee *not*[86] *with corruptible things, as silver and gold, but with the precious bloud of his own Sonne?*

How dangerous a matter it is to bee at odds with God, old *Eli* sheweth by this maine argument: *If*[87] *one man sinne against another, the Iudge shall judge him: but if a man sinne against the Lord, who shall plead* or *intreat for him?* and *Iob,* before him. *He*[88] *is not a man as I am, that I should answer him, and we should come together in judgement: neither is there any Days-man or Vmpire betwixt us, that may lay his hand upon us both.* If this generall should admit no manner of exception, then were we in a wofull case, and cause to weep much more then S. *Iohn* did in the Revelation; when none[89] *was found in heaven, nor in earth, nor under the earth, that was able to open the booke* which he saw in the right hand of him that sate upon the Throne, *neither to looke thereon.* But as S. *Iohn* was wished there, to refraine his weeping, because the[90] *Lyon of the tribe of* Juda, *the root of* David, *had prevailed to open the booke, and to loose the seven seals thereof:* so he himselfe elsewhere giveth the like comfort unto all of us in particular. *If*[91] *any man sin, we have an Advocate with the Father, Iesus Christ the righteous: and he is a propitiation for our sins; and not for ours only, but also for the sins of the whole world.*

---

83. Heb. 11:16.
84. Heb. 2:13.
85. Deut. 32:6.
86. I Peter 1:17, 18, 19.
87. I Sam. 2:25.
88. Job 9:32, 33.
89. Rev. 5:3, 4.
90. Rev. 5:5.
91. I John 2:1, 2.

For as there[92] is *one God,* so is there *one Mediator between God and men, the man Christ Iesus: who gave himselfe a ransome for all;* and in discharge of this his office of mediation, as the only fit umpire to take up this controversie, was to lay his hand aswell upon God the party so highly offended, as upon *Man* the party so basely offending. In things concerning God, the *Priesthood* of our Mediator is exercised; *For[93] every high Priest is taken from among men, and ordained for men in things pertaining to God.* The parts of his Priestly function are two; *Satisfaction* and *Intercession:* the former whereof giveth contentment to Gods *justice;* the latter solliciteth his *mercy,* for the application of this benefit to the children of God in particular. Whereby it commeth to passe, that God in shewing[94] mercy upon whom he will shew mercy, is yet for his justice no looser: being both *just,[95] and the justifier of him which beleeveth in Iesus.*

By vertue of his *Intercession,* our Mediatour appeareth[96] in the presence of God for us, and maketh[97] request for us. To this purpose, the Apostle noteth, in the IIIIth to the *Hebrewes,* I. *That we have a great high Priest, that is passed into the heavens, Iesus the Son of God.* (vers. 14.) II. That *we have not an high Priest which cannot be touched with the feeling of our infirmities, but was in all things tempted as we are; yet without sin.* (vers. 15.) Betwixt the *having* of such, and the *not having* of such an Intercessor, betwixt the *height* of him in regard of the one, and the *lowlinesse* in regard of his other nature, standeth the comfort of the poore sinner. He must be such a sutor as taketh our case to heart: and therefore in[98] *all things it behoved him to be made like unto his brethren, that he might be a mercifull and faithfull high Priest.* In which respect as it was needfull he should partake with our flesh and bloud, that he might be tenderly affected unto his brethren: so likewise for the obtaining of so great a sute, it behoved he should be most deare to God the Father, and have so great an interest in him, as he might always be sure to be heard[99] in his requests: who therefore could be no other, but

---

92. I Tim. 2:5, 6.
93. Heb. 5:1; 2:17.
94. Rom. 9:15, 16.
95. Rom. 3:26.
96. Heb. 9:24.
97. Rom. 8:34; Heb. 7:25.
98. Heb. 2:17.
99. John 11:42.

he of whom the Father testified from heaven; *This*[100] *is my beloved Son, in whom I am well pleased.* It was fit our Intercessor should be Man, like unto our selves; that we might *boldly*[101] come to him, *and find grace to help in time of need:* it was fit he should be God, that he might *boldly* goe to the Father, without any way disparaging him; as being his *fellow,*[102] and *equall.*[103]

But such was Gods *love* to justice, and *hatred* to sinne; that he would not have his *justice* swallowed up with mercy, nor *sinne* pardoned without the making of fit reparation. And therefore our Mediatour must not looke to procure for us a simple *pardon* without more adoe; but must be a *propitiation*[104] for our sinnes, and redeem us by fine and *ransome:*[105] and so not onely be the master of our *requests,* to intreat the Lord for us; but also take upon him the part of an *Advocate,*[106] to plead full *satisfaction* made by himselfe, as our *surety,*[107] unto all the debt wherewith we any way stood chargeable. Now the *satisfaction* which our surety bound himselfe to perform in our behalfe, was a double *debt:* the principall, and the accessory. The principall debt is obedience to Gods most holy Law: which man was bound to pay as a perpetuall tribute to his Creator, although he had never sinned; but, being now by his owne default became bankrupt, is not able to discharge in the least measure. His surety therefore being to satisfie in his stead, none will be found fit to undertake such a payment, but he who is both God and man. . . .

And now are wee come to that part of Christs mediation, which concerneth the conveyance of the[108] *redemption of* this *purchased possession* unto the sons of men. A deare purchase indeed, which was to bee redeemed with no lesse price than the bloud of the Sonne of God: but what should the purchase of a stranger have beene to us? or what should we have been the better for all this; if we could not derive our descent from the purchaser, or raise some good title whereby wee might estate our selves in his purchase? Now this was

100. Matt. 3:17.
101. Heb. 4:16.
102. Zech. 13:7.
103. Phil. 2:6.
104. Rom. 3:25; I John 2:2; 4:10.
105. Matt. 20:28; I Tim. 2:6. See Job 33:24.
106. I John 2:1.
107. Heb. 7:22.
108. Eph. 1:14.

the manner in former time in *Israel*, concerning redemptions: that unto him who was the next of kinne, belonged the right of being *Goël*,[109] or the *Redeemer*. And *Iob* had before that left this glorious profession of his faith unto the perpetuall memory of all posterity. *I*[110] *know that my Goël or Redeemer liveth, and at the last shall arise upon the dust* (or, *stand upon the earth.) And after this my skin is spent; yet in my flesh shall I see God. Whom I shall see for my selfe, and mine eyes shall behold, and not another* for me. Whereby we may easily understand, that his and our Redeemer was to bee the invisible God; and yet in his assumed flesh made visible even to the bodily eyes of those whom he redeemed. For if he had not thus assumed our *flesh;* how should we have been of his bloud, or claimed any kindred to him? and unlesse the *Godhead* had by a personall union been unseparably conjoyned unto that flesh; how could he therein have been accounted our *next* of kinne?

For the better clearing of which last reason; wee may call to minde that sentence of the Apostle. *The*[111] *first man is of the earth earthy: the second man is the Lord from heaven.* Where, notwithstanding there were many millions of men in the world betwixt these two; yet wee see our Redeemer reckoned *the second man.* and why? but because these two were the onely men who could be accounted the prime fountaines from whence all the rest of mankinde did derive their existence and being. For as all men in the world by meane descents doe draw their first originall *from the first man:* so in respect of a more immediate influence of efficiency and operation doe they owe their being unto *the second man,* as hee is *the Lord from heaven.* This is Gods owne language from *Ieremy. Before*[112] *I formed thee in the belly, I knew thee.* and this is *Davids* acknowledgment, for his part. *Thy*[113] *hands have made me and fashioned me; thou*[114] *hast covered mee in my mothers womb: thou*[115] *art he that took me out of my mothers bowels.* and *Iobs*, for his also. *Thy*[116] *hands have made me and fashioned me together round about: thou hast cloathed me with skin and flesh, and hast fenced me with bones and sinews.* and

---

109. Ruth 3:12; 4:1, 3, 4, 7.
110. Job 19:25, 26, 27.
111. I Cor. 15:47.
112. Jer. 1:5.
113. Ps. 119:73.
114. Ps. 139:13.
115. Ps. 71:6.
116. Job 10:8, 11.

the Apostles[117] for us all: *In him we live, and move, and have our being.* who inferreth also thereupon, both that *we are the off spring or generation of God;* and that *he is not farre from every one of us.* this being to bee admitted for a most certaine truth (notwithstanding the opposition of all gaine-sayers) that God[118] doth more immediately concurre to the generation and all other motions of the creature, then any naturall agent doth or can doe. And therefore, *if*[119] *by one mans offence, death reigned by one; much more they which receive abundance of grace and of the gift of righteousnesse, shall reigne in life by one, Iesus Christ.* Considering that this *second* man is not onely as universall a principle of all our beings, as was that *first,* and so may sustaine the common person of us all, as well as he; but is a farre more immediate agent in the production thereof: not, as the *first,* so many generations removed from us, but more neere unto us then our very next progenitors; and in that regard justly to be accounted our next of kinne, even before them also.

Yet is not this sufficient neither: but there is an other kinde of generation required, for which wee must bee beholding unto *the second man, the Lord from Heaven;* before we can have interest in this purchased *Redemption.* For as the guilt of the *first mans* transgression is derived unto us by the meanes of carnall generation: so must the benefit of the *second mans* obedience be conveyed unto us by spirituall regeneration. And this must be laid downe as a most undoubted verity: that, *except*[120] *a man bee borne againe, hee cannot see the kingdome of God;* and that every such must bee *borne,*[121] *not of bloud, nor of the will of the flesh, nor of the will of man, but of God.* Now, as our Mediator in respect of the Adoption of Sonnes, which hee hath procured for us, is not ashamed to call us *Brethren:*[122] so in respect of this new birth, whereby hee begetteth us to a spirituall and everlasting life, he disdaineth not to owne us as his *Children.* When *thou*[123] *shalt make his seed an offering for sinne, hee shall see his seed:* saith the Prophet *Esaias. A*[124] *seed shall serve him; it*

---

117. Acts 17:27, 28, 29.
118. See Bradwardin. de causâ Dei, lib. 1. cap. 3. et 4.
119. Rom. 5:17.
120. John 3:3.
121. John 1:13.
122. Heb. 2:11.
123. Isa. 53:10.
124. Ps. 22:30.

shall be accounted to the Lord for a generation: saith his Father *David* likewise of him. And he himselfe, of himselfe: *Behold*[125] *I, and the children which God hath given me.* Whence the Apostle deduceth this conclusion: *Forasmuch*[126] *then as the children are partakers of flesh and bloud, he also himselfe likewise took part of the same.* He himself, that is, he who was God equall to the Father: for who else was able to make this *new*[127] *creature,* but the same God[128] that is the Creator of all things? (no lesse power being requisite to the effecting of this, then was at the first to the producing of all things out of nothing:) and these new babes[129] being to be *born*[130] *of the Spirit;* who could have power to send the *Spirit,* thus to beget them, but the Father and the Son from whom hee proceeded? the same blessed Spirit, who framed the naturall body of our Lord in the womb of the Virgin, being to new mould and fashion every member of his mysticall body unto his similitude and likenesse.

For the further opening of which mystery (which went beyond the apprehension of *Nicodemus,*[131] though a *master of Israel*) we are to consider; that in every perfect generation, the creature produced receiveth two things from him that doth beget it: *Life* and *Likenesse.* A curious Limmer draweth his own sons pourtraicture to the life (as we say:) yet because there is no true life in it, but a likenesse onely; hee cannot be said to be the begetter of his Picture, as he is of his Son. And some creatures there be that are bred out of mud or other putrid matter: which although they have life, yet because they have no correspondence in likenesse unto the principle from whence they were derived, are therefore accounted to have but an improper and equivocall generation. Whereas in the right and proper course of generation (others being esteemed but monstrous births that swarve from that rule) every creature begetteth his life:

> ———*nec imbellem feroces*
> *Progenerant aquilae columbam.*

Now touching our spirituall death and life, these sayings of the

---

125. Heb. 2:13.
126. Heb. 2:14.
127. II Cor. 5:17; Eph. 2:10; Gal. 6:15.
128. John 1:13; James 1:18; I Peter 1:3; I John 5:1.
129. I Peter 2:2 with 1:22.
130. John 3:5, 6, 8.
131. John 3:4, 9, 10.

Apostle would be thought upon. *We*[132] *thus judge, that if one dyed for all, then were all dead: and that he dyed for all, that they which live, should not henceforth live unto themselves, but unto him which dyed for them and rose again. God*[133] *who is rich in mercy, for his great love wherwith he loved us, even when we were dead in our sins, hath quickned us together with Christ. And*[134] *you being dead in your sins, and the uncircumcision of your flesh, hath he quickned together with him, having forgiven you all trespasses. I*[135] *am crucified with Christ. Neverthelesse I live, yet not I, but Christ liveth in mee: and the life which I now live in the flesh, I live by the faith of the Sonne of God, who loved mee and gave himselfe for me.* From all which wee may easily gather, that if by the obedience and sufferings of a bare man, though never so perfect, the most soveraigne medicine that could be thought upon should have beene prepared for the curing of our wounds: yet all would bee to no purpose, wee being found dead, when the medicine did come to be applyed.

Our Physitian therefore must not onely bee able to restore us unto health, but unto life it selfe: which none can doe but the Father, Son, and holy Ghost; one God, blessed for ever. To which purpose, these passages of our Saviour also are to be considered. *As*[136] *the Father hath life in himselfe: so hath he given to the Son to have life in himselfe. As*[137]*the living Father hath sent me, and I live by the Father: so he that eateth me, even he shall live by me. I*[138] *am the living bread, which came downe from heaven; if any man eat of this bread, he shall live for ever: and the bread that I will give, is my flesh, which I will give for the life of the world.* The substance whereof is briefly comprehended in this saying of the Apostle: *The*[139] *last Adam was made a quickening spirit.* An *Adam* therefore and perfect Man must he have been; that his flesh, given for us upon the Crosse, might be made the conduict to conveigh life unto the world: and *a quickning spirit* he could not have been, unlesse he were *God,* able to make that flesh an effectuall instrument of life by

---

132. II Cor. 5:14, 15.
133. Eph. 2:4, 5.
134. Col. 2:13.
135. Gal. 2:20.
136. John 5:26.
137. John 6:57.
138. John 6:51.
139. I Cor. 15:45.

the operation of his blessed Spirit. For, as himselfe hath declared, *It*[140] *is the spirit that quickneth;* without it, *the flesh would profit nothing.*

As for the point of similitude and likenesse: we reade of *Adam,* after his fall, that he *begat*[141] *a sonne in his own likenesse, after his image.* and generally, as well touching the carnall as the spirituall generation, our Savior hath taught us this lesson, *That*[142] *which is borne of the flesh, is flesh; and that which is borne of the spirit, is spirit.* Whereupon the Apostle maketh this comparison betwixt those who are borne of that first man, who is of the earth earthy, and of the second man, who is the Lord from heaven. *As*[143] *is the earthy, such are they that are earthy; and as is the heavenly, such are they also that are heavenly: and as wee have borne the image of the earthy, wee shall also beare the image of the heavenly.* We shall indeed hereafter beare it in full perfection: when *the*[144] *Lord Iesus Christ shall change our base body, that it may be fashioned like unto his glorious body; according to the working, whereby he is able even to subdue all things unto himselfe.* Yet in the meane time also, such a conformity is required in us unto that heavenly man, that *our*[145] *conversation must be in heaven, whence we looke for* this Saviour: and that we must *put*[146] *off, concerning the former conversation, that old man, which is corrupt according to the deceitfull lusts, and bee renued in the spirit of our mind; and put on the new man, which after God is created in righteousnesse and true holinesse.* For as in one particular point of domesticall authority, *the*[147] *Man is said to be the image and glory of God, and the Woman the glory of the man:* so in a more universall manner is *Christ* said to bee *the*[148] *image of God,* even *the*[149] *brightnesse of his glory, and the expresse image of his person;* and we *to*[150] *be conformed to his image, that he might be the first-*

---

140. John 6:63.
141. Gen. 5:3.
142. John 3:6.
143. I Cor. 15:48, 49.
144. Phil. 3:21.
145. Phil. 3:20.
146. Eph. 4:22, 23, 24.
147. I Cor. 11:7.
148. II Cor. 4:4.
149. Heb. 1:3.
150. Rom. 8:29.

borne among those *many brethren,* who in that respect are accounted *the*[151] *glory of Christ.*

We read in the holy story, that God *tooke*[152] *of the spirit which was upon* Moses, *and gave it unto the seventy Elders;* that they might beare the burden of the people with him, and that hee might not beare it, as before he had done, himselfe alone. It may be, his burden being thus lightned, the abilities that were left him for government were not altogether so great, as the necessity of his former imployment required them to have been: and in that regard, what was given to his assistants, might perhaps be said to be taken from him. But we are sure the case was otherwise in him of whom now we speake: unto whom *God*[153] *did not* thus *give the Spirit by measure.* And therefore although so many millions of beleevers doe continually receive this *supply*[154] *of the Spirit of Iesus Christ;* yet neither is that fountaine any way exhausted, nor the plenitude of that well-spring of grace any whit impaired or diminished: it being Gods pleasure *That*[155] *in him should all fulnesse dwell;* and that *of*[156] *his fulnesse all we should receive, grace for grace.* That as in the naturall generation there is such a correspondence in all parts betwixt the begetter and the Infant begotten; that there is no member to be seen in the Father, but there is the like answerably to be found in the childe, although in a farre lesse proportion: so it falleth out in this spirituall, that for every grace which in a most eminent manner is found in Christ, a like grace will appeare in Gods Childe, although in a farre inferiour degree; similitudes and likenesses being defined by the Logicians to bee comparisons made in *qualitie,* and not in *quantitie.*

Wee are yet further to take it into our consideration, that by thus enlivening and fashioning us according to his owne image, Christs purpose was not to raise a seed unto himselfe, dispersedly and distractedly, but to *gather*[157] *together in one, the Children of God that were scattered abroad;* yea and to *bring*[158] *all unto one head by himselfe, both them which are in Heaven and them which are on the Earth.*

---

151. II Cor. 8:23.
152. Num. 11:17, 25.
153. John 3:34.
154. Phil. 1:19.
155. Col. 1:19.
156. John 1:16.
157. John 11:52.
158. Eph. 1:10.

that as in the Tabernacle, *the*[159] *vaile divided between the Holy place and the most Holy;* but the curtaines which covered them both were so coupled together with the taches, that it might still *be*[160] *one Tabernacle:* so the Church Militant and Triumphant, typified thereby, though distant as farre the one from the other as Heaven is from Earth, yet is made but one Tabernacle in Jesus Christ; *in*[161] *whom all the building fitly framed together groweth unto an holy Temple in the Lord,* and *in whom all of us are builded together for an habitation of God through the Spirit.*

The bond of this mysticall union betwixt Christ and us (as elsewhere[162] hath more fully been declared) is on his part that *quickning*[163] *Spirit,* which being in him as the Head, is from thence diffused to the spirituall animation of all his Members: and on our part *Faith,*[164] which is the prime act of life wrought in those who are capable of understanding by that same Spirit. Both whereof must bee acknowledged to be of so high a nature, that none could possibly by such ligatures knit up so admirable a body, but hee that was God Almighty. And therefore although we did suppose such a man might be found who should performe the Law for us, suffer the death that was due to our offence and overcome it; yea and whose obedience and sufferings should be of such value, that it were *sufficient* for the redemption of the whole world: yet could it not be *efficient* to make us live by faith, unlesse that Man had been able to send Gods Spirit to apply the same unto us.

Which as no bare Man or any other Creature whatsoever can doe; so for *Faith* we are taught by S. *Paul,*[165] that it is the *operation of God,* and a *worke* of his *power,* even of that same power wherewith Christ himselfe was raised from the dead. Which is the ground of that prayer of his, that the eyes[166] of our understanding being enlightned, wee might know *what is the exceeding greatnesse of his power to us-ward who beleeve; according to the working of his mighty power, which he wrought in Christ when hee raised him from the dead, and set him at his owne right hand in the heavenly places farre*

159. Exod. 26:33.
160. Exod. 26:6, 11.
161. Eph. 2:21, 22.
162. Sermon to the Commons house of Parliament, *anno* 1620.
163. John 6:63; I Cor. 6:17; 15:45; Phil. 2:1; Rom. 8:9; I John 3:24; 4:13.
164. Gal. 2:20; 5:5; 3:11; Eph. 3:17.
165. Col. 2:12; II Thess. 1:11.
166. Eph. 1:19, 20, &c.

above all Principality, and power, and Might, and every Name that is named not onely in this world, but also in that to come: and hath put all things under his feet, and gave him to be head over all things to the Church, which is his body, the fulnesse of him that filleth all in all.

Yet was it fit also, that this *Head* should bee of the same nature with the *Body* which is knit unto it: and therefore that he should so be God, as that hee might partake of our flesh likewise. *For*[167] *wee are members of his body,* saith the same Apostle; *of his flesh, and of his bones.* And, *except*[168] *yee eate the flesh of the Son of man,* saith our Saviour himselfe, *and drinke his blood; yee have no life in you. Hee*[169] *that eateth my flesh, and drinketh my blood, dwelleth in mee, and I in him.* Declaring thereby, *first,* that by this misticall and supernaturall union, wee are as truely conjoyned with him, as the meat and drinke wee take is with us; when by the ordinary worke of Nature, it is converted into our own substance. *Secondly,* that this conjunction is immediately made with his humane nature. *Thirdly,* that the *Lambe*[170] *slaine,* that is, *Christ*[171] *crucified,* hath by that death of his, made his flesh broken, and his blood powred out for us upon the Crosse, to bee fit food for the spirituall nourishment of our soules; and the very well-spring from whence, by the power of his Godhead, all life and grace is derived unto us.

Vpon this ground it is, that the Apostle telleth us, that wee *have*[172] *boldnesse to enter into the Holiest by the blood of Iesus; by a new and living way which hee hath consecrated for us, through the vaile, that is to say, his flesh.* That as in the Tabernacle, there was no passing from the Holy to the most Holy place, but by the vaile: so now there is no passage to bee looked for from the Church Militant to the Church Triumphant, but by the *flesh* of him, who hath said of himself; *I*[173] *am the way, the truth and the life, no man commeth unto the Father but by mee.* Jacob in his dream beheld *a*[174] *ladder set upon the Earth, the top whereof reached to Heaven, and the Angels of God ascending and descending on it,* the *Lord* himselfe

---

167. Eph. 5:30.
168. John 6:53.
169. John 6:56.
170. Rev. 5:12; 13:8.
171. I Cor. 1:23; 2:2.
172. Heb. 10:19, 20.
173. John 14:6.
174. Gen. 28:12, 13.

standing above it. Of which vision none can give a better interpretation than hee, who was prefigured therein, gave unto *Nathaneel. Hereafter*[175] *you shall see heaven opened, and the Angels of God ascending and descending upon the Son of man.* Whence wee may well collect, that the onely meanes whereby God standing above and his *Israel* lying here below are conjoyned together, and the onely ladder whereby Heaven may be scaled by us, is the *Sonne of man.* the type of whose flesh, the *veile,* was therefore commanded to be made[176] with *Cherubims;* to shew that we come *to*[177] *an innumerable company of Angels,* when we come *to Iesus, the Mediator of the New Testament:* who as the head of the Church hath power to *send*[178] *forth all those ministring spirits, to minister for them who shall be Heires of salvation.*

Lastly, we are to take into our consideration, that as in things concerning God, the maine execution of our Saviours *Priesthood* doth consist; so in things concerning man, hee exerciseth both his *Propheticall* office, whereby hee openeth the will of his Father unto us, and his *Kingly,* whereby he ruleth and protecteth us. It was indeed a part of the *Priests* office in the Old Testament,[179] to instruct the people in the Law of God, and yet were they[180] distinguished from *Prophets:* like as in the New Testament also, *Prophets*[181] as well as *Apostles,* are made a different degree from ordinary *Pastours* and *Teachers,* who received not their doctrine by immediate inspiration from Heaven; as those other *Holy*[182] *men of God* did, *who spake as they were moved by the Holy Ghost.* Whence S. *Paul* putteth the Hebrewes in minde, that *God*[183] *who in sundry parts and in sundry manners spake in time past unto the Fathers by the Prophets, hath in these last dayes spoken unto us by his Son* Christ Jesus: whom therefore he stileth *the*[184] *Apostle,* as well as *the High Priest of our profession; who was faithfull to him that appointed him, even as Moses was in all his house.*

---

175. John 1:51.
176. Exod. 26:31; 36:35.
177. Heb. 12:22, 24.
178. Heb. 1:14.
179. Deut. 33:10; Hag. 2:11; Mal. 2:7.
180. Isa. 28:7; Jer. 6:13; 8:10; 14:18; 23:11, 33, 34; Lam. 2:10.
181. Eph. 4:11.
182. II Peter 1:21.
183. Heb. 1:1.
184. Heb. 3:1, 2.

Now *Moses,* wee know, had a singular preheminence above all the rest of the Prophets: according to that ample testimony which God himselfe giveth of him. *If[185] there bee a Prophet among you, I the Lord will make my selfe knowne unto him in a vision, and will speake unto him in a dreame. My servant Moses is not so, who is faithfull in all mine house: with him will I speake mouth to mouth, even apparently and not in darke speeches; and the similitude of the Lord shall hee behold.* And therefore wee finde, that our Mediatour in the execution of his Propheticall office is in a more peculiar manner likened unto *Moses:* which hee himselfe also did thus foretell. *The[186] Lord thy God will raise up unto thee a Prophet from the midst of thee, of thy Brethren, like unto me; and unto him yee shall hearken. According to all that thou desirest of the Lord thy God in* Horeb, *in the day of the assembly, saying, Let mee not heare againe the voyce of the Lord my God; neither let me see this great fire any more, that I dye not. And the Lord said unto me, They have well spoken, that which they have spoken. I will raise them up a Prophet from among their brethren, like unto thee, and will put my words in his mouth, and he shall speak unto them all that I shall command him. And it shall come to passe, that whosoever will not hearken unto my words, which hee shall speak in my Name, I will require it of him.*

Our *Prophet* therefore must be a Man raised from among his Brethren the *Israelites,* (*of[187] whom, as concerning the flesh,* he came) who was to performe unto us, that which the Fathers requested of *Moses:* *Speake[188] thou to us and we will heare; but let not God speak with us, lest we dye.* And yet (that in this also we may see, how our Mediator had the preheminence) when *Aaron,*[189] and all the children of *Israel* were to receive from the mouth of *Moses* all that the Lord had spoken with him in Mount *Sinai, they were afraid to come nigh him,* by reason of the glory of his shining countenance: so that he was faine to put a *vaile* over his face, while he spake unto them that which he was commanded. But that which for a time was thus *made[190] glorious, had no glory in respect of the glorie that excelleth;* and both the *glory* thereof, and the *vaile* which covered it, are

185. Num. 12:6, 7, 8.
186. Deut. 18:15, 16, &c.; Acts 3:22, 23.
187. Rom. 9:5.
188. Exod. 20:19; Deut. 5:25, 27.
189. Exod. 34:30, 32, 33.
190. II Cor. 3:7, 10, 11, 13.

now abolished in *Christ*: the vaile of whose flesh doth so over-shadow *the*[191] *brightnesse of his glorie,* that yet under it we may *behold*[192] *his glory, as the glory of the onely begotten of the Father;* yea, and *we*[193] *all with open face, beholding as in a glasse the glorie of the Lord, are changed into the same Image, from glorie to glorie, even as by the Spirit of the Lord.*

And this is daily effected by the power of the Ministery of the Gospel, instituted by the authority, and seconded by the power, of this our great Prophet: whose transcendent excellency beyond *Moses* (unto whom, in the execution of that function he was otherwise likened) is thus set forth by the Apostle. He is *counted*[194] *worthy of more glory then* Moses, *in as much as he who hath builded the house hath more honour than the house. For every house is builded by some one: but he that built all things is God. And* Moses *verily was faithfull in all his house, as a servant, for a testimony of those things which were to be spoken after: but* Christ, *as the Sonne, over his owne house.* This house of God is no other then *the*[195] *Church of the living God:* whereof as hee is the onely *Lord,* so is he also properly the onely *Builder.* Christ therefore being both the *Lord* and the *Builder*[196] of his Church, must bee God as well as Man: which is the cause, why wee finde all the severall mansions of this *great*[197] *house* to carry the title indifferently of the *Churches*[198] *of God,* and the *Churches*[199] *of Christ.*

True it is, that there are other ministeriall *builders,* whom Christ employeth in that service: this being not the least of those gifts which hee bestowed upon men at his triumphant ascension into Heaven, that he gave not onely ordinary *Pastours*[200] and *Teachers,* but *Apostles* likewise, and *Prophets,* and *Evangelists;* for the *perfecting of the Saints, for the worke of the ministerie, for the edifying of the body of Christ.* Which, what great power it required, he himself doth fully express

191. Heb. 1:3.
192. John 1:14.
193. II Cor. 3:11.
194. Heb. 3:3, 4, 5, 6.
195. I Tim. 3:15.
196. Matt. 16:18.
197. II Tim. 2:20.
198. I Cor. 11:16.
199. Rom. 16:16.
200. Eph. 4:11, 12.

in passing the grant of this high Commission unto his Apostles. *All*[201] *power is given unto me in Heaven and in Earth. Goe yee therefore and teach all Nations, baptizing them in the name of the Father, and of the Son, and of the holy Ghost; teaching them to observe all things, whatsoever I have commanded you: and lo, I am with you alway, even unto the end of the World. Amen.*

S. *Paul* professeth of himselfe, that he *laboured*[202] *more abundantly then* all the rest of the Apostles: *yet not I,* saith he, *but the grace of God which was with me.* And therefore although *according*[203] *to that grace of God which was given unto him,* he denyeth not but that, *as a wise Master-builder, he had laid the foundation;* yet hee acknowledgeth that they upon whom he had wrought, were *Gods building, as well as Gods husbandrie.* For *who,* saith hee,[204] *is* Paul, *and who is* Apollo, *but Ministers by whom you beleeved, even as the Lord gave to every man? I have planted, Apollo watered: but God gave the increase. So then, neither is he that planteth any thing, neither he that watereth: but God that giveth the encrease.*

Two things therefore we finde in our great *Prophet,* which doe farre exceed the ability of any bare Man; and so doe difference him from all the *Holy*[205] *Prophets, which have been since the world began.* For *first,* we are taught; that *no*[206] *man knoweth the Father, save the Sonne, and he to whomsoever the Sonne will reveale him:* and that *no*[207] *man hath seen God at any time;* but *the onely begotten Son, which is in the bosome of the Father, he hath declared him.* Being in his *bosome,* he is become conscious of his secrets, and so out of his owne immediate knowledge, inabled to discover the whole will of his Father unto us. whereas all other Prophets and Apostles receive their revelations at the second hand, and according to the grace given unto them by the Spirit of Christ. Witnesse that place of S. *Peter,* for the Prophets: *Of*[208] *which salvation the Prophets have enquired, and searched diligently, who prophesied of the grace that should come unto you; searching what or what manner of time* THE SPIRIT OF CHRIST

---

201. Matt. 28:18, 19, 20.
202. I Cor. 15:10.
203. I Cor. 3:9, 10.
204. I Cor. 3:5, 6, 7.
205. Luke 1:70.
206. Matt. 11:27.
207. John 1:18.
208. I Peter 1:10, 11.

WHICH WAS IN THEM *did signifie, when it testified before hand the sufferngs of Christ, and the glory that should follow*. and for the Apostles, those heavenly words which our Saviour himself uttered unto them, whilst he was among them. *When*[209] *the Spirit of Truth is come, he will guide you into all truth: for hee shall not speak of himselfe, but whatsoever he shall heare, that shall he speake; and he will shew you things to come. He shall glorifie me: for he shall receive of mine, and shew it unto you. All things that the Father hath, are mine: therefore said I, that he shall take of mine, and shall shew it unto you.*

Secondly, all other Prophets and Apostles can doe no more (as hath beene said) but plant and water; onely *God* can give the increase: they may teach indeed and baptize; but unlesse Christ were with them by the powerfull presence of his Spirit, they would not bee able to save one soule by that ministerie of theirs. *Wee*[210] *as lively stones, are built up a spirituall house:* but, *except*[211] *the Lord doe build this house, they labour in vaine that build it.* For who is able to breathe the spirit of life into those dead stones, but he, of whom it is written; *The*[212] *houre is coming, and now is,* when the dead shall *heare the voice of the Son of God; and they that heare it shall live.* and againe: *Awake*[213] *thou that sleepest, and arise from the dead; and Christ shall give thee light.* Who can awake us out of this dead sleep, and give light unto these blinde eyes of ours; but the Lord our God, unto whom we pray, that he would *lighten*[214] *our eyes, lest we sleep* the sleep *of death.*

And as a blinde man is not able to conceive the distinction of colours, although the skilfullest man alive should use all the art he had to teach him; because he wanteth the sence whereby that object is discernable: so *the*[215] *naturall man perceiveth not the things of the Spirit of God (for they are foolishnesse unto him;) neither can he know them, because they are spiritually discerned.* Whereupon the Apostle concludeth, concerning himselfe and all his fellow-labourers, that *God*[216] *who commanded the light to shine out of darknesse, hath*

---

209. John 16:13, 14, 15.
210. I Peter 2:5.
211. Ps. 127:1.
212. John 5:25.
213. Eph. 5:14.
214. Ps. 13:3.
215. I Cor. 2:14.
216. II Cor. 4:6, 7.

shined in our hearts; to give *the light of the knowledge of the glory of God, in the face of Iesus Christ: but we have this treasure in earthen vessels; that the excellency of the power may bee of God, and not of us.* Our Mediatour therefore (who must *be*[217] *able to save them to the uttermost that come unto God by him*) may not want *the excellency of the power,* whereby hee may make us capable of this high knowledge of the things of God, propounded unto us by the ministry of his servants: and consequently, in this request also, must be *God* as well as *Man.*

There remaineth the *Kingdome* of our Redeemer: described thus by the prophet *Esay. Of*[218] *the increase of his government and peace there shall be no end, upon the throne of* David, *and upon his Kingdome; to order it, and to establish it with judgement and with justice, from henceforth even for ever.* and by Daniel: *Behold,*[219] *one like the Son of man came with the clouds of Heaven, and came to the Ancient of dayes; and they brought him near before him. And there was given him Dominion, and Glory, and a Kingdome, that all People, Nations and Languages should serve him: his dominion is an everlasting dominion, which shall not passe away; and his kingdome* that *which shall not be destroyed.* and by the Angell *Gabriel,* in his ambassage to the blessed Virgin. *Behold,*[220] *thou shalt conceive in thy wombe, and bring forth a Son, and thou shalt call his name Iesus. He shall be great, and shall be called the Son of the Highest; and the Lord God shall give him the Throne of his Father* David. *And he shall reigne over the house of* Jacob *for ever; and of his kingdome there shall bee no end.*

This is that new *David*[221] our King, whom God hath raised up unto his owne *Israel:*[222] who was in Truth, that which Hee was called; the Son of *Man,* and the Son of the *Highest.* That in the one respect, we[223] may say unto him, as the *Israelites* of old did unto their *David; Behold,*[224] *we are thy bone and thy flesh:* and in the

---

217. Heb. 7:25.
218. Isa. 9:7.
219. Dan. 7:13, 14.
220. Luke 1:31, 32, 33.
221. Jer. 30:9; Hos. 3:5; Ezek. 34:23; 37:24.
222. Gal. 6:16.
223. Eph. 5:30.
224. II Sam. 5:1.

other, sing of him as *David* himselfe did; *The*[225] *Lord said unto my Lord, Sit thou at my right hand, untill I make thine enemies thy foot-stoole.* So that the promise made unto our first Parents, that *the*[226] *seed of the Woman should bruise the Serpents head*, may well stand with that other saying of Saint *Paul*; that *the*[227] *God of peace shall bruise Satan under our feet.* Seeing for this very *purpose*[228] *the Son of God was manifested* in the flesh, *that*[229] *he might destroy the works of the Devill.* And still that foundation of God will remaine unshaken: *I*[230] *even I am the Lord, and beside me there is no Saviour. Thou*[231] *shalt know no God but me: for* there is *no Saviour beside me.*

Two speciall branches there be of this Kingdome of our Lord and Saviour: the one of *Grace*, whereby that part of the Church is governed which is Militant upon Earth; the other of *Glory*, belonging to that part which is Triumphant in Heaven. Here up on Earth, as by his Propheticall Office he worketh upon our Minde and Understanding, so by his Kingly, he ruleth our Will and Affections; *casting*[232] *downe imaginations and every high thing that exalteth it selfe against the knowledge of God, and bringing into captivity every thought to the obedience of Christ.* Where, as we must needs acknowledge, that *it*[233] *is* GOD *which worketh in us both to will and to doe*, and that it is he which *sanctifieth*[234] *us* wholly: so are we taught likewise to beleeve, that *both*[235] *he who sanctifieth, and they who are sanctified, are all of one*, namely of one and the selfsame nature; that the sanctifier might *not be ashamed to call* those, who are sanctified by him, his *brethren.* that as their nature was corrupted, and their bloud tainted in the first *Adam*, so it might be restored again in the second *Adam*; and that as from the one a corrupt, so from the other a pure and undefiled nature might be transmitted unto the heirs of salvation.

---

225. Ps. 110:1; Matt. 22:43, 44; Acts 2:34, 35.
226. Gen. 3:15.
227. Rom. 16:20.
228. I John 3:8.
229. I Tim. 3:16.
230. Isa. 43:11.
231. Hos. 13:4.
232. II Cor. 10:5.
233. Phil. 2:13.
234. II Thess. 5:23.
235. Heb. 2:11.

The same God[236] that giveth *grace*, is he also that giveth *glory:* yet so, that the streames of both of them must run to us through the golden pipe of our Saviours humanity. *For*[237] *since by man* came *death;* it was fit that *by man also* should come *the resurrection of the dead.* Even by that man, who hath said: *Who*[238] *so eateth my flesh, and drinketh my blood, hath eternall life; and I will raise him up at the last day.* Who then, shall come[239] *to be glorified in his Saints, and to be made marvellous in all them that beleeve:* and shall change[240] *this base body of ours, that it may be fashioned like unto his owne glorious body; according to the working, whereby he is able even to subdue all things unto himselfe.* Unto him therefore that hath thus loved[241] *us, and washed us from our sins in his owne bloud, and hath made us Kings and Priests unto God and his Father; to him be glory and dominion for ever and ever,* AMEN.

PHIL. 3:8

I COUNT ALL THINGS BUT LOSSE, FOR
THE EXCELLENCY OF THE KNOWLEDGE
OF CHRIST JESUS MY LORD.

---

236. Ps. 84:11.
237. I Cor. 15:21.
238. John 6:54.
239. II Thess. 1:10.
240. Phil. 3:21.
241. Rev. 1:5, 6.

William Perkins
1558-1602

7

Salvation: Introduction

William Perkins, an outstanding preacher, made great contributions to the Puritan movement despite the shortness of his life. He was born in Warton, Warwickshire, and educated in Christ College, Cambridge. In his early years he demonstrated scholarly ability, but his personal life was wild and sinful. After his conversion he became a strong exponent of Calvinism and always dealt sympathetically with those in spiritual need. He became a fellow at the college in 1578.

Perkins was later ordained and began his ministry preaching to prisoners in the Cambridge jail. He is said to have encountered a young condemned prisoner who was terrified not so much of death as of the impending judgment of God. The Puritan preacher knelt beside him to "show what the grace of God can do to strengthen thee." He showed him that Christ is the means of salvation by the grace of God and urged him with tears to believe in Him and experience the remission of his sins. The youth did so and was able to face his execution with composure, a glorious display of God's sovereign grace. This incident should be kept in mind while studying Perkins's chart of election and reprobation. It shows that his theology did not make him cold and heartless when dealing with sinners in need of a Savior.

Around 1585 Perkins was chosen rector of St. Andrews, Cambridge, and continued there until his death in 1602. His individual writings consisted mainly of treatises on the Apostle's Creed and the Lord's Prayer, and expositions of Galatians 1-5, Matthew 5-7, and Hebrews 11. He wrote the practical *Cases of Conscience*. His writings were popularly received and were translated into Latin, French, Dutch, and Spanish. They were collected in the three-volume *The Works of William Perkins* (1616-1618).

Perkins's "Golden Chain" is a basic guide to Puritan theology and preaching. Though not every Puritan preacher agreed with each detail of Perkins's Chain, it does represent Reformed doctrine as generally interpreted by the Puritans. His analysis and organization of soteriology is amazing, especially in relating the work of Christ to the elect believer. Perkins considers faith the result of God's effectual call rather than of sinful man's "free will." He also considers true repentance to result from sanctification and to lead to complete obedience.

Perhaps the most interesting feature of the "Golden Chain" is the religious zealot whose penitence is only temporary and arises from his sinful heart. In the twentieth century we need, more than ever before, to realize that such individuals are still unconverted and not merely "out of fellowship." Perkins's concept appears again in the selection on ecclesiology by Richard Baxter. The Puritans never considered church members saved just because they met outward requirements like baptism, confession of a creed, and response to an altar call. They preached the perseverance of true believers in obedience and good works as the result of true conversion. They were careful not to give people a false sense of assurance. The great problem of worldliness in our churches today can be solved only with this kind of preaching. Thus the emotional but false repentance of a Saul or Judas must not be taken as a sign of true conversion.

The Puritans generally also were wary of those "converts" who showed extreme religious "zeal." Not that they opposed spiritual zeal, but they recognized it could be a "cover-up" for deep, unrepented sin. Modern psychologists verify that many people with great religious or social zeal are attempting to sublimate guilt and anxiety. Again, today's ministers must urge their people to be as concerned about what they are as about what they are doing. In today's churches we see much activity but little real spiritual growth and godly living.

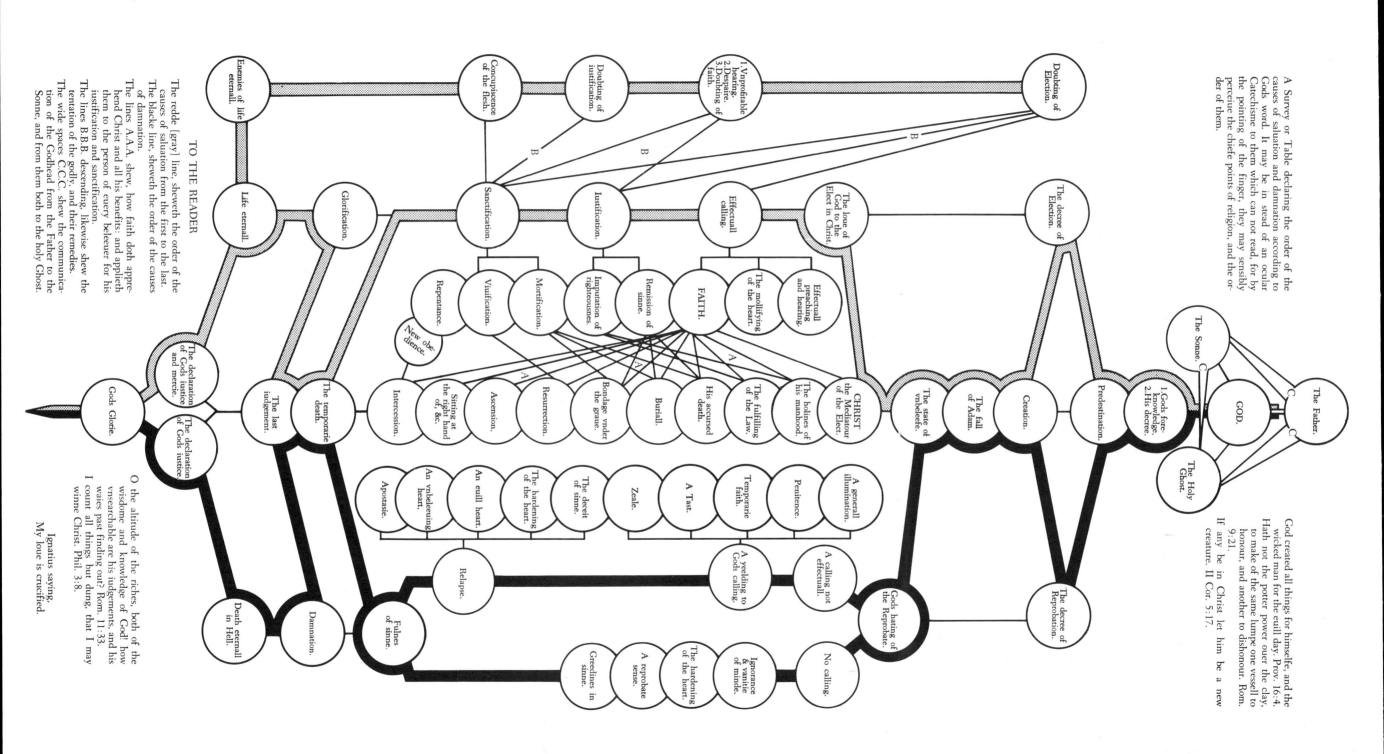

A Survey or Table declaring the order of the causes of saluation and damnation according to Gods word. It may be in stead of an ocular Catechisme to them which can not read, for by the pointing of the finger, they may sensibly perceiue the chiefe points of religion, and the order of them.

God created all things for himselfe, and the wicked man for the euill day. Prov. 16:4. Hath not the potter power ouer the clay, to make of the same lumpe one vessell to honour, and another to dishonour. Rom. 9:21.

If any be in Christ let him be a new creature. II Cor. 5:17.

TO THE READER

The redde [gray] line, sheweth the order of the causes of saluation from the first to the last.

The blacke line, sheweth the order of the causes of damnation.

The lines A.A.A. shew, how faith doth apprehend Christ and all his benefits: and applieth them to the person of euery beleeuer for his iustification and sanctification.

The lines B.B.B. descending, likewise shew the tentation of the godly, and their remedies.

The wide spaces C.C.C. shew the communication of the Godhead from the Father to the Sonne, and from them both to the holy Ghost.

O the altitude of the riches, both of the wisdome and knowledge of God! how vnsearchable are his iudgements, and his waies past finding out? Rom. 11:33.

I count all things but dung, that I may winne Christ. Phil. 3:8.

Ignatius saying,
My loue is crucified.

John Owen
1616-1683

8

The Atonement

John Owen was unquestionably one of the greatest Puritan divines. He was born at Stradhampton, Oxfordshire, the son of a country minister. At the age of twelve he entered Queen's College, Oxford, receiving a B.A. in 1632 and M.A. in 1635. He was ordained in the Anglican church while still at Oxford, but he later refused to submit to William Laud's High Church discipline. He left Oxford in 1637 and was a private chaplain for the next six years.

He went to Fordham, Essex, in 1643 when he was still Presbyterian (cf. his *Duty of Pastors and People Distinguished* [1643]). Soon after taking the Presbyterian congregation at Coggeshall, Essex, Owen introduced and espoused independent church government. At about the same time (1646), he preached before Long Parliament, clearly advocating his Independent and Parliamentarian views. He continued to preach before Parliament, and at its request he preached there in 1649, the day after Charles I was executed. Owen eventually became the chaplain of Cromwell.

During these stormy years, Owen was actively involved in political affairs, and during the Protectorate he was at the head of Oxford University, appointed dean of Christ Church in 1651 and vice chancellor of the university in 1652. In 1653 he was awarded the D.D.

by Oxford. In 1658, however, he separated from Cromwell, opposing Cromwell's desire for kingship, and left Oxford to take a leading role in the Savoy Assembly. His contribution to the university had been the improvement of its scholarship and discipline.

During these years Owen poured forth volumes of sermons, tracts, controversial pamphlets, commentaries, and doctrinal studies. The value and significance of Owen's writings is unsurpassed. After the Restoration in 1660, he was greatly respected by the royal government and became the leader of the Independents. After declining a call to the pastorate in Boston, Massachusetts, as well as an offer to be president of Harvard College, Owen became pastor in 1673 of a large congregation at Leadenhall Street Chapel and remained there until his death in 1683.

Among Owen's main works were *Display of Arminianism* (1642), *The Death of Death in the Death of Christ* (1648), *The Doctrine of the Saint's Perseverance* (1654), *Vindiciae Evangelicae* (1655), *On the Mortification of Sin* (1656), *A Primer for Children* (1660), the four-volume *Exposition of the Epistle to the Hebrews* (1668-1684), *Discourse on the Holy Spirit* (1674), *Christology* (1679), *Vindication of the Nonconformists* (1680), and *True Nature of a Gospel Church* (1689). Owen's entire works were edited by William Orme and published in twenty-three volumes in 1820. A twenty-four-volume edition, edited by William Goold, was published in 1850 and reprinted by the Banner of Truth Trust of London from 1965 to 1968.

The following selection is part of Owen's discussion of chapter 20 of Thomas More's *The Universality of God's Free Grace*. It is one of the finest statements anywhere of the doctrine of limited atonement. Owen takes almost every conceivable objection to the doctrine and convincingly refutes it from Scripture. He discusses such objections as these: at least some Biblical phrases concerning those for whom Christ died are unlimited; salvation is to be preached to the whole world; all will confess that Christ is Lord; God desires that none should perish; God is merciful to all men. Owen's replies are relevant both to conservative non-Calvinists who object that limited atonement is unfair, and to those neo-orthodox theologians who teach that, because atonement is universal and because ultimately all creatures will acknowledge Christ, salvation is universal.

Owen's strongest arguments are that More assumes indefinite expressions to be universal and that he fails to prove that the universal offer of salvation necessitates a universal atonement. As a true scholar, Owen challenges the Christian reader to evaluate both the arguments for and those against the doctrine of limited atonement.

It should be noted that no one ever attempted to refute Owen as thoroughly as he had refuted More.

The *title*[1] pretends satisfaction to them who desire to have reason satisfied: which, that it is a great undertaking, I easily grant; but for the performance of it, "hic labor, hoc opus." That ever Christian reason, rightly informed by the word of God, should be satisfied with any doctrine so *discrepant* from the word, so full of contradiction in itself and to its own principles, as the doctrine of universal redemption is, I should much marvel. Therefore, I am persuaded that the author of the arguments following (which, lest you should mistake them for others, he calleth *reasons*), will fail of his intention with all that have so much reason as to know how to make use of reason, and so much grace as not to love darkness more than light. The only reason, as far as I can conceive, why he calls this collection of all the arguments and texts of Scripture which he had before cited and produced at large so many *reasons,* being a supposal that he hath given them a logical, argumentative form in this place, I shall briefly consider them; and, by the way, take notice of his skill in a regular framing of arguments, to which here he evidently pretends. His first reason, then, is as followeth:—

I. "That which the Scripture oft and plainly affirmeth in plain words is certainly true and to be believed, Prov. 22:20, 21; Isa. 8:20; II Peter 1:19, 20;

"But that Jesus Christ gave himself a ransom, and by the grace of God tasted death for every man, is oft and plainly affirmed in Scripture, as is before shown, chap. 7-13:

"Therefore, the same is certainly a truth to be believed, John 20:31; Acts 26:27."

First, the proposition of this argument is clear, evident, and acknowledged by all professing the name of Christ; but yet universally with this caution and proviso, that by *the Scripture affirming any thing in plain words that is to be believed,* you understand the plain sense of those words, which is clear by rules of interpretation so to be. It is the thing signified that is to be believed, and not the words only, which are the sign thereof; and, therefore, the *plain sense and meaning* is that which we must inquire after, and is intended when

---

1. The title here referred to is *The Universality of God's Free Grace* ..., a book written by Thomas More and published in 1643. —*Ed.*

we speak of believing plain words of the Scripture. But now if by *plain words* you understand the literal importance of the words, which may perhaps be *figurative,* or at least of *various signification,* and capable of extension or restriction in the interpretation, then there is nothing more false than this assertion; for how can you then avoid the blasphemous folly of the Anthropomorphites, assigning a body and human shape unto God, the *plain words of the Scripture* often mentioning his eyes, hands, ears, etc., it being apparent to every child that the true importance of those expressions answers not at all their gross carnal conception? Will not also transubstantiation, or its younger brother consubstantiation, be an article of our creed? With this limitation, then, we pass the proposition, with the places of Scripture brought to confirm it; only with this observation, that there is not one of them to the purpose in hand,—which, because they do not relate to the argument in consideration, we only leave to men's silent judgments.

Secondly, The assumption, or minor proposition, we absolutely deny as to some part of it; as that Christ should be said to give himself a ransom for every man, it being neither often, nor once, nor plainly, nor obscurely affirmed in the Scripture, nor at all proved in the place referred unto: so that this is but an empty flourishing. For the other expression, of "tasting death for every man," we grant that the words are found Heb. 2:9; but we deny that *every man* doth always necessarily signify *all and every man in the world.* Νουθετοῦντες πάντα ἄνθρωπον, καὶ διδάσκοντες πάντα ἄνθρωπον, Col. 1:28—"Warning every man, and teaching every man." *Every man* is not there every man in the world; neither are we to believe that Paul warned and taught every particular man, for it is false and impossible. So that *every man,* in the Scripture, is not universally collective of all of all sorts, but either distributive, for some of all sorts, or collective, with a restriction to all of some sort; as in that of Paul, *every man,* was only of those to whom he had preached the gospel. Secondly, In the original there is only ὑπὲρ παντός, *for every,* without the substantive *man,* which might be supplied by other words as well as *man,*—as elect, or believer.

Thirdly, That *every one* is there clearly restrained to all the members of Christ, and the children by him brought to glory, we have before declared. So that this place is no way useful for the confirmation of the assumption, which we deny in the sense intended; and are sure we shall never see a clear, or so much as a probable, testimony for the confirming of it.

To the conclusion of the syllogism, the author, to manifest his skill in disputing in such an argumentative way as he undertaketh, addeth some farther proofs. Conscious, it seems, he was to himself that it had little strength from the propositions from which it is enforced; and, therefore, thought to give some new supportments to it, although with very ill success, as will easily appear to any one that shall but consult the places quoted, and consider the business in hand. In the meantime, this new logic, of filing proofs to the conclusion which are suitable to neither proposition, and striving to give strength to that by new testimony which it hath not from the premises, deserves our notice in this age of learned writers. "Heu quantum est sapere." Such logic is fit to maintain such divinity. And so much for the first argument.

II. "Those whom Jesus Christ and his apostles, in plain terms, without any exception or restraint, affirm that Christ came to save, and to that end died, and gave himself a ransom for, and is a propitiation for their sin, he certainly did come to save, and gave himself a ransom for them, and is the propitiation for their sins, Matt. 26:24; John 6:38; I Cor. 15:3, 4; Heb. 10:7; John 8:38, 45; II Peter 1:16; Heb. 2:3, 4;

"But Jesus Christ and his apostles have, in plain terms, affirmed that 'Christ came to save sinners,' I Tim. 1:15; the 'world,' John 3:17; that he died for the 'unjust,' I Peter 3:18; the 'ungodly,' Rom. 5:6; for 'every man,' Heb. 2:9; 'gave himself a ransom for all men,' I Tim 2:6; and is the 'propitiation for the sins of the whole world,' I John 2:2; and every one of these affirmations without any exception or restraint, all being unjust, ungodly, sinners, and men, and of the world, Rom. 3:10, 19, 20, 23; Eph. 2:1-3; Titus 3:3; John 3:4, 6:

"Therefore, Jesus Christ came to save, died, and gave himself a ransom for all men, and is the propitiation for their sins, John 1:29."

To the proposition of this argument I desire only to observe, that we do not affirm that the Scripture doth, in any place, lay an exception or restraint upon those persons for whom Christ is said to die, as though in one place it should be affirmed he died for all men, and in another some exception against it, as though some of those *all men* were excluded,—which were to feign a repugnancy and contradiction in the word of God; only, we say, one place of Scripture interprets another, and declares that sense which before in one place was ambiguous and doubtful. For instance: when the Scripture showeth that Christ died or gave himself a ransom for *all,* we believe it; and when, in another place, he declares that *all* to be his *church,* his *elect,* his *sheep,* all *believers,*—some of all sorts, *out of all kindreds, and nations, and tongues, under heaven;* this is not to lay an exception or restraint upon what was said of *all* before, but only to declare that the *all* for which he gave himself a ransom were all his church, all his elect, all his sheep, some of all sorts: and so we believe that he died for all. With this observation we let pass the proposition, taking out its meaning as well as the phrase whereby it is expressed will afford it, together with the vain flourish and pompous show of many texts of Scripture brought to confirm it, whereof not one is any thing to the purpose; so that I am persuaded he put down names and figures at a venture, without once consulting the texts, having no small cause to be confident that none would trace him in his flourish, and yet that some eyes might dazzle at his supernumerary quotations. Let me desire the reader to turn to those places, and if any one of them be any thing to the purpose or business in hand, let the author's credit be of weight with him another time. O let us not be as many, who corrupt the word of God! But perhaps it is a mistake in the impression, and for Matt. 26:24, he intends verse 28, where Christ is said to shed his blood for many. In John 6, he mistook verse 38 for 39, where our Saviour affirms that he came to save that which his Father gave him,—that none should be lost; which certainly are the elect. In I Cor. 15:3, 4, he was not much amiss, the apostle conjoining in those verses the death and resurrection of Christ, which he saith was for us; and how far this advantageth his cause in hand, we have before declared. By Heb. 10:7, I suppose he meant verse 10 of the chapter, affirming that by the will of God, which Christ came to do, we are sanctified, even through the offering of the body of Jesus,—ascribing our sanctification to his death, which is not effected in all and every one; though perhaps he may suppose the last clause of the verse, "once for all," to make for him. But some charitable man, I hope, will undeceive him, by letting him know the meaning of the word ἐφάπαξ. The like may be observed of the other places,—that in them is nothing at all to the proposition in hand, and nigh them at least is enough to evert it. And so his proposition in sum is:—"All those for whom the Scripture affirms that Christ did die, for them he died"; which is true, and doubtless granted.

The assumption affirms that Christ and his apostles in the Scriptures say that he died to save *sinners, unjust, ungodly,* the *world, all;* whereupon the conclusion ought barely to be, "Therefore Christ died for sinners, unjust, ungodly, the world, and the like." To which we say,—First, That this is the very same argument, for substance, with that which went before, as also are some of those that follow; only some words are varied, to change the outward appearance, and so to make show of a number. Secondly, That the whole strength of this argument lies in turning indefinite propositions into universals, concluding that because Christ died for sinners, therefore he died for all sinners; because he died for the unjust, ungodly, and the world, that therefore he died for every one that is unjust, or ungodly, and for every one in the world; because he died for all, therefore for all and every one of all sorts of men. Now, if this be good arguing, I will furnish you with some more such arguments against you have occasion to use them:—*First,* God "justifieth the ungodly," Rom. 4:5; therefore, he justifieth every one that is ungodly. Now, "whom he justifieth, them he also glorifieth"; and therefore every ungodly person shall be glorified. *Secondly,* When Christ came, "men loved darkness rather than light," John 3:19; therefore, all men did so, and so none believed. *Thirdly,* "The world knew not Christ," John 1:10; therefore, no man in the world knew him. *Fourthly,* "The whole world lieth in wickedness," I John 5:19; therefore, every one in the world doth so. Such arguments as these, by turning indefinite propositions into universals, I could easily furnish you withal, for any purpose that you will use them to. Thirdly, If you extend the words in the conclusion no farther than the intention of them in the places of Scripture recited in the assumption, we may safely grant the whole,— namely, that Christ died for sinners and the world, for sinful men in their several generations living therein; but if you intend a universality collective of all in the conclusion, then the syllogism is sophistical and false, no place of Scripture affirming so much that is produced, the assignation of the object of the death of Christ in them being in terms indefinite, receiving light and clearness for a more restrained sense in those places where they are expounded to be meant of all his own people, and the children of God scattered throughout the world. Fourthly, For particular places of Scripture urged, I Tim. 1:15; I Peter 3:18; Rom. 5:6, in the beginning of the assumption, are not at all to the purpose in hand. John 3:17; Heb. 2:9; I John 2:2, have been already considered. Rom. 3:10, 19, 20, 23; Eph. 2:1-3; Titus 3:3; John 3:4, 6, added in the close of the same proposition, prove that all are sinners and children of wrath; but of Christ's dying for all sinners, or for all those children of wrath, there is not the least intimation. And this may suffice in answer to the first two arguments, which might easily be retorted upon the author of them, the Scripture being full and plain to the confirmation of the position which he intends to oppose.

III. "That which the Scripture layeth forth as one end of the death of Christ, and one ground and cause of God's exalting Christ to be the Lord and Judge of all, and of the equity of his judging, that is certainly to be believed, Ps. 12:6; 18:130; 119:4;

"But the Scripture layeth forth this for one end of the death and resurrection of Christ, that he might be the Lord of all, Rom. 14:9; II Cor. 5:14, 15. And for that cause (even his death and resurrection) hath God exalted him to be the Lord and Judge of all men, and his judgments shall be just, Rom. 14:9, 11, 12; II Cor. 5:10; Phil. 2:7-11; Acts 17:31; Rom. 2:16:

"Therefore, that Christ so died, and rose again for all, is a truth to be believed, I Tim. 2:6."

First, The unlearned framing of this argument, the uncouth expressions of the thing intended, and failing in particulars, by the by, being to be ascribed to the person and not the cause, I shall not much trouble myself withal; as,—*First,* To his artificial regularity in bringing his minor proposition, namely, Christ being made Lord and Judge of all, into the major; so continuing one term in all three propositions, and making the whole almost unintelligible. *Secondly,* His interpreting, "For this cause God exalted Christ," to be his death and resurrection, when his resurrection, wherein he was "declared to be the Son of God with power," Rom. 1:4, was a glorious part of his exaltation. To examine and lay open the weakness and folly of innumerable such things as these, which everywhere occur, were to be lavish of precious moments. Those that have the least taste of learning or the way of reasoning do easily see their vanity; and for the rest, especially the poor admirers of these foggy sophisms, I shall not say, "Quoniam hic populus vult decipi, decipiatur," but, "God give them understanding and repentance, to the acknowledgment of the truth."

Secondly, To this whole argument, as it lies before us, I have nothing to say but only to entreat Mr More, that if the misery of our times should be calling upon him to be writing again, he would cease expressing his mind by syllogisms, and speak in his own manner; which, by its own confusion in innumerable tautologies, may a little puzzle his reader. For, truly, this kind of arguing here used,—for want of logic, whereby he is himself deceived, and delight in sophistry, whereby he deceiveth others,—is exceedingly ridiculous; for none can be so blind but that, at first reading of the argument, he will see that he asserts and infers that in the conclusion, strengthening it with a new testimony, which was not once dreamed of in either of the premises; they speaking of the exaltation of Christ to be judge of all, which refers to his own glory; the conclusion, of his dying for all, which necessarily aims at and intends their good.

Were it not a noble design to banish all human learning, and to establish such a way of arguing in the room thereof? "Hoc Ithacus velit et magno mercentur Atridae."

Thirdly, The force and sum of the argument is this:—"Christ died and rose again that he might be Lord and Judge of all; therefore, Christ died for all." Now, ask what he means by dying for all, and the whole treatise answers that it is a paying a ransom for them all, that they might be saved. Now, how this can be extorted out of Christ's dominion over all, with his power of judging all committed to him, which also is extended to the angels for whom he died not, let them that can understand it rejoice in their quick apprehension; I confess it flies my thoughts.

Fourthly, The manner of arguing being so vain, let us see a little whether there be any more weight in the matter of the argument. Many texts of Scripture are heaped up and distributed to the several propositions. In those out of Ps. 12:6; 18:30 (as I suppose it should be, not 130, as it is printed); 119:4, there is some mention of the precepts of God, with the purity of his word and perfection of his word; which that they are any thing to the business in hand I cannot perceive. That of II Tim. 2:6, added to the conclusion, is one of those places which are brought forth upon every occasion, as being the supposed foundation of the whole assertion, but causelessly, as hath been showed oft. [Among] those which are annexed to the minor proposition, [is] II Cor. 5:14, 15: as I have already cleared the mind of the Holy Ghost in it, and made it manifest that no such thing as universal redemption can be wrested from it, so unto this present argument it hath no reference at all, not containing any one syllable concerning the judging of Christ and his power over all, which was the medium insisted on. Phil. 2:7-11; Acts 17:31; Rom. 2:16, mention, indeed, Christ's exaltation, and his judging all at the last day; but because he shall judge all at the last day, therefore he died for all, will ask more pains to prove than our adversary intends to take in this cause.

The weight, on the whole, must depend on Rom. 14:9, 11, 12; which being the only place that gives any colour to this kind of arguing, shall a little be considered. It is the lordship and dominion of Christ over all which the apostle, in that place, at large insists on and evidenceth to believers, that they might thereby be provoked to walk blameless, and without offence one towards another, knowing the terror of the Lord, and how that all men, even themselves and others, must come to appear before his judgment-seat, when it will be but a sad thing to have an account to make of scandals and offences.

Farther to ingraft and fasten this upon them, he declares unto them the way whereby the Lord Christ attained and came to this dominion and power of judging, all things being put under his feet, together with what design he had, as to this particular, in undertaking the office of mediation, there expressed by "dying, rising, and reviving,"— to wit, that he might have the execution of judging over all committed to him, that being part of the "glory set before him," which caused him to "endure the cross and despise the shame," Heb. 12:2.

So that all which here is intimated concerning the death of Christ is about the end, effects, and issue that it had towards himself, not any thing of what was his intention towards them for whom he died. To die for others does at least denote to die for their good, and in the Scripture always to die in their stead. Now, that any such thing can be hence deducted as that Christ died for all, because by his death himself made way for the enjoyment of that power whereby he is Lord over all, and will judge them all, casting the greatest part of men into hell by the sentence of his righteous judgment, I profess sincerely that I am no way able to perceive. If men will contend and have it so, that Christ must be said to die for all, because by his death and resurrection he attained the power of judging all, then I shall only leave with them these three things:—*First,* That innumerable souls shall be judged by him for not walking according to the light of nature left unto them, directing them to seek after the eternal power and Godhead of their Creator, without the least rumour of the gospel to direct them to a Redeemer once arriving at their ears, Rom. 2:12; and what good will it be for such that Christ so died for them? *Secondly,* That he also died for the devils, because he hath, by his death and resurrection, attained a power of judging them also. *Thirdly,* That the whole assertion is nothing to the business in hand; our inquiry being about them whom our Saviour intended to redeem and save by his blood; this return, about those he will one day judge: "quaestio est de alliis, responsio de cepis."

IV. "That which the Scripture so sets forth in general for the world of mankind, as a truth for them all, that whosoever of the particulars so believe as to come to Christ and receive the same shall not perish, but have everlasting life, is certainly a truth to be believed, Acts 5:20;

"But that God sent forth his Son to be the Saviour of the world is in Scripture so set forth in general for all men, that whosoever of the particulars so believe as they come to Christ and receive the same, they shall not perish, but have everlasting life, John 3:16-18, 36; 1:4, 11, 12:

"Therefore, that God sent his Son to be the Saviour of the world is a certain truth, I John 4:14."

I hope no ingenuous man, that knows any thing of the controversy in hand, and to what head it is driven between us and our adversary, or is in any measure acquainted with the way of arguing, will expect that we should spend many words about such poor flourishes, vain repetitions, confused expressions, and illogical deductions and argumentations, as this pretended new argument (indeed the same with the first two, and with almost all that follow), will expect that I should cast away much time or pains about them. For my own part, I were no way able to undergo the tediousness of the review of such things as these, but that "eundum est quo trahunt fata ecclesiae." Not, then, any more to trouble the reader with a declaration of that in particulars which he cannot but be sufficiently convinced of by a bare overlooking of these reasons,—namely, that this author is utterly ignorant of the way of reasoning, and knows not how tolerably to express his own conceptions, nor to infer one thing from another in any regular way, I answer,—First, That whatsoever the Scripture holds forth as a truth to be believed is certainly so, and to be embraced. Secondly, That the Scripture sets forth the death of Christ, to all whom the gospel is preached [unto], as an all-sufficient means for the bringing of sinners unto God, so as that whosoever believe it and come in unto him shall certainly be saved. Thirdly, What can be concluded hence, but that the death of Christ is of such infinite value as that it is able to save to the utmost every one to whom it is made known, if by true faith they obtain an interest therein and a right thereunto, we cannot perceive. This truth we have formerly confirmed by many testimonies of Scripture, and do conceive that this innate sufficiency of the death of Christ is the foundation of its promiscuous proposal to elect and reprobate. Fourthly, That the conclusion, if he would have the reason to have any colour or show of an argument, should at least include and express the whole and entire assertion contained in the proposition,—namely, "That Christ is so set forth to be the Saviour of the world, that whosoever of the particulars believe," etc. And then it is by us fully granted, as making nothing at all for the universality of redemption, but only for the fulness and sufficiency of his satisfaction. Of the word *world* enough hath been said before.

V. "That which God will one day cause every man confess to the glory of God is certainly a truth, for God will own no lie for his glory, John 3:33; Rom. 3:3, 4;

"But God will one day cause every man to confess Jesus (by virtue of his death and ransom given) to be the Lord, even to the glory of God, Phil. 2:7-11; Isa. 45:22, 23; Rom. 14:9, 11, 12; Ps. 86:9:

"Therefore, it is certainly a truth that Jesus Christ hath given himself a ransom for all men, and hath thereby the right of lordship over them; and if any will not believe and come into this government, yet he abideth faithful, and cannot deny himself, but will one day bring them before him, and cause them to confess him Lord, to the glory of God; when they shall be denied by him, for denying him in the days of his patience, II Tim. 2:12-14; Matt. 10:32, 33; II Cor. 5:10."

Ans. The conclusion of this argument ought to be thus, and no otherwise, if you intend it should receive any strength from the premises: "Therefore, that Jesus Christ is the Lord, and to be confessed to the glory of God, is certainly a truth." This, I say, is all the conclusion that this argument ought to have had, unless, instead of a syllogism, you intend three independent propositions, every one standing upon his own strength. That which is inserted concerning his giving himself a ransom for all, and that which follows of the conviction and condemnation of them who believe not nor obey the gospel, confirmed from II Cor. 5:10; II Tim. 2:12-14, is altogether heterogeneous to the business in hand. Now, this being the conclusion intended, if our author suppose that the deniers of universal redemption do question the truth of it, I wonder not at all why he left all other employment to fall a-writing controversies, having such apparent advantages against his adversaries as such small mistakes as this are able to furnish his conceit withal. But it may be an act of charity to part him and his own shadow,—so terribly at variance as here and in other places; wherefore, I beseech him to hear a word in his heat, and to take notice,—[First,] That though we do not ascribe a fruitless, ineffectual redemption to Jesus Christ, nor say that he loved any with that entire love which moved him to lay down his life, but his own church, and that all his elect are effectually redeemed by him, yet we deny not but that he shall also judge the reprobates,—namely, even all them that know not, that deny, that disobey and corrupt the truth of his gospel,—and that all shall be convinced that he is Lord of all at the last day: so that he may spare his pains of proving such unquestionable things. Something else is extremely desirous to follow, but indignation must be bridled. Secondly, For that clause in the second proposition, "By virtue of his death and ransom given," we deny that it is anywhere in the Scripture once intimated that the ransom paid by Christ in his death for us was the cause of his exaltation to be Lord of all:

it was his obedience to his Father in his death, and not his satisfaction for us, that is proposed as the antecedent of this exaltation;
as is apparent, Phil. 2:7-11.

VI. "That which may be proved in and by the Scripture, both
by plain sentences therein and necessary consequences imported
thereby, without wrestling, wrangling, adding to, taking from, or
altering the sentences and words of Scripture, is a truth to be believed,
Matt. 22:29, 32; Rom. 11:2, 5, 6;

"But that Jesus Christ gave himself a ransom for all men, and by
the grace of God tasted death for every man, may be proved in and
by the Scripture, both by plain sentences therein and necessary consequences imported thereby, without wresting, wrangling, adding,
or taking away, or altering the words and sentences, as is already
showed, chap. 7, 13, which will be now ordered into several proofs:

"Therefore, that Jesus Christ gave himself for all men, and by the
grace of God tasted death for every man, is a truth to be believed,
Mark 1:15; 16:15, 18; I John 4:14.

Ans. First, The meaning of this argument is, that universal redemption may be proved by the Scripture; which, being the very
thing in question, and the thesis undertaken to be proved, there is
no reason why itself should make an argument, but only to make
up a number: and, for my part, they should pass without any other
answer, namely, that they are a number, but that those *who are the
number* are to be considered.

Secondly, Concerning the argument itself (seeing it must go for
one), we say,—*First,* To the first proposition, that laying aside the
unnecessary expressions, the meaning of it I take to be this: "That
which is affirmed in the Scripture, or may be deduced from thence
by just consequence, following such ways of interpretation, of af-
firmation, and consequences, as by which the Spirit of God leadeth
us into the knowledge of the truth, is certainly to be believed"; which
is granted of all, though not proved by the places he quoteth, Matt.
22:29, 32; Rom. 11:2, 5, 6, and is the only foundation of that article
of faith which you seek to oppose. *Secondly,* To the second, that
Christ gave himself a ransom ὑπὲρ πάντων, for all, and tasted death
ὑπὲρ παντός, for all, is the very word of Scripture, and was never
denied by any. The making of *all* to be all men and every man, in
both the places aimed at, is your addition, and not the Scripture's
assertion. If you intend, then, to prove that Christ gave himself a
ransom for all, and tasted death for all, you may save your labours;
it is confessed on all hands, none ever denied it. But if you intend
to prove those *all* to be all and every man, of all ages and kinds,

elect and reprobate, and not all his children, all his elect, all his sheep, all his people, all the children given him of God,—some of all sorts, nations, tongues, and languages only, I will, by the Lord's assistance, willingly join issue with you, or any man breathing, to search out the meaning of the word and mind of God in it; holding ourselves to the proportion of faith, essentiality of the doctrine of redemption, scope of the places where such assertions are, comparing them with other places, and the like ways,—labouring in all humility to find the mind of the Lord, according to his own appointment. And of the success of such a trial, laying aside such failings as will adhere to my personal weakness, I am, by the grace of God, exceedingly confident; having, by his goodness, received some strength and opportunity to search into and seriously to weigh whatever the most famous assertors of universal redemption, whether Lutherans or Arminians, have been able to say in this cause. For the present, I address myself to what is before me; only desiring the reader to observe, that the assertion to be proved is, "That Jesus Christ, according to the counsel and will of his Father, suitable to his purpose of salvation in his own mind and intention, did, by his death and oblation, pay a ransom for all and every man, elect and reprobate,— both those that are saved and those that perish,—to redeem them from sin, death, and hell, [and] to recover salvation, life, and immortality for them; and not only for his elect, or church, chosen to an inheritance before the foundation of the world." To confirm this we have divers proofs produced; which, by the Lord's assistance, we shall consider in order.

Proof 1 *of argument* 6. "God so loved the world, that he gave his Son to be the Saviour of the world, I John 4:14; and sends his servant to bear witness of his Son, that all men through him might believe, John 1:4, 7; that whosoever believes on him might have everlasting life, John 3:16, 17. And he is willing that all should come to the knowledge of the truth, I Tim. 2:4, and be saved, I Tim. 1:15. Nor will he be wanting in the sufficiency of helpfulness to them, if, as light comes, they will suffer themselves to be wrought on and to receive it, Prov. 1:23; 8:4, 5. And is not this plain in Scripture?"

Ans. First, The main, yea, indeed, only thing to be proved, as we before observed, is, that those indefinite propositions which we find in the Scripture concerning the death of Christ are to be understood universally,—that the terms *all* and *world* do signify in this business, when they denote the object of the death of Christ, all and every man in the world. Unless this be done, all other labour is altogether useless and fruitless. Now, to this there is nothing at all urged in this pretended proof, but only a few ambiguous places barely recited, with a false collection from them or observation upon them, which they give no colour to.

Secondly, I John 4:14, God's sending his Son to be the "Saviour of the world," and his servant to testify it, is nothing but to be the Saviour of men living in the world; which his elect are. A hundred such places as these, so clearly interpreted as they are in other places, would make nought at all to the purpose. The next thing is from John 1:4, 7. Verse 4 is, that Christ was the "life of men"; which is most true, no life being to be had for any man but only in and through him. This not being at all to the question, the next words of verse 7 [are], "That all men through him might believe"; which words being thrust in, to piece-up a sense with another fraction of Scripture, seem to have some weight, as though Christ were sent that all men through him might believe. A goodly show! seeming no less to make for universal redemption than the Scripture cited by the devil, after he had cut off part of it, did for our Saviour's casting himself from the pinnacle of the temple. But if you cast aside the sophistry of the old serpent, the expression of this place is not a little available to invalidate the thesis sought to be maintained by it. The words are, "There was a man sent from God, whose name was John. The same came for a witness, to bear witness of the light, that all men through him might believe." Now, who do you think is there meant by δι' αὐτοῦ, "through him"? Is it Christ, think you, the light? or John, the witness of the light? Certainly John, as almost all expositors do agree, except certain among the Papists, and Grotius,— that Ishmael. So the Syriac interpreter, reading, "By his hand or ministry." So the word infers; for we are not said to believe διὰ Χρίστου, "by Christ," or, as it should be here, διὰ τοῦ φωτός, "by the light"; but εἰς τὸ φῶς, John 12:36, "in the light," not *by* it. And ἐπὶ τὸν Κύριον, Acts 9:42, "believed in the Lord"; so also, Rom. 9:33, Καὶ πᾶς ὁ πιστεύων ἐπ' αὐτῷ, "Every one that believeth on him." So ἐν Χριστῷ, in divers places, *in him*; but no mention of believing *by him*, which rather denotes the instrument of believing, as is the ministry of the word, than the object of faith, as Christ is. This being apparent, let us see what is affirmed of John, why he was sent "that all through him might believe." Now, this word *all* here hath all the qualifications which our author requireth for it, to be always esteemed a certain expression of a collective universality, that it is spoken of God, etc. And who, I pray you, were these *all*, that were intended to be brought to the faith by the ministry of John? Were they not only all those that lived throughout the world in his days, who preached (a few years) in Judea only, but also all those that were dead before his nativity, and that were born after his death, and shall be to the end of the world in any place under heaven? Let them that can believe it enjoy their persuasion, with this assurance that I will never be their rival; being fully persuaded that by *all men* here is meant only some of all sorts, to whom his word did come. So that the necessary sense of the word *all* here is wholly destructive to the proposition.

For what, thirdly, is urged from John 3:16, 17, that God so sent his Son, that "whosoever believeth on him might have everlasting life," as far as I know is not under debate, as to the sense of it, among Christians.

Fourthly, For God's willingness that all should be saved, from I Tim. 2:4 (to which a word is needlessly added to make a show, the text being quite to another purpose, from I Tim. 1:15), taking *all men* there for the universality of individuals, then I ask,—*First,* What act it is of God wherein this his willingness doth consist? Is it in the eternal purpose of his will that all should be saved? Why is it not accomplished? "Who hath resisted his will?" Is it in an antecedent desire that it should be so, though he fail in the end? Then is the blessed God most miserable, it being not in him to accomplish his just and holy desires. Is it some temporary act of his, whereby he hath declared himself unto them? Then, I say, Grant that salvation is only to be had in a Redeemer, in Jesus Christ, and give me an instance how God, in any act whatsoever, hath declared his mind and revealed himself to all men, of all times and places, concerning his willingness of their salvation by Jesus Christ, a Redeemer, and I will never more trouble you in this cause. *Secondly,* Doth this will equally respect the *all* intended, or doth it not? If it doth, why hath it not equal effects towards all? what reason can be assigned? If it doth not, whence shall that appear? There is nothing in the text to intimate any such diversity. For our parts, by *all men* we understand some of all sorts throughout the world, not doubting but that, to the equal reader, we have made it so appear from the context and circumstances of the place, the will of God there being that mentioned by our Saviour, John 6:40. That which follows in the close of this proof, of God's "not being wanting in the sufficiency of helpfulness to them who, as light comes, suffer themselves to be wrought upon and receive it," is a poisonous sting in the tail of the serpent, wherein is couched the whole Pelagian poison of free-will and Popish merit of congruity, with Arminian sufficient grace, in its whole extent and universality; to neither of which there is the least witness given in the place produced.

The sum and meaning of the whole assertion is, that there is a universality of sufficient grace granted to all, even of grace subjective, enabling them to obedience, which receives addition, increase, degrees, and augmentation, according as they who have it do make use of what they presently enjoy; which is a position so contradictory to innumerable places of Scripture, so derogatory to the free grace of God, so destructive to the efficacy of it, such a clear exaltation of the old idol free-will into the throne of God, as any thing that the decaying estate of Christianity hath invented and broached. So far is it from being "plain and clear in Scripture," that it is universally repugnant to the whole dispensation of the new covenant revealed to us therein; which, if ever the Lord call me to, I hope very clearly to demonstrate: for the present, it belongs not immediately to the business in hand, and therefore I leave it, coming to—

Proof 2. "Jesus Christ, the Son of God, came into the world to save the world, John 12:47; to save sinners, I Tim. 1:15; to take away our sins, and destroy the works of the devil, I John 3:5, 8; to take away the sins of the world, John 1:29; and therefore died for all, II Cor. 5:14, 15; and gave himself a ransom for all, I Tim. 2:6; to save that which was lost, Matt. 18:11. And so his propitiation was made for the world, II Cor. 5:19; the whole world, I John 2:2. And all this is full and plain in Scripture."

Ans. Those places of this proof where there is mention of *all* or *world,* as John 12:47; 1:29; II Cor. 5:14, 15; I Tim. 2:6; II Cor. 5:19; I John 2:2, have been all already considered, and I am unwilling to trouble the reader with repetitions. See the places, and I doubt not but you will find that they are so far from giving any strength to the thing intended to be proved by him, that they much rather evert it. For the rest, I Tim. 1:15; Matt. 18:11; I John 3:5, 8, how any thing can be extracted from them to give colour to the universality of redemption I cannot see; what they make against it hath been declared. Pass we then to—

Proof 3. "God in Christ doth, in some means or other of his appointment, give some witness to all men of his mercy and goodness procured by Christ, Ps. 19:4; Rom. 10:18; Acts 14:17; and therethrough, at one time or other, sendeth forth some stirrings of his Spirit, to move in and knock at the hearts of men, to invite them to repentance and seeking God, and so to lay hold on the grace and salvation offered: and this not in a show or pretence, but in truth and good-will, ready to bestow it on them. And this is all fully testified in Scripture, Gen. 6:3; Isa. 45:22; Acts 17:30, 31; John 1:19."

Ans. First, "Parvas habet spes Troja, si tales habet." If the universality of redemption have need of such proofs as these, it hath indeed great need and little hope of supportment. *Universal vocation* is here asserted, to maintain *universal redemption*. "Manus manum fricat," or rather, "Muli se mutuo scabiunt"; this being called in oftentimes to support the other; and they are both the two legs of that idol free-will, which is set up for men to worship, and when one stumbles the other steps forward to uphold the Babel. Of *universal vocation* (a gross figment) I shall not now treat; but only say, for the present, that it is true that God at all times, ever since the creation, hath called men to the knowledge of himself as the great Creator, in those things which of him, by the means of the visible creation, might be known, "even his eternal power and Godhead," Rom. 1:19, 20; Ps. 19:1, 2; Acts 14:17. Secondly, That after the death of Christ, he did, by the preaching of the gospel extended far and wide, call home to himself the children of God, scattered abroad in the world, whereas his elect were before confined almost to one nation; giving a right to the gospel to be preached to "every creature," Mark 16:15; Rom. 10:18; Isa. 45:22; Acts 17:30, 31. But, thirdly, That God should at all times, in all places, in all ages, grant means of grace or call to Christ as a redeemer, or to a participation of his mercy and goodness in him manifested, with strivings and motions of his Spirit for men to close with those invitations, is so gross and groundless an imagination, so opposite to God's distinguishing mercy, so contradictory to express places of Scripture and the experience of all ages, as I wonder how any man hath the boldness to assert it, much more to produce it as a proof of an untruth more gross than itself. Were I not resolved to tie myself to the present controversy, I should not hold from producing some reasons to evert this fancy; something may be done hereafter, if the Lord prevent not. In the meantime, let the reader consult Ps. 147:19, 20; Matt. 11:25; 22:14; Acts 14:16; 16:7; Rom. 10:14, 15. We pass to—

Proof 4. "The Holy Ghost, that cometh from the Father and the Son, shall reprove the world of sin (even that part of the world that refuseth now to believe that they are under sin), because they believe not on Christ, and that it is their sin that they have not believed on him. And how could it be their sin not to believe in Christ, and they for that cause [be] under sin, if there were neither enough in the atonement made by Christ for them, nor truth in

God's offer of mercy to them, nor will nor power in the Spirit's moving in any sort sufficient to have brought them to believe, at one time or other? And yet is this evident in Scripture, and shall be by the Holy Spirit, to be their great sin, that fastens all other sins on them, John 3:18, 19; 8:24; 12:48; 15:22, 24; 16:7-11.

Ans. The intention of this proof is, to show that men shall be condemned for their unbelief, for not believing in Christ; which, saith the author, cannot be unless three things be granted,—First, That there be enough in the atonement made by Christ for them. Secondly, That there be truth in God's offer of mercy to them. Thirdly, That there be sufficient will and power given them by the Spirit, at some time or other, to believe. Now, though I believe no man can perceive what may be concluded hence for the universality of redemption, yet I shall observe some few things: and to the first thing required do say, That if, by "Enough in the atonement for them," you understand that the atonement, which was made for them, hath enough in it, we deny it; not because the atonement hath not enough in it for them, but because the atonement was not for them. If you mean that there is a sufficiency in the merit of Christ to save them if they should believe, we grant it, and affirm that this sufficiency is the chief ground of the proposing it unto them (understanding those to whom it is proposed, that is those to whom the gospel is preached). To the second, That there is truth, as in all the ways and words of God, so in his offer of mercy to whomsoever it is offered. If we take the command to believe, with the promise of life upon so doing, for an offer of mercy, there is an eternal truth in it; which is, that God will assuredly bestow life and salvation upon all believers, the proffers being immediately declarative of our duty; secondly, of the concatenation of faith and life, and not at all of God's intention towards the particular soul to whom the proffer is made: "For who hath known the mind of the Lord, and who hath been his counsellor?" To the third, the Spirit's giving will or power, I say,—First, That ye set the cart before the horse, placing will before power. *Secondly,* I deny that any internal assistance is required to render a man inexcusable for not believing, if he have the object of faith propounded to him, though of himself he have neither power nor will so to do, having lost both in Adam. *Thirdly,* How a man may have given him a will to believe, and yet not believe, I pray, declare the next controversy ye undertake. This being observed, I shall take leave to put this proof into such form as alone it is capable of, that the strength thereof may appear, and it is this: "If the Spirit shall convince all those of sin to whom the gospel is preached, that do not believe, then Christ died for all men, both those that have the gospel preached unto them and those that have not; but the first is true, for their unbelief is their great sin: ergo, Jesus Christ died for all." Which, if any, is an argument "a baculo ad angulum," "from the beam to the shuttle." The places of Scripture, John 3:18, 19; 8:24; 12:48; 15:22, 24, prove that unbelief is a soul-condemning sin, and that for which they shall be condemned in whom it is privative, by their having the gospel preached to them. But *quid ad nos?*

One place is more urged, and consequently more abused, than the rest, and therefore must be a little cleared; it is John 16:7-11. The words are, "I will send the Comforter to you. And when he is come, he will reprove the world of sin, and of righteousness, and of judgment: of sin, because they believe not in me; of righteousness, because I go to my Father, and ye see me no more; of judgment, because the prince of this world is judged." First, It is uncertain whether our author understands the words of the Spirit in and with Christ at the last day, or in and with the ministry of the word now in the days of the gospel. If the first, he is foully mistaken; if the latter, then the conviction here meant intends only those to whom the gospel is preached,—and what that will advantage universal redemption, which compriseth all as well before as after the death of Christ, I know not. But, secondly, It is uncertain whether he supposeth this conviction of the Spirit to attend the preaching of the gospel only, or else to consist in strivings and motions even in them who never hear the word of the gospel; if he mean the latter, we wait for a proof. Thirdly, It is uncertain whether he supposeth those thus convinced to be converted and brought to the faith by that conviction and that attending effectualness of grace, or no.

But omitting those things, that text being brought forth and insisted on, farther to manifest how little reason there was for its producing, I shall briefly open the meaning of the words. Our Saviour Christ intending, in this his last sermon, to comfort his apostles in their present sad condition, whereto they were brought by his telling them that he must leave them and go to his Father,—which sorrow and sadness he knew full well would be much increased when they should behold the vile, ignominious way whereby their Lord and Master should be taken from them, with all those reproaches and persecutions which would attend them so deprived of him,—bids them not be troubled, nor filled with sorrow and fear, for all this; assuring them that all this loss, shame, and reproach should be abundantly made up by what he would do for them and bestow upon them when his bodily presence should be removed from them. And as to that particular, which was the head of all, that he should be so vilely rejected and taken out of the world as a false teacher and seducer, he telleth them he will send them ἄλλον παράκλητον, John 14:16, "another Comforter," one that shall "vicariam navare operam," as Tertul.,—be unto them in his stead, to fill them with all that consolation whereof by his absence they might be deprived; and not only so, but also to be present with them in other greater things than any he had as yet employed them about. This again he puts them in mind of, chap. 16:7. Now, ὁ παράκλητος, who is there promised, is properly "an advocate,"—that is, one that pleadeth the cause of a person that is guilty or accused before any tribunal,—and is opposed τῷ κατηγόρῳ, Rev. 12:10; and so is this word by us translated, I John 2:1. Christ, then, here telleth them, that as he will be their advocate with the Father, so he will send them an advocate to plead his cause, which they professed, with the world; that is, those men in the world, which had so vilely traduced and condemned him as a seducer, laying it as a reproach upon all his followers. This, doubtless, though in some respect it be continued to all ages in the ministry of the word, yet it principally intended the plentiful effusion of the Spirit upon the apostles at Pentecost, after the ascension of our Saviour; which also is made more apparent by the consideration of what he affirmeth that the advocate so sent shall do, namely,—1. "He shall reprove," or rather, evidently, "convince, the world of sin, because they believed not on him"; which, surely, he abundantly did in that sermon of Peter, Acts 2, when the enemies themselves and haters of Christ were so reproved and convinced of their sin, that, upon the pressing urgency of that conviction, they cried out, "Men and brethren, what shall we do to be saved?" Then was the world brought to a voluntary confession of the sin of murdering Jesus Christ. 2. He shall do the same of "righteousness, because he went to his Father";— not of its own righteousness, to reprove it for that, because it is not; but he shall convince the men of the world, who condemned Christ as a seducer, of his righteousness,—that he was not a blasphemer, as they pretended, but the Son of God, as himself witnessed: which they shall be forced to acknowledge when, by the effusion and pouring out of the Spirit upon his apostles, it shall be made evident that he is gone to and received of his Father, and owned by him, as the centurion did presently upon his death. 3. He shall "convince the world of judgment, because the prince of this world is judged"; manifesting to all those of whom he speaketh, that he whom they despised as the carpenter's son, and bade come down from the cross if he could, is exalted to the right hand of God, having all judgment committed to him, having beforehand, in his death, judged, sentenced, and overcome Satan, the prince of this world, the chief instigator of his crucifiers, who had the power of death. And this I take to be the clear, genuine meaning of this place, not excluding the efficacy of the Spirit, working in the same manner, though not to the same degree, for the same end, in the majesty of the word, to the end of the world. But what this is to universal redemption, let them that can understand it keep it to themselves, for I am confident they will never be able to make it out to others.

Proof 5. "God hath testified, both by his word and his oath, that he would that his Son should so far save as to work a redemption for all men, and likewise that he should bring all to the knowledge of the truth, that there-through redemption might be wrought in and upon them, I Tim. 2:4, with John 3:17. So he willeth not, nor hath any pleasure in, the death of him (even the wicked) that dieth, but rather that he turn and live, Ezek. 18:23, 32; 33:11. And dare any of us say, the God of truth saith and sweareth that of which he hath no inward and serious meaning? O far be such blasphemy from us!"

Ans. First, This assertion, "That God testifieth, by his word and oath, that he would that Christ should so far save us," etc., is a bold calling of God to witness that which he never affirmed, nor did it ever enter into his heart; for he hath revealed his will that Christ should save to the utmost them that come to him, and not save so far or so far, as is boldly, ignorantly, and falsely intimated. Let men beware of provoking God to their own confusion; he will not be a witness to the lie of false hearts. Secondly, "That Christ should so bring all to the knowledge of the truth, that there-through redemption might be wrought in and upon them," is another bold corruption of the word, and false-witness-bearing in the name of God. Is it a small thing for you to weary and seduce men? will you weary our God also? Thirdly, For places of Scripture corrupted to the sense imposed: In John 3:17, God is said to "send his Son, that the world through him might be saved"; not be saved so far or so far, but saved "from their sins," Matt. 1:21, and "to the uttermost," Heb. 7:25: so that the world of God's elect, who only are so saved, is only there to be understood, as hath been proved. In I Tim. 2:4, there is something of the will of God for the saving of all sorts of men, as hath been declared; nothing conducing to the bold assertion used in this place. Fourthly, To those are added that of Ezek. 18:23, that God hath no "pleasure at all that the wicked should die"; and, verse 32, "no pleasure in the death of him that dieth." Now, though these texts are exceeding useless to the business in hand, and might probably have some colour of universal vocation, but none possibly of universal redemption, there being no mention of Christ or his death in the place from whence they are cited; yet because our adversaries are frequently knitting knots from this place to inveigle and hamper the simple, I shall add some few observations upon it to clear the meaning of the text, and demonstrate how it belongs nothing at all to the business in hand.

First, then, let us consider to whom and of whom these words are spoken. Is it to and of all men, or only to the house of Israel? Doubtless these last; they are only intended, they only are spoken to: "Hear now, O house of Israel," verse 25. Now, will it follow that because God saith he delights not in the death of the house of Israel, to whom he revealed his mind, and required their repentance and conversion, that therefore he saith so of all, even those to whom he never revealed his will by such ways as to them, nor called to repentance, Ps. 147:19, 20? So that the very ground-work of the whole conclusion is removed by this first observation. Secondly, "God willeth not the death of a sinner," is either, "God purposeth and determineth he shall not die," or, "God commandeth that he shall do those things wherein he may live." If the first, why are they not all saved? why do sinners die? for there is an immutability in the counsel of God, Heb. 6:17; "His counsel shall stand, and he will do all his pleasure," Isa. 46:10. If the latter way, by commanding, then the sense is, that the Lord commandeth that those whom he calleth should do their duty, that they may not die (although he knows that this they cannot do without his assistance); now, what this makes to general redemption, I know not. Thirdly, To add no more, this whole place, with the scope, aim, and intention of the prophet in it, is miserably mistaken by our adversaries, and wrested to that whereof there is not the least thought in the text. The words are a part of the answer which the Lord gives to the repining Jews, concerning their proverb, "The fathers have eaten sour grapes, and the children's teeth are set on edge." Now, about what did they use this proverb? Why, "concerning the land of Israel," verse 2, the land of their habitation, which was laid waste by the sword (as they affirmed) for the sins of their fathers, themselves being innocent. So that it is about God's temporal judgments in overturning their land and nation that this dispute is; wherein the Lord justifieth himself by declaring the equity of these judgments by reason of their sins, even those sins for which the land devoured them and spewed them out; telling them that his justice is, that for such things they should surely die, their blood should be upon them, verse 13,—they shall be slain with the sword, and cut off by those judgments which they had deserved: not that the shedding of their blood and casting out of their carcasses was a thing in itself so pleasurable or desirable to him as that he did it only for his own will, for let them leave their abominations, and try whether their lives were not prolonged in peace. This being the plain, genuine scope and meaning of this place, at the first view presenting itself to every unprejudiced man, I have often admired how so many strange conclusions for a general purpose of showing mercy to all, universal vocation and redemption, have been wrested from it; as also, how it came to be produced to give colour to that heap of blasphemy which our author calleth his fifth proof.

Proof 6. "The very words and phrases used by the Holy Ghost in Scripture, speaking of the death of Christ, and the ransom and propitiation, to whom it belongs, and who may seek it, and in believing find life, implies no less than all men. As to instance: "All nations," Matt. 28:19, 20; "the ends of the earth," Isa. 45:22; 49:6; "every creature," Mark 16:15; "all," II Cor. 5:14, 15; I Tim. 2:6; "every man," Heb. 2:9; "the world," John 3:16, 17; II Cor. 5:19; "the whole world," I John 2:2; "that which was lost," Luke 19:10; "sinners," Matt. 9:13; "unjust," I Peter 3:18; "ungodly," Rom. 5:6; and that whosoever of these repent and believe in Christ shall receive his grace, John 3:16, 18; Acts 10:43. Now, all these so often and indifferently used, were it not pride and error to devise glosses to restrain the sense the Scripture holdeth forth, so full and large for all men?"

Ans. First, This argument, taken from the words and phrases whereby the object of the death of Christ is in the Scripture expressed, is that which filleth up both pages of this book, being repeated, and most of the places here cited urged, a hundred times over; and yet it is so far from being any pressing argument, as that indeed it is nothing but a bare naked repetition of the thing in debate, concluding according to his own persuasion; for the main *quaere* between us is, whether the words *all* and *the world* be to be taken universally? He saith so, and he saith so; which is all the proof we have, repeating over the thing to be proved instead of a proof. Secondly, For those places which affirm Christ to die for "sinners," "ungodly," "that which was lost," etc.,—as Luke 19:10; Matt. 9:13; I Peter 3:18; Rom. 5:6,—I have before declared how exceedingly unserviceable they are to universal redemption. Thirdly, For those places where the words "all," "every man," "the world," "the whole world," are used, we have had them over and over; and they likewise have been considered. Fourthly, For those expressions of "all nations," Matt. 28:19, 20, "every creature," Mark 16:15, used concerning them to whom the gospel is preached, I say,—*First*, That they do not comprise all individuals, nay, not all nations at all times, much less all singular persons of all nations if we look upon the accomplishment and fulfilling of that command; neither, *de facto,* was the gospel ever so preached to all, although there by a fitness and a suitableness in the dispensation thereof to be so preached to all, as was declared. *Secondly*, The command of preaching the gospel to all doth not in the least manner prove that Christ died with an intention to redeem all; but it hath other grounds and other ends, as hath been manifested. *Thirdly*, That the ransom belongs to all to whom it is proposed we deny; there be other ends of that proposal; and Christ will say to some of them that he never knew them: therefore, certainly, he did not lay down his life for them. *Fourthly*, "The ends of the earth," Isa. 45:22, are those that look up to God from all parts, and are saved; which surely are not all and every one. And Christ being given to be a "salvation unto the end of the earth," chap. 49:6, is to do no more among the Gentiles than God promiseth in the same place that he shall do for his own people,—even "gather the preserved of Israel"; so shall he bear forth the salvation of God, and gather the preserved remnant of his elect to the ends of the earth.

And now, I hope, I need not mind the intelligent reader that the author of these collections could not have invented a more ready way for the ruin of the thesis which he seeks to maintain than by producing those places of Scripture last recounted for the confirmation of it, granting that *all* and *the world* are no more than "all the ends of the earth," mentioned in Isa. 45:22; 49:6; it being evident beyond denial that by these expressions, in both these places, only the elect of God and believers are clearly intimated: so that, interpreting the one by the other, in those places where *all* and *the world* are spoken of, those only are intended. "If pride and error" had not taken full possession of the minds of men, they could not so far deny their own sense and reason as to contradict themselves and the plain texts of Scripture for the maintenance of their false and corrupt opinions.

Proof 7. "That whereas there are certain high and peculiar privileges of the Spirit contained in the New Testament, sealed by the blood of Christ, which belong not to all men, but only to the saints, the called and chosen of the Lord, and when they are alone distinctly mentioned, they are even so spoken of as belonging to them only, Matt. 13:11; John 14:17, 21-23; 16:13-15; 17:19, 20; Acts 2:38,

39; I Cor. 2:9, 14; Heb. 9:15; 8; I Peter 2:3, 9; yet many of these peculiar privileges are so spoken of as joined together with the ransom and propitiation, which belongs to all. Then are they not spoken of in such a restraining and exclusive manner, or with such appropriating words, but so, and with such words, as room is left to apply the ransom to all men, in speech; and withal, so hold out the privileges to them that believe that are proper to them, that they may both have their comfort and especial hope, and also hold forth the ransom and keep open the door for others, in belief and receipt of the propitiation, to come in and partake with them. And so it is said for his "sheep," and for "many"; but nowhere but only for his sheep, or but only for many: which is a strong proof of the ransom for all men, as is shown, chap. 3, 10."

Ans. The strength of this proof, as to the business in hand, is wholly hid from me; neither do I perceive how it may receive any such tolerable application as to deserve the name of a proof, as to the main thesis intended to be maintained. The force which it hath is in an observation which, if it hath any sense, is neither true nor once attempted to be made good; for,—First, That there are peculiar high privileges belonging to the saints and called of God is a thing which needs no proof. Amongst these is the death of Christ for them, not as saints, but as elect, which, by the benefit of that death and blood-shedding, are to be made saints, and accounted to be the holy ones of God: for "he redeemed his church with his own blood," Acts 20:28; he "loved and gave himself for it," Eph. 5:25; even "us," Titus 2:14;—even as divers of those [privileges] here intimated are expressly assigned unto them, as elect, such as those, John 17:19, 20; amongst which also, as in the same rank with them, is reckoned Jesus' "sanctifying himself for their sakes," that is to be an oblation, verse 19. In a word, all peculiar saving privileges belong only to God's elect, purchased for them, and them alone, by the blood of Jesus Christ, Eph. 1:3, 4. Secondly, For the other part of the observation, that where mention is made of these together with the ransom, there is room left to extend the ransom to all, I answer,—First, This is said, indeed, but not once attempted to be proved. We have but small cause to believe the author, in any thing of this importance, upon his bare word. Secondly, For the "leaving of room for the application," I perceive that if it be not left, ye will make it, though ye justle the true sense of the Scripture quite out of its place. Thirdly, I have already showed that where "many" are mentioned, the ransom only (as ye use to speak) is expressed, as also where "sheep" are spoken of; the like is said where the word "all" is used;—so that there is not the least difference. *Fourthly,* In divers places the ransom of Christ and those other peculiar privileges (which indeed are fruits of it) are so united together, as it is impossible to apply the latter to *some* and the other to *all,* being all of them restrained to his saved ones only, Rev. 5:9, 10. The redemption of his people by the ransom of his blood, and their making kings and priests, are united, and no room left for the extending of the ransom to all, it being punctually assigned to those saved crowned ones, distinguished from the rest of the nations and languages from among whom they were taken, who were passed by in the payment of the ransom; which is directly opposite to all the sense which I can observe in this observation. *Fifthly,* Of "sheep, and sheep only," enough before.

Proof 8. "The restoration wrought by Christ in his own body for mankind is set forth in Scripture to be as large and full for all men, and of as much force, as the fall of the first Adam, by and in himself, for all men; in which respect the first Adam is said to have been a figure of Christ, the second Adam, Rom. 3:22-25; 5:12, 14, 18; I Cor. 15:21, 22, 45-47: as is before shown, chap. 8."

Ans. First, It is most true that Christ and Adam are compared together (in respect of the righteousness of the one, communicated to them that are his, and the disobedience and transgression of the other, in like manner communicated to all them that are of him) in some of the places here mentioned, as Rom. 5:12, 18. But evidently the comparison is not instituted between the righteousness of Christ and the disobedience of Adam *extensively,* in respect of the *object,* but *intensively,* in respect of the *efficacy* of the one and the other; the apostle asserting the effectualness of the righteousness of Christ unto justification, to answer the prevalency of the sin of Adam unto condemnation,—that even as the transgression of Adam brought a guilt of condemnation upon all them that are his natural seed, so the righteousness of Christ procured the free gift of grace unto justification towards all them that are his, his spiritual seed, that were the children given unto him of his Father.

Secondly, I Cor. 15:21, 22, speaketh of the resurrection from the dead, and that only of believers; for though he mentions them all, verse 22, "In Christ shall all be made alive," yet, verse 23, he plainly interprets those *all* to be all that are "Christ's": not but that the other dead shall rise also, but that it is a resurrection to glory, by virtue of the resurrection of Christ, which the apostle here treats of; which certainly all shall not have.

Thirdly, The comparison between Christ and Adam, verse 45 (to speak nothing of the various reading of that place), is only in respect of the principles which they had, and were intrusted withal to communicate to others: "Adam a living soul," or a "living creature"; there was in him a principle of life natural, to be communicated to his posterity;—"Christ a quickening Spirit," giving life, grace, and spirit to his. And here I would desire that it may be observed, that all the comparison that is anywhere instituted between Christ and Adam still comes to one head, and aims at one thing,—namely, that they were as two common stocks or roots, communicating to them that are ingrafted into them (that is, into Adam *naturally,* by generation; into Christ *spiritually,* by regeneration) that wherewith they were replenished;—Adam, sin, guilt, and disobedience; Christ, righteousness, peace, and justification. [As] for the number of those that do thus receive these things from one and the other, the consideration of it is exceedingly alien from the scope, aim, and end of the apostle in the places where the comparison is instituted.

Fourthly, It is true, in Rom. 3:23, it is said, "All have sinned, and come short of the glory of God," which the apostle had at large proved before, thereby to manifest that there was no salvation to be attained but only by Jesus Christ; but if ye will ask to whom this righteousness of Christ is extended, and that redemption which is in his blood, he telleth you plainly, it is "unto all and upon all them that believe," verse 22, whether they be Jews or Gentiles, "for there is no difference."

Proof 9. "The Lord Jesus Christ hath sent and commanded his servants to preach the gospel to all nations, to every creature, and to tell them withal that whoever believeth and is baptized shall be saved, Matt. 28:19, 20; Mark 16:15, 16: and his servants have so preached to all, II Cor. 5:19; Rom. 10:13, 18. And our Lord Jesus Christ will make it to appear one day that he hath not sent his servants upon a false errand, nor put a lie in their mouths, nor wished them to dissemble, in offering that to all which they knew belonged but to some, even to fewest of all, but to speak truth, Isa. 44:26; 61:8; I Tim. 1:12."

Ans. The strength of this proof is not easily apparent, nor manifest wherein it lieth, in what part or words of it: for,—First, It is true, Christ commanded his apostles to "preach the gospel to all nations and every creature,"—to tell them "that whosoever believeth shall be saved," Matt. 28:19, 20; Mark 16:15, 16; that is, without distinction of persons or nations, to call all men to whom the providence of God should direct them, and from whom the Spirit of God should not withhold them (as from them, Acts 16:6, 7), warning them to repent and believe the gospel. Secondly, It is also true, that, in obedience unto this command, his servants did beseech men so to do, and to be reconciled unto God, even all over the nations, without distinction of any, but where they were forbidden, as above, labouring to spread the gospel to the ends of the earth, and not to tie it up to the confines of Jewry, II Cor. 5:19, 20; Rom. 10:18. Most certain also it is, that the Lord Jesus Christ sent not his servants with a lie, to offer that to all which belonged only to some, but to speak the truth; of which there needs no proof. But now, what can be concluded from hence for universal redemption is not easily discernible.

Perhaps some will say it is in this, that if Christ did not die for all to whom the word is preached, then how can they that preach it offer Christ to all? A poor proof, God wot! For,—First, The gospel was never preached to all and every one, nor is there any such thing affirmed in the places cited; and ye are to prove that Christ died for all, as well those that never hear of the gospel as those that do. Secondly, What do the preachers of the gospel offer to them to whom the word is preached? Is it not life and salvation through Christ, upon the condition of faith and repentance? And doth not the truth of this offer consist in this, that every one that believeth shall be saved? And doth not that truth stand firm and inviolable, so long as there is an all-sufficiency in Christ to save all that come unto him? Hath God intrusted the ministers of the gospel with his intentions, purpose, and counsels, or with his commands and promises? Is it a lie, to tell men that he that believeth shall be saved, though Christ did not die for some of them? Such proofs as these had need be well proved themselves, or they will conclude the thing intended very weakly.

Proof 10. "The Lord willeth believers to pray even for the unjust and their persecutors, Matt. 5:44, 48; Luke 6:28; yea, even 'for all men'; yea, even 'for kings and all in authority,' when few in authority loved Christianity. Yet he said not, some of that sort, but, 'For all in authority'; and that on this ground,—it is good in the sight of God, 'who will have all men saved, and come to the knowledge of the truth,' Luke 10:5; I Tim. 2:1-4. Surely there is a door of life opened for all men, II Tim. 1:10; for God hath not said to the seed of Israel, 'Seek ye me in vain,' Isa. 44:19. He will not have his children pray for vain things."

Ans. The strength of this proof lieth in supposing,—First, That *indefinite* assertions are to be interpreted as equivalent to *universal;* which is false, Rom. 4, 5. Secondly, That by "all," I Tim. 2:1, is not meant all sorts of men, and the word *all* is not to be taken distributively, when the apostle, by an enumeration of divers sorts, gives an evident demonstration of the distribution intended. Thirdly, That we are bound to pray for every singular man that he may be saved; which,—1. We have no warrant, rule, precept, or example for;

2. It is contrary to the apostolical precept, I John 5:16; 3. To our Saviour's example, John 17:9; 4. To the counsel and purpose of God, in the general made known to us, Rom. 9:11, 12, 15; 11:7, where evidently our praying for all is but for all sorts of men, excluding none, and that those may believe who are ordained to eternal life. Fourthly, It supposeth that there is nothing else that we are to pray for men but that they may be saved by Christ; which is apparently false, Jer. 29:7. Fifthly, That our ground of praying for any is an assurance that Christ died for them in particular; which is not true, Acts 8:22, 24. Sixthly, It most splendidly takes for granted that our duty is to be conformed to God's secret mind, his purpose and counsel. Until every one of these supposals be made good, (which never a one of them will be very suddenly), there is no help in this proof nor strength in this argument, "We must pray for all; therefore God intends by the death of Christ to save all and every one," its sophistry and weakness being apparent. From our duty to God's purpose is no good conclusion, though from his command to our duty be most certain. . . .

And these are the proofs which this author calls *"plain* and according to Scripture," being a recapitulation of almost all that he hath said in his whole book; at least, for the argumentative part thereof, there is not any thing of weight omitted: and therefore this chapter I fixed on to return a full and punctual answer unto. Now, whether the thing intended to be proved, namely, *The paying of a ransom by Christ for all and every man, be plainly, clearly, and evidently* from the Scripture *confirmed,* as he would bear us in hand; or whether all this heap of words, called arguments, reasons, and proofs, be not, for their manner of expression, obscure, uncouth, and ofttimes unintelligible,—for their way of inference, childish, weak, and ridiculous,—in their allegations and interpretations of Scripture, perverse, violent, mistaken, through ignorance, heedlessness, and corruption of judgment, in direct opposition to the mind and will of God revealed therein,— is left to the judgment of the Christian reader that shall peruse them, with the answers annexed.

Samuel Hopkins
1721-1803

9

Regeneration and Conversion

Samuel Hopkins was born at Waterbury, Connecticut, 17 September 1721 and was set apart by his father for the ministry. He entered Yale College in 1737 when New Haven was being moved by the Calvinistic preaching of George Whitefield and Gilbert Tennent, and Hopkins was converted under their preaching. Upon graduation he began studying theology under Jonathan Edwards and was greatly influenced by him. In 1741 Hopkins began preaching with great embarrassment and humility. Two years later he was ordained minister of a new church of only five members at Housatanick. He remained there for twenty-five years while the church membership grew to 116, despite the interruptions of two great wars. From 1744 to 1763 the French and Indian War raged in the area, and Hopkins often had to flee with his family.

During his ministry Hopkins was criticized for many things: for reading Scripture portions in the Sunday services in addition to preaching; for delivering his sermons without notes; for evangelizing the Indians; for advocating strong Calvinistic doctrine; and for forbidding non-Christians to take communion. He also alienated the Tories with his patriotism to the Colonial cause. Some of his parishioners, despite his fidelity to Scripture, gave nothing to support him, and others had nothing to give. In poverty he left the church in 1769 and went to one at Newport, Rhode Island, a commercial center that then rivaled New York. During his first year at Newport Hopkins was visited by Whitefield. In 1776 the town was captured by the British, who held it for three years, and Hopkins fled to Newburyport to assist his friend Samuel Spring.

In 1779 Hopkins returned to Newport to preach despite the congregation's inability to pay him a regular salary. It was at this time, and in the capital of the New England slave market, that Hopkins preached his famous sermons against slavery and wrote the widely read *Dialogue Concerning the Slavery of the Africans* and *Address to Slaveholders*. He became a leading Abolitionist—probably the first American clergyman to promote that cause.

It was as a theologian, though, that Hopkins became best known. He developed a modified form of Calvinism that came to be identified as "Hopkinsianism." He attempted to blend Calvinism with revivalism, and in so doing he made all sin equal selfishness; he modified the doctrine of imputation; and he made repentance a necessary prerequisite of faith, rather than vice versa.

The following excerpt comprises a cogent discussion of regeneration and exemplifies American Puritan teaching on this subject. Hopkins's main thesis is that the Holy Spirit sovereignly regenerates the unbeliever. He attacks the Catholic concept of synergism, whereby man cooperates with God in salvation and sanctification. Hopkins identifies regeneration as the work of God alone through the Holy Spirit.

Also included is a very interesting discussion of the role of Scripture in the process of regeneration. Hopkins denies the Catholic and Lutheran sacramental concept of the Bible's role. His position is this: in the actual process of regeneration, God works directly through the Holy Spirit; the Scripture acts as a catalyst in the process, being indispensable *(sine qua non)* to the reaction without actually entering into it.

Hopkins distinguishes between a general illumination by the Word and regeneration by the Holy Spirit. He also discusses the matter of the sinner "seeking" God by using divine "means" (i.e., Scripture), saying, like Manton, that "seeking" is a preparatory step in the process of regeneration.

John 1:13—*Which were born, not of blood, nor of the will of the flesh, nor of the will of man, but of God.*

In the words preceding these, we are told in what way persons become the sons of God, viz., by receiving Christ, or believing on his name. It is by virtue of their union of heart to Christ the eternal Son of God, which consists in cleaving to him and trusting in him, in the character of Mediator between God and man, that they are received into the relation of sons, and made heirs of God, and joint heirs with Jesus Christ.

In the text we are told by whom they who thus become the sons of God are brought into this state of union to Jesus Christ and made to exist in this relation, or who is the cause or author of their thus receiving Christ or believing in him, by which they become the sons of God, which is here called *a being born*. When a child is born into the world, there is some cause of this production, this living, perfect child; so, when any person becomes a new creature, and in a sense enters into a new world, even into the kingdom of God, by believing on the name of Jesus Christ, there is some agent which is the cause of this.

"God hath made of one blood all nations of men," (Acts 17:26); that is, he hath produced all nations by natural descent from one man. The evangelist here tells us that the birth he speaks of is quite a different thing from this; it is not produced by natural generation or descent from father to son; it does not thus run in the blood, and is not transmitted from generation to generation in this way. Men do not become the sons of God, they are not regenerated, and do not become believers in Christ by any thing derived from their natural parents, by their descent from them, and near relation to them, by which the blood of the parents does, as it were, run in their veins. The piety or holiness of the parents has no influence or hand in this production, as a cause; it does nothing towards regenerating, or producing faith in the child. The child of the most holy parent is by nature as corrupt and as far from this birth, and always will be so, without some other cause or influence, as are the children of the ungodly.

In this assertion there seems to be a particular design to contradict and oppose a then prevailing notion among the Jews—that they were the sons of God by blood, as they were the children of Abraham. Of this they boast to our Savior, and say that they were Abraham's seed, and, therefore, that God was their father; as if by being the children of Abraham they were the sons of God. (John 8:33, 41; Rom. 8:1-9; Gal. 5:17) In opposition to this notion of theirs, John Baptist says to them, "Begin not to say within yourselves, We have Abraham to our father; for I say unto you, that God is able of these

stones to raise up children unto Abraham." (Luke 3:8; I Cor. 2:14, 15)
Nor of the will of the flesh. By flesh is meant man in his natural,
corrupt state, as he is antecedent to regeneration. This is the meaning
of *flesh* as it is used in many places in Holy Scripture; which is
evident, among other things, by its being frequently put in opposition
to the Spirit; and to be in the flesh, and to walk after the flesh, or
to be carnal, is spoken of as directly opposite to being spiritual, having the spirit of Christ, and walking after the Spirit, and as if there
was no medium between them. (John 3:1, 6) What is here asserted
then is, that persons are not regenerated by any inclinations, choice,
or exertions of their own, while they were in a state of unregeneracy.
They do not, by the exercise of their own wills, or by their endeavors,
do any thing towards their being born again; nor do they coöperate
in the least degree with the efficient cause. So far from this, that all
their inclinations, and every act of will and exertion of theirs, is in
direct opposition to it, for the flesh always lusteth against the Spirit.

It is, indeed, as great an absurdity as can be thought of, to suppose
that the corrupt, vicious heart does any thing towards its becoming
holy, or exercises any will or choice that has the least tendency to it;
as absurd as to suppose that the exercise of perfect selfishness has a
tendency to produce benevolence, or that the heart is made better
and becomes holy by the constant exercise of lust and wickedness.
For all the exercises and volitions of the corrupt, unregenerate heart
are certainly the exercises of sin. It was, nevertheless, of importance
that this should be particularly observed by the evangelist, when
treating of this matter; seeing, however plain it is, and though the
contrary is so very absurd, men are ready to imagine they may be
born again by the will of the flesh, or, at least, that by the exertions
of their own wills and endeavors they may do something towards it.
In this delusion I suppose all men naturally are, and that no man
heartily and really gives up this point until he is taught of God. And
multitudes of professing Christians do persist in expressly opposing
what is here asserted all their days. But of this more will be said,
before I have done.

Nor of the will of man; that is, not by the power and influence
of others. No one person is born again by the will and endeavors
of others. However pious and wise they are, and how much soever
they exert themselves to bring others to holiness, they do in no degree produce the effect. If all the angels and saints in heaven and
all the godly on earth should join their wills and endeavors, and
unitedly exert all their powers to regenerate one sinner, they could
not effect it; yea, could do nothing towards it. It is an effect infi-

nitely beyond the reach of finite wisdom and power. "Paul planted, and Apollos watered; but God giveth the increase. So, then, neither he that planteth is any thing, neither he that watereth, but God that giveth the increase." (I Cor. 3:6, 7)

St. John, having declared what is not the cause of the new birth, proceeds to say in one word what it is—*but of God.* God is the only efficacious agent or efficient cause in this affair. It is all to be wholly ascribed to him.

What I propose now is, particularly to inquire into this change here spoken of and called *a being born;* to consider the nature of it, and wherein it consists, and especially how, and in what sense, God is the author of it.

And, for the more distinct and clear treating this matter, I would observe, that in this change, taken in its full extent, there is the agency both of God, the cause and author of it, and of man, who is the subject of the change. God, by his Spirit, is the efficient cause; by his agency and influence the change is produced. Man's agency in the affair is in consequence of the divine agency and influence, and is an effect and fruit of it, and consists in those views and exercises of heart in which the regenerate repent, turn to God, believe on Jesus Christ, which is comprised in true Christian holiness, or the new creature. The divine agency and operation, which is first, and lays the foundation for all right views and exercises in the person who is the subject, is called by divines *regeneration.* The holy views and exercises of the subject, in which he receives Christ, or believes on his name, is called *conversion,* and sometimes *active conversion,* to distinguish it from that previous operation and change wrought by the Spirit of God, in which God is the only agent, and man, the subject, does not act, but is perfectly passive.

This subject, I conceive, cannot be properly illustrated, and so as to be well understood, without a distinct and particular attention to each of these in their nature, dependence, and connection. This is, therefore, what I would now attempt.

Regeneration

First, then, let us consider the divine agency, the work of the Spirit of God, by which persons are regenerated or born of God, and which lays the only foundation for conversion or holy exercises in the subject.

Concerning this the following things may be observed:—

I. The only ground and reason of regeneration, or of the necessity of the regenerating influences of the Spirit of God, in order to men's converting and embracing the gospel, is the total depravity and corruption of the heart of man in his natural, fallen state.

By total corruption of the heart, I mean its being wholly without any degree of right disposition or principles that should be a foundation for holy exercises, but altogether under the dominion of a contrary disposition and principle; so that there is no right exercise of heart, but every notion or act of the will is wrong, corrupt, and sinful. If this was not the case with man, there would be no need of his beginning a new kind of life, of his being created anew, and made quite a new creature, by having a new principle implanted in order to his salvation; there would be no necessity of that work of regeneration of which I am now speaking in order to man's believing on Jesus Christ. Was not man wholly corrupt, he would naturally, as I may say, believe on Christ, without any new, special operation on his heart by the Spirit of God, and would need nothing but to have the disposition and principles which are naturally in his heart strengthened and increased by exercise, in order to his salvation. But if this is really the case with man,—if he is so far sunk into corruption that he has not naturally the least degree of disposition to that which is good, but his heart is wholly and perfectly opposite to it,—then no possible means and external applications will be sufficient to bring him to the least degree of right disposition and exercise, or do any thing towards it. This can be effected only by the power and Spirit of God, which at first created all things out of nothing, and implanted a right disposition in man when he was first made. It is as absurd to suppose that in this case right disposition and exercises do take place in the heart without the all-creating influence of the Spirit of God, as it is to suppose that the whole world came into existence without creating power, or from no cause at all.

Therefore, since the ground of the necessity of the regenerating influences of the Spirit of God is the perfect corruption and wickedness of the heart of man, he is wholly to blame for being and continuing unregenerate, or for that in which unregeneracy consists. If mankind are under any law at all, and are in the least to blame for any thing, they are required to love God with all their hearts, and their neighbor as themselves; and are wholly to blame for every degree in which they come short of this, for every defect in their hearts of this kind, and for every degree of contrary disposition. Therefore, to be perfectly indisposed to that which God's law requires, and wholly inclined to that which is contrary to it, is altogether and most perfectly inexcusable, and man is wholly to blame for all this, and criminal in proportion to the degree in which it takes place, if there is any such thing as criminalness or blame in the universe. I desire this may be particularly observed and borne in mind through all the following discourse; for many, I perceive, are apt to make a mistake here, by which this matter is often set in a wrong and most absurd light. It is common for persons who believe they must be born again in order to be saved to think themselves not at all to blame that their hearts are not holy, or for that in which their unregeneracy consists; "for," say they, "we cannot change our own hearts; this is the work of God." And it has been common to represent man's depravity and moral impotency in such a light as to be inconsistent with his being directly to blame for not being holy, or not believing on Christ, etc.; and, consequently, they have represented the whole duty of the unregenerate to consist in those endeavors and doings which are antecedent to regeneration, and do not imply any real holiness or conformity to the law of God.

The absurdity of this appears so clearly, even in stating the matter, that it seems needless further to expose it. This is to turn the tables indeed, and to make man's duty wholly to lie not in obedience to God's law, but in something which is consistent with perfect obedience; and his sin to consist, not in want of love to God and opposition of heart to him, but in something else; so that a person may be perfectly sinless—yea, really and perfectly holy, for he does the whole of his duty—without a spark of true holiness, or the least degree of real conformity to the law of God.

I would forewarn my hearers, that I am about to teach no regeneration but what consists in the removal of that from man's heart for which he is altogether to blame and criminal for having it there, and the implantation of the principles of that life and holiness which man is always under infinite obligations to have and exercise at all times. And the more need men stand in of this regeneration by the Spirit of God, the more criminal and blameworthy they are. I proceed to observe,—

II. This regeneration of which I am speaking consists in a change of the will or heart. The truth of this observation appears from the foregoing, as it is a plain consequence from it. If the depravity and corruption of the heart is the only ground of the necessity of regeneration, then regeneration consists in removing this depravity, and introducing opposite principles, and so laying a foundation for holy exercises. But depravity or sin lies wholly in the heart, and not in the intellect or faculty of understanding, considered as distinct from the will, and not including that. So far as the will is renewed or set right, the whole mind is right; for sin and holiness lie wholly in this. If moral depravity does not lie in, or properly belong to, the faculty of the understanding or the intellect, as distinguished from the will, or heart, then that operation of the Spirit of God, by which this is in some measure removed and moral rectitude introduced, does not immediately respect the understanding, but the will or heart, and immediately produces a change in the latter, not in the former. It is allowed by all, I suppose, that regeneration does not produce any new *natural* capacity or faculty in the soul. These remain the same after regeneration that they were before, so far as they are *natural*. The change produced is a moral change, and, therefore, the will or heart must be the immediate subject of this change, and of the operation that effects it; for every thing of a moral nature belongs to the will or heart.

As depravity or sin began in the will, and consists wholly in the irregularity and corruption of that, so regeneration, or a recovery from sin in the renovation of the mind, must begin here, and wholly consists in the change and renewal of the will. There is not, nor can there be, any need of any other change, in order to the complete renovation of the depraved mind, and its recovery to perfect holiness. Therefore, I think I have good grounds to assert, that in regeneration the will or heart is the immediate subject of the divine operation, and so of the moral change that is effected hereby. The Spirit of God in regeneration gives a new heart, an honest and good heart. He begets a right and good taste, temper, or disposition, and so lays a foundation for holy exercises of heart.

But let us go on to the next particular.

III. In this change of which I am now speaking the Spirit of God is the only agent; and man, the subject, is wholly passive, does not act, but is acted upon.

In conversion man is active, and it wholly consists in his act; but in regeneration the Spirit of God is the only active cause. What has been said already brings this truth into view. This change lays the only foundation for all right views and exercises of the heart, and is, therefore, antecedent to all such. To suppose that the person is not wholly positive in this change, therefore, is to make him active before he begins to act. The man who is the subject of this change is, indeed, active antecedent to it; but by the supposition all the exertions and exercises of his heart are corrupt and wrong, and in direct opposition to the Spirit of God. Before this change the heart is wholly sinful,—a heart of stone, an impenitent, rebellious heart,— and all the exercises of it are acts of rebellion, in opposition to God, his Spirit, and law. This change is, therefore, wrought in the heart by the Spirit of God, in direct opposition to all its biases, inclinations, and exertions, by which they are, in a measure, overcome and destroyed, and a new and opposite principle and inclination created or implanted. Man is, therefore, so far from being active in producing this change, or having any hand in it by voluntarily falling in with, or submitting to, the divine operation, or coöperating with the Spirit of God, that the whole strength of his heart opposes it, until it is effected and actually takes place; he is, therefore, most perfectly passive. When Adam was created, and his mind formed, prepared, ·and disposed to right and holy action, it is easy to see he was altogether passive until he began first to act in consequence of his being thus formed, for which action a foundation was laid in his creation. This is a parallel with the case before us; only with this difference, that what is caused to take place in the mind in regeneration is in direct opposition to all that was in the heart before; whereas, in the formation of Adam's heart to right exercises and action, there was nothing to be opposed or counteracted.

IV. This change is wrought by the Spirit of God *immediately;* that is, it is not effected by any medium or means whatsoever.

The operation of the Spirit of God in this case is as immediate, or as much without any means, as that by which Adam's mind was at first formed. In that there was no medium, no means made use of in creating the mind formed and disposed to right action. God said, "Let it be," and it was. The Almighty first produced it immediately, or without any coöperating means. So it is in this case; there is no conceivable medium by which this change is wrought any more than there is in creation out of nothing. The sinner's own thoughts, exercises, and endeavors cannot be a means of this change; for they are all in direct opposition to it, as has been just observed.

I would particularly observe here, that light and truth, or the word of God, is not in any degree a means by which this change is effected. It is not wrought by light.

This change is most certainly not effected by light, because it is by this change that the mind is illuminated; by this the way is prepared for the light to have access to the mind, so as to become the means of any effect. This operation of the Spirit of God by which a new heart is given is necessary in order to the illumination of the mind, and, indeed, is the very thing in which it consists, as it is the opening of the eyes of the blind. It is depravity or corruption of heart that holds the mind in darkness and shuts out the light. And this corruption of heart is that in which unregeneracy consists, as has been observed; and, in truth, spiritual darkness, or blindness of mind, consists in this, too. In order to the mind's being enlightened, that must be removed in which blindness consists, or which shuts light out of the mind; but that in which unregeneracy consists does blind the mind, and shuts out the light, or, rather, is the blindness itself. Therefore, men must be regenerated, and the corruption of their hearts in some measure removed, in order to the removal of their darkness and the illumination of their mind; for this is nothing else than giving them eyes to see, and can be done in no other possible way. Consequently, men are not illuminated before regeneration; but they are first regenerated, in order to introduce light into the mind. Therefore, they are not regenerated by light, or the truths of God's word. . . .

V. This change, which we are now considering, is instantaneous, wrought at once, and not gradually.

The heart does not grow more and more disposed to that which is good before regeneration, but remains the same corrupt, rebellious heart, a heart of stone, until God takes it in hand and speaks the powerful word; and it immediately, or at once, becomes a heart of flesh, a new, regenerate heart. There is no possible medium between these two opposites,—a regenerate and unregenerate heart,—as there can be none between death and life, or non-existence and existence. The unregenerate heart, therefore, is in no degree well disposed or has the least right inclination, but is as far from all right disposition, till the instant in which it is regenerated, as it ever was. And it exists a new heart as instantaneously as did the mind of Adam when God created him. Nothing that precedes regeneration does any thing towards it by altering the bent and bias of the heart so as to time it towards holiness in the least degree. But the heart continues to oppose that to which it is brought in regeneration till that instant in which it becomes a new heart; and it takes no time to effect this change. The change is, indeed, imperfect at first, the heart is renewed but in part; and after this renovation is begun, it is carried on gradually to greater degrees, until the heart is perfectly renewed, in a work of sanctification. But this new life is first begun instantaneously.

VI. This operation of the Spirit of God, by which men are regenerated, is altogether unperceivable.

The subjects of this change know nothing what is done, or that any thing is done, with respect to their hearts, and are not sensible of any operation and change in any other way but by the effect and consequence of it. We are conscious or sensible of nothing in our own mind; we feel and perceive nothing but our own ideas, thoughts, and exercises; but, as has been observed, the active change or conversion consists in these, and they are the fruit and effect of regeneration, or that work of the Spirit of God, of which I am now speaking. That which takes place with respect to our minds antecedent to the views and exercises we have, as the foundation and cause of them, is, by the supposition, perfectly unexperienced; but this is true of the operation and change now under consideration. All the notice we can have of this operation and change, and all the evidence there can be that our minds are the subjects of it, is by perceiving that which is the fruit and consequence of it by our own views and exercises, which are new, and we find to be of such a nature and kind that we have ground to infer that they are the effect of the operation of the Spirit of God, or the fruits of the Spirit, by which we are become new creatures.

When Adam was created a living soul, the immediate divine operation was not perceived by him, for he had no perception of any thing until he actually existed and the work of his creation was finished: he did not begin to be conscious of any thing until this was over, and then he perceived nothing but what was the fruit and consequence of the divine operation. So it is in the new creature, by which men are born of the Spirit of God.

I make this remark partly to detect and expose the delusion of those who think they feel the motions of the Spirit of God on their hearts, somewhat as one body is sensibly touched and impressed by another, antecedent to all exercises of their own and independent of them, and place great part of their religion in those feelings or impulses which they call the operation of the Spirit of God, and which immediately suggests to them what is truth, and what is duty, which they think is to be led by the Spirit. We have no way to determine what is the cause of the ideas and sensations of our hearts, whether we are influenced by the Spirit of God or by a wicked spirit, but by considering their nature and tendency, whether they are such as the Scripture tells us are the fruits of the Spirit.

VII. In the work of regeneration, by which men are born of the Spirit, God acts as a sovereign.

When I speak of God's acting in a sovereign way, I do not mean that he acts above or without all reason and motive, or merely because he will, for God never acts so in any instance whatsoever. Such sovereignty and arbitrariness is in no case to be ascribed to God, for this would be to dishonor and reproach him as acting without any wisdom or holiness. The sovereignty of God consists in his being above all obligation to his creatures, and so infinitely above any direction, influence, and control from them in any thing that he does. In this sense, God is an infinite sovereign; he does just as he pleases, not being influenced by any obligation he is under to any one, any further than he has been pleased to oblige himself by promise or some other way.

Sovereignty is, therefore, in a peculiar manner, essential to all acts of grace, or grace in all cases is sovereign grace, and what is not so is no grace at all; for, whatever good is bestowed, if he that grants it is under any original obligation to do it, or is obliged to do it from the reason and nature of things, and so owes it to him that receives it, it is only an act of justice, and the nature of paying a debt, and there is no grace in it; for grace is free, unobliged, undeserved favor, and that which is not so is not grace.

In the case before us, God acts in the highest sense and degree as a sovereign, he being not only under no obligation to grant such a favor to any one when he does it, but there is in the sinner something infinitely contrary to this, even infinite unworthiness of the favor granted, and desert of infinite evil. Therefore, whenever God changes and regenerates the heart of a sinner, he does what he was under no sort of obligation to the sinner to do, but might justly leave him to the hardness of his own heart to perish in his sins forever. So that God in determining to whom he will grant this infinite favor, and in giving it to some and withholding it from others, "has mercy on whom he will have mercy, and whom he will he hardeneth." What the sinner does before he is regenerated does not lay God under any degree of obligation to him by promise or any other way, for he complies with none of God's commands or offers in the least degree. He is not so much as willing to accept of offered mercy, but opposes God and his grace with all his heart, however anxious he may be about his eternal interest, and how much soever he prays and cries for mercy and continues a perfect enemy to the just God and the Savior, until his heart is renewed, and the enmity slain by the regenerating influence of God's Spirit.

I should now proceed to consider this change in which men are born of God, as it implies, and consists in, that in which they are active, in the views and exercises of their own hearts, for which that which I have been speaking of lays the foundation, were it not that a question may probably arise in the minds of some upon what has been said, which it may be proper to attend to and answer here.

QUESTION. If these things are so,—if men are not active, but perfectly passive, in regeneration, and the work is wrought by the Spirit of God without means, and God in this acts as a sovereign, having mercy on whom he will have mercy, and leaving whom he will to perish, whatever are the sinner's circumstances, whatever means are used, and notwithstanding all the pains the sinner takes for his own salvation,—then what encouragement and what reason is there for the sinner's using any means, or for others to take any pains or use means with him for his salvation?

ANSWER. If what has been now said is agreeable to the truth, there is certainly no reasonable encouragement to the use of means from a view to lay God under any obligation hereby to sinners to regenerate and save them, for God will be under none, nor can he be; he is infinitely far from this.

Nor is there any reason and encouragement to use means with a view that they shall in any degree effect this change, or do any thing towards it, or properly be any means of changing the heart, for this change is wrought immediately.

Neither is there any encouragement to use means in order to make the sinner's heart better antecedent to regeneration, or that his case may hereby be made less miserable, if he finally perishes in his sins. None, surely, will imagine that if the sinner continues impenitent, and dies in his sins, the means that have been used for his salvation will be of any advantage to him. It is certain they will not, but the contrary; for this, as well as every thing else, will, in this case, turn against him. The more means are used with the sinner, the greater advantages he enjoys, the more instruction is given him, and the more light and conviction he has in his own conscience, and the greater sense he has of the reality and importance of invisible things, of the worth of his soul, and of eternal happiness, and of the dreadfulness of eternal damnation,—I say, the more there is of these things the more miserable he will be, if he continues impenitent and perishes after all; for all these things do greatly aggravate the crime of his continuing in sin, so are the occasion of his being more guilty than if they had not taken place. The preaching of the gospel, and so all means of salvation, are a savor of death unto death to them that perish. (II Cor. 2:17) It is most unreasonable, therefore, to use any means with a sinner in order to his salvation, with a view that they shall be to his advantage, if he continues impenitent and abuses them; for to such they will have directly the contrary effect. (See Matt. 11:20-24.)

And the use of means is so far from making their hearts better, more inclined to obedience and holiness, or less obstinate, while they continue impenitent and unregenerate, that it is the occasion of the contrary to a very great degree. The heart, by resisting means and opposing light and truth, rather grows harder than softer. And the more means are used, and the more the mind is awakened to attention, and the greater light and conviction it has, while the heart continues perfectly impenitent and obstinate in opposition to all this, the more strong and vigorous, as well as more aggravated and criminal, are the sinful exertions of it; for the more the powers of the mind—which is wholly corrupt—are awakened and roused, the more strong and active are the sinful principles of the heart; and it requires a greater degree of opposition of heart to resist and continue impenitent under ten degrees of light and conviction than it does to continue so under but one degree of this.

Pharaoh, under all the rousing, softening, powerful means used with him to induce and persuade him to obey Jehovah and let the people of Israel go from under his oppressive hand, and all the attention he gave to that matter under all the conviction he had in his own mind, and the trouble and distress with which he was exercised, grew harder rather than more pliable; and the corruption of his heart was exercised in a much higher degree, and was much more aggravated and criminal, than if no means had been used with him, and he had remained without any light and conviction of conscience. But this instance of Pharaoh is very parallel with that of a sinner under conviction, with whom special means are used to bring him to a submission to God, who, notwithstanding, absolutely refuses, and continues in impenitence, as might easily be shown; and it was doubtless designed to be an image of this. All means used with unregenerate sinners, if they live and die so, will have the same effect and consequence with respect to them that they had in Pharaoh. Therefore, if it was known concerning any one that he would certainly persist and perish in impenitence, there could be no reasonable inducement and motive to use any means with him in order to bring him to repentance, with a view and design of any benefits to him. They who continue impenitent and perish will have no good by any thing; but all their enjoyments and advantages of every kind, all the means used with them for their good, and all the light and conviction of their own consciences will turn against them, and be the occasion of their greater destruction.

Why, then, are means to be used? What reason and encouragement to do it? is still the question. I therefore proceed to a positive answer.

I. The use of means with sinners may answer great and important ends, even though they continue impenitent and perish more dreadfully than if no such means had been used; which might easily be proved, was there need. God answered his own wise and glorious ends in the means he used with Pharaoh, notwithstanding he continued obstinate. But,—

II. Means are absolutely necessary in order to the conversion and salvation of men, as much so as if there was no other agent except the subject, and nothing done but what was effected by means. For,—

First. Means are necessary to be used in order to prepare persons for regeneration; for, consistent with all that has been said, a preparatory work is as important and necessary as on any plan whatsoever. God can, indeed, just as easily regenerate one as another; he has power to regenerate the most stupid, benighted heathen on earth, or the most ignorant, or deluded, erroneous person in the Christian world, at any moment he pleases, without the use of any means. But as this would not be wise and proper, in this sense it cannot be done, because God never did, and never will, do any thing which is not wise and proper to be done. The reason why it is not wise and suitable to give a person a new heart in such circumstances and without the use of means is, that in such a case there is no foundation, provision, or opportunity for right views and exercises, if a new heart should be given, therefore no good end answered by it. This would be like creating a monster without any parts or capacity whereby he might live and act in any proper way, but so as to act monstrously, and even counteract and destroy itself; or as if a man should be made without feet or hands, or without any mouth to take the food necessary to support life; or as if an animal should be made in such a situation and circumstances as that it is impossible for him to come at the things necessary for the support of his existence and life.

When God causes this moral change in any man, it is in order to new life and action; therefore, he will not do it where there is no opportunity and means for the support and exercise of this new life; for, though men are not regenerated by means, yet means must be antecedently used, in order to persons' being prepared to act properly when regenerated. For instance, the many errors and delusions that all adult, uninstructed persons, and even all careless sinners are in, must be, at least in a good degree, removed, and there must be some considerable degree of speculative knowledge about the things of religion, in order to the proper exercise of holiness or the new creature; and there must be more knowledge than a careless, secure sinner ever attains to, whatever instruction he has, and however much he is given to speculations on the things of religion. The things necessary to be known in order to the proper exercise of Christian holiness are never understood by a secure sinner as they may be by an unregenerate sinner, when, in the use of means, his attention and conscience are thoroughly awakened, and as they must be understood in order to the mind's being properly prepared for the exercise of grace. Such an awakened sinner will commonly learn more of those truths that are most necessary to be known, in a very short time, than others will ever learn under the best instruction. . . .

SECONDLY. The use of means is absolutely necessary in order to any exercise of the new heart or of Christian holiness at any time. If we set aside the consideration of a preparatory work, and the necessity of that, in order to regeneration, in the view that has been given of it under the former particular, yet there will be a reason for the use of means, and a necessity of them, in order to salvation. If there is no truth set before the mind objectively, or by way of external exhibition, in any sense and degree, and if there is no attention of the mind and application in the use of any means whatever, the new heart must lie dormant, if there is one, and there can be no possible right exercise. For it is written, "Faith cometh by hearing, and hearing by the word of God." Therefore, means are necessary in order to conversion, or the exercise of faith and holiness, without which men cannot be saved. He, therefore, who lives and dies in the neglect of the use of means must perish. The use of means, then, is of as great importance to men as is their salvation; and the motives and encouragement to a constant attendance on them, in this view of the matter, are equal to the importance and worth of salvation.

Conversion

We come now to the second thing proposed, which is to consider the change that is included in being born of God, in which men are active, and consists in the views and exercises of heart, which are the genuine fruit and effect of the divine operation and change of which I have been speaking, and which is called active conversion.

We have been so lengthy on the other head, that we must be shorter here, and give only a general view of it, without descending into all those particulars that might be mentioned and enlarged upon.

When the mind is regenerated, and a new heart given, divine things will appear in a new light, and the heart will exercise itself in quite a new manner. The first thing that now presents itself to the mind is the omnipresent and glorious God, the sum of all being and excellence. Now the heart sees and feels that there is a God with a conviction and assurance that it never had before, and is entertained and fixed in a calm, sweet view and sense of greatness, majesty, wisdom, justice, goodness, excellence, glory, with which it is captivated and charmed. Now the person finds himself surrounded with Deity, and sees God manifesting himself every where and in every thing. The sun, moon, and stars, the clouds, the mountains, the trees, the fields, the grass, and every creature and thing conspire in silent yet clear, powerful, and striking language to declare to him the being, perfections, and glory of God. Now he sees he never before really believed there was a God. He never had any idea and sense of such a Being before, nor received the abundant and all-convincing evidence of his being and perfections.

In this view he sinks into nothing, as it were, before this great and glorious Being, and his heart is filled with a sense of the glorious greatness and excellence of God, and his infinite worthiness to be loved, obeyed, and honored by all intelligent creatures. Now, therefore, he sees the reasonableness and excellence of that law which requires all to love him with all their hearts; so the divine law comes into view, in all its justice, goodness, and glory. His heart approves of it as most worthy to be maintained and honored, while it requires perfect, persevering love and obedience, on pain of eternal damnation. He, therefore, now sees the infinite evil of sin, its infinite odiousness and ill desert, and, in this view, sees his own sinfulness and vileness, and sinks down, as it were, infinitely low, in a sense of his own infinite odiousness and guilt; and hates, judges, and condemns himself, heartily acknowledging the justice of his condemnation, feeling himself most righteously cast off forever into eternal misery, and, therefore, in himself, wholly lost and infinitely miserable.

And when he sees what he has done, how he has broken and dishonored the divine law, and despised and contemned God, and trampled on his most sacred authority, how infinitely unreasonable and injurious to the divine character he has been, he desires and wishes with all his heart that the mighty breach could be made up, and the injury repaired and removed; that the blot he has cast on the glorious character of God might be wiped off, and full recompense and atonement made; and he has not the least wish that he might be pardoned and obtain the favor of God in any other way; and he immediately sees and feels that he is infinitely far from any possibility of doing this himself; that he is infinitely in debt, and has nothing to pay; has nothing but infinite vileness, unworthiness, and guilt to offer, which can only pull down divine vengeance on his head; that his repentance, however sincere, can do nothing towards making up the breach, or in the least degree atone for the least sin. He is, therefore, far from any disposition or thought to attempt to offer any thing of his own, by which he might obtain the forgiveness of his sins and the favor of God, which now appear infinitely important and desirable. Thus the law comes, sin revives, and he dies.

And now he is prepared to receive the good news reported in the gospel, "Behold the Lamb of God, which taketh away the sins of the world!" This is to him "good tidings of great joy." Behold, the Son of God, who is equal with God, and is God, who himself made the world, has become a man; has been in the world, and, by his own obedience and sufferings unto death, has made full reparation and atonement for sin, is risen from the dead, and exalted to the right hand of the Majesty on high, to give repentance and remission of sins, and is ready to pardon and save all that come unto him, to which all, even the most guilty and vile, are freely excited. Now the light of the knowledge of the glory of God in the face of Jesus Christ shines in his heart, and the character of the Mediator appears to him in all its fulness and glory; and the way of salvation by Christ appears wise, excellent, and glorious, and pleases, rejoices, and charms his heart; and in a sense of his own infinite unworthiness, vileness, and guilt, he puts his whole trust in him for pardon and salvation, deliverance from the guilt and power and pollution of sin, "desiring to be found in him, not having his own righteousness, which is of the law, but that which is through the faith of Christ, the righteousness which is of God by faith."

And while he attends to the dignity and excellence of Christ's person, and sees what he has done and suffered to obey and honor the divine law and make atonement for sin, and sees and tastes the wonderful, amazing goodness of God and the Redeemer, exercised and manifested in this redemption, his sense of the worthiness of the law of God and the infinite vileness of sin rises higher and higher; and his heart is more and more warmed with love to God and the Redeemer, and filled with hatred and abhorrence of sin, and is especially broken in repentance and self-abhorrence, in a sense of his amazing ingratitude and vileness in neglecting and opposing this way of salvation, and slighting and rejecting such a Savior.

And now, with all his heart he renounces the ways of sin, and with pleasure and strength of soul gives himself up to God through Jesus Christ, to serve and obey him forever, feeling it to be the happiest thing in the world, the greatest privilege he can imagine, to be wholly devoted to God in all the ways of strict and pure religion and holy obedience.

In these views and exercises of heart, active conversion from sin to God does consist; and all this is implied in faith in Jesus Christ, or receiving him, and believing on his name; and every one in whose mind these things do not take place, in the sum and substance of them, is not converted or born of God. Though I pretend not to say that the views and exercises of every one that is converted do sensibly take place exactly in the order and connection in which I have now placed them,—so that every true convert shall be able to recollect that these things passed in his mind just so, and in this order, from step to step,—yet he must be sensible that all this has taken place in his heart and abides with him; and it may be demonstrated that they do in fact take place in this connection and order, and that there is no other possible way, though all may be so much at once, as it were, and the exercises of the mind may be so quick as not to be attended with any consciousness of their being in this particular arrangement.

But to proceed.

The person of whom I am speaking is now become a truly humble person, in a sense of his own meanness, vileness, and infinite unworthiness and guilt, and his absolute dependence on God for strength and righteousness. This lays him low before God, and he is disposed to walk humbly with him, working out his own salvation with fear and trembling, i.e., in a sense of his own nothingness, weakness, and insufficiency with respect to any good thing, and his perfect, continual, and, as it were, infinite dependence on God, who alone worketh in him to will and to do; and as he has a more full, clear, and constant view and sense of his own amazing vileness and misery than he can have of others, he is naturally disposed in lowliness of mind to prefer others to himself, and led to a meek and humble conduct and behavior among men.

And he has now a new view and sense of the truth, divinity, excellence, and sweetness of the Word of God; and he delights in the Holy Scriptures, and is disposed to meditate therein day and night. They are more precious to him than much fine gold, and sweeter than the honey and the honeycomb. He now becomes a devout and zealous worshipper of God. With pleasure he daily enters into his closet, and prays to and praises Him who sees in secret, and would not be deprived of this privilege for all the kingdoms of the world. He loves to join with Christians in social prayer and religious conversation; and his feet run with constancy and eagerness to the place of public worship, where he devoutly joins in prayer and praise, and with great attention hears the word preached, receives instruction, and is quickened thereby.

And as he has given himself up to God sincerely and without reserve, he is from hence naturally led to desire to do it publicly, by espousing the cause of God, and appearing on his side, as a disciple and follower of Christ before the world, by a public profession of religion. And it appears to him to be a great privilege to be among the number of God's visible people, to be united with them, and have the advantage of their Christian watch and care; and without delay he joins with them, and attends on all Christ's holy institutions.

And in this change he becomes a friend to mankind, and his heart is filled with love to them. This effectually, and at once, cures him of all the ways of deceit, injustice, and injuriousness in his concerns and dealings with his neighbor, of which the world is so full, and which are so common among professing Christians; and he is immediately possessed with that harmlessness, honesty, sincerity, truth, integrity, and faithfulness of heart which is peculiar to a true Christian; and he is not only just and upright, but his heart is full of goodness, kind affection, tenderness, and mercy, which prompts him to do good to all as he has opportunity, especially to seek and promote, in all the ways he can, the welfare of their souls in their eternal salvation.

In a word, he heartily devotes himself to the service of God and his fellow-men, as his whole and only business, and to this end is faithful and diligent in his own proper station and calling; "not slothful in business, but fervent in spirit, serving the Lord." And in these things he perseveres and makes progress to the end of life; for conversion is but the beginning of the same thing which is carried on and makes advances unto perfect holiness.

This is a short, imperfect sketch of the true convert, the new man, who is born of the Spirit of God. I will conclude with two or three reflections on the whole.

I. The view we have had of this matter may serve to teach us what it is to be led by the Spirit of God, which is spoken of as a privilege common to all Christians. (Rom. 8:14; Gal. 5:18) It is not to be influenced and guided by any unaccountable impulses, or immediate suggestions to the mind of some new truth not contained in divine revelation, or of particular texts or passages of Scripture. But the Christian is led by the Spirit of God, by the Spirit's dwelling in him as a principle of new life and action, begetting, maintaining, and increasing a right taste and temper of mind, and thus preparing and disposing the heart to attend to, and discern, the truths revealed in God's word, or exercise itself in a wise and holy manner, in a view and sense of the truths contained in divine revelation. This is all the leading and influence the Christian wants from the Spirit of God. If he has a right taste and disposition of heart to a sufficient degree, he will want nothing further from the immediate influences of the divine Spirit in order to be led into all truth, and know and do his duty in every branch of it.

II. We may hence learn what persons are to inquire after in order to determine whether they are born of God or not; viz., what are the views and exercises of their own hearts, and what influence and effect these have in practice. By this, my hearers, you are to determine whether you have the Spirit of God or not, even by considering and finding out whether you have the discerning and exercises in which conversion consists, even all those holy exercises by which men do first turn from sin to God, and believe on the name of Jesus Christ, and in which they persevere in a holy life, which are in Scripture called the fruit of the Spirit.

Therefore, what has now been said in the description of conversion may be applied as matter of examination and trial by all those who are desirous to know what their state is, whether they are born of God or not. They who are in any good degree engaged to get satisfaction in this interesting point, have been hearing with self-application, in this view. And I recommend it to all seriously, and with impartiality, to apply what has been said—so far as it appears to them to be agreeable to the Word of God—to themselves, by way of self-examination. And may the Lord give us understanding and discerning to determine this important question according to truth.

And have any of you good and satisfying evidence that you are born of God; give all the glory to his sovereign grace, and remember that this is but the beginning of something very great and glorious. "Think not that ye have already attained, or are already perfect, but follow after, that you may apprehend that for which you are apprehended of Christ Jesus. Forgetting those things which are behind, and reaching forth unto those which are before, press toward the mark for the prize of the high calling of God in Christ Jesus." "As newborn babes, desire the sincere milk of the word, that ye may grow thereby."

III. They who find themselves in an unregenerate state may most reasonably be concerned about themselves, in a view of the infinitely miserable condition they are in. Your case is shockingly dreadful. There is nothing good or right in your hearts; but you are perfectly corrupt and wicked, devoted to that which is your destruction. And you are wholly and perfectly to blame for all this, and, therefore, infinitely guilty and odious in God's sight, and most unworthy of the least pity and mercy from him; so that you are eternally undone, unless God shall exercise that distinguishing sovereign grace towards you which you have been always refusing and opposing, and which he may most justly refuse to grant.

Say not within yourselves, "We are utterly unable to help ourselves; we can do nothing towards our salvation; God must do all; why do you blame us? it signifies nothing for us to take any pains about the matter. If God is pleased to regenerate and save us, he will do it in his own time. Why, then, do you call upon us, and give us any trouble about the matter?" As well may the man who has turned rebel against his sovereign, and by this means has undone himself, and is apprehended and condemned to the most cruel torture and death, and is exposed to be executed every hour; at the same time, the prince whom he has offended and injured offers to pardon him, and put him into most happy circumstances, if he will only make his submission to him and be willing to be his friend and servant, and is sending persons to treat with him about this matter, and urge him by all imaginable arguments and motives to accept of the kind and advantageous offer, so that all the difficulty of obtaining complete deliverance is his disposition to justify himself in his rebellion, and unwillingness to comply with the most reasonable and kind proposals,—I say, as well may such a one reply, "I cannot help myself; unless the prince give me a new heart, and incline me to accept of his offer as well as make it to me, the proposal will do me no good. I am, therefore, not to blame; I will not give myself the least trouble about it, let come what will." And as reasonably might a man use this language who has set his own house on fire, which is burning down over his head, and he sits easy and secure in the midst of it, or is busy throwing oil into the flame, and increasing the fire, while he is called upon and urged to escape for his life.

It is your indispensable duty, your highest interest, immediately to repent, believe on the name of the Lord Jesus Christ, and give yourselves up to God. Nothing can possibly be the least excuse for your neglecting it one minute; you have all the opportunity and advantage you can desire; and motives are set before you which are, I may say, infinitely weighty and forcible. And if divine, eternal vengeance should fall on your heads immediately, for the hardness of your hearts and continued rebellion, in these circumstances, God will be just, and you most justly miserable forever. And how soon this will be your case, you know not.

It is certain this will come upon you soon, unless you wake up and attend to your case and fly to the only refuge. "Cleanse your hands, ye sinners; and purify your hearts, ye double-minded." "Be afflicted and mourn, and weep; let your laughter be turned into mourning, and your joy into heaviness. Humble yourselves in the sight of the Lord, and he shall lift you up. Repent ye, therefore, and be converted, that your sins may be blotted out. Believe on the name of the Lord Jesus Christ, and ye shall be saved."

George Downame
1560?-1634

10

Justification

George Downame (also Downham) was born at Chester, where his father was a bishop. He studied at Cambridge and was elected fellow of Christ College in 1585. Later he was appointed professor of logic and granted the D.D. degree. In 1616 he became bishop of Derry. Though not as well known as some of the Puritan divines, his writings were as sound as any. His *A Treatise of Justification,* published in 1639, was his most outstanding work. He died in 1634 after a long and faithful preaching ministry.

Downame's other writings included: *A Treatise Concerning Antichrist* (1603), *An Abstract of the Duties Commanded in the Law of God* (1635), *The Christian's Freedom* (1635), and *A Godly and Learned Treatise of Prayer* (1640).

The following excerpt is from *A Treatise of Justification* and examines Robert Bellarmine's arguments for the Catholic doctrine of justification by inherent righteousness. It is a brilliant refutation. Downame argues that man is corrupt because of imputed sin, not inherent sin, and therefore man is made righteous by imputation of Christ's righteousness. Downame accepts the "federal headship" view of Adam, and many contemporary evangelicals unfortunately have failed to see the importance of this view. Its antithesis, the entrance of sin into the human race by inherent corruption, leads to the Roman Catholic concept of salvation by inherent righteousness—good works and self-effort. Downame shows from Scripture that the total depravity of the sinner precludes the concept of inherent righteousness.

··

I. Now I am to examine *Bellarmines* proofes.[1] And first hee alleageth *Rom.* 5:17, 18, 19. out of which place he would prove, that *to bee justified by Christ is not to be accounted or pronounced just, but to be truly made and constituted just by obtaining inherent righteousnesse; and that, a righteousnesse not unperfect, but absolute and perfect: for, that to justifie, in this place, is to make just, and not to pronounce just, appeareth; first, out of those words, verse 19. many shall be constituted or made just,* unto which allegation I have heretofore answered in his due place[2] so much as concerneth the signification of the word, and have maintained the exceptions of *Calvin* and *Chemnitius,*[3] against his cavils. His second reason is *from the Antithesis of Adam unto Christ. For thus,* saith he, *the Apostle writeth. As we are made unjust through the disobedience of Adam, so we are made just through the obedience of Christ.*

> *But it is certaine, that through Adams disobedience we are made unjust by injustice inherent, and not imputed:*[4]
> *Therefore through the obedience of Christ we are made just by righteousnesse inherent, and not imputed.*

Answ. Wee confesse, that as from the first *Adam* we receive inherent corruption in our carnall generation: so from the second *Adam* wee receive inherent grace in our spirituall regeneration, but this is not our justification, but our sanctification, whereof the Apostle speaketh not in this place, whereas therefore he assumeth, that wee are made unjust through *Adams* disobedience by inherent injustice onely not imputed, I deny the assumption, and returne the argument upon the Adversary.

> As we are made sinners, that is, guilty of sinne and damnation by *Adams* disobedience or transgression: so wee are justified, that is, not onely absolved from the guilt of sinne, and damnation,

---

1. *De iustif, lib.* 2. *cap.*3.
2. *Lib.* 2. *c.*5. §.1.
3. *Ibid.* §.2.3,&c.
4. *Non in iustitia Adami nobis imputata.*

but also accepted as righteous unto salvation, by the obedience of Christ.

But wee are made sinners, that is guilty of sinne and damnation by imputation of *Adams* disobedience, or transgression:

Therefore wee are justified, that is, not onely absolved from the guilt of sinne, but also accepted as righteous, by imputation of Christs obedience.

As touching the proposition: that the word *sinners* doth in this place signifie guilty of sinne, and obnoxious to condemnation; it is testified by *Chrysostome*,[5] τί οὖν ἐνταῦθα τὸ ἁμαρτωλοὶ, ἐμοὶ δοκεῖ, τὸ ὑπεύθυνοι κολάσει, καὶ καταδεδικασμένοι θανάτῳ, what then is the word sinners in this place? it seemeth to mee, that it is to be subject or obnoxious to punishment, and condemned to death: by *Oecumenius* ἁμαρτωλοὶ τοῦτέστιν ὑπεύθυνοι θανάτῳ καὶ κολάσει, and by *Theophylact* likewise, sinners; that is obnoxious to punishments and guilty of death, which exposition is plainely confirmed by the verses going before, where the same opposition betweene the first and second *Adam* being made, the former part is expressed in these words, that the κρῖμα, or guilt of *Adams* transgression came upon his posterity εἰς κατάκριμα unto condemnation, especially, *vers.* 16. and 18.

II. The assumption, though gaine-said by *Bellarmine* in this place yet is taught not only by other Papists, who fully contradict *Bellarmines* Assumption but elsewhere also by *Bellarmine* himselfe. For *Durandus, Pighius,*[6] *Catharinus,*[7] doe hold originall sinne to be nothing else, but the guilt of *Adams* fall, or the disobedience of *Adam* imputed unto us, which opinion also *Occam* professeth, that he would hold, if he were not hindered by the authority of the Fathers. *Yea,* saith *Bellarmine*[8] *it seemeth to have beene the opinion of some of the ancient, as* Peter Lombard,[9] *reporteth.* In refuting this opinion *Bellarmine* justly findeth fault with them,[10] that they held originall sinne to be nothing else, but the guilt of *Adams* disobedience imputed, it being also the depravation of our nature following thereupon. But in that they say, originall sinne is the disobedience of *Adam* imputed unto us, that he doth approve. *For Adam alone did indeed commit*

---

5. *In locum.*

6. *Controv. a. de orig. peccat.*

7. *In Rom. 5. in opusc. de lapsu hominis & orig. peccat. c.6.*

8. *De amiss. gratiae & stat pec. l.5. c.16.*

9. *2 Sent. dist. 30.*

10. *De amiss. gratiae & stati. peccat. l.5. c.17.*

that sinne by actuall will. but[11] *to us it is communicated by genera-tion* eo modo quo communicari potest id quod transiit, nimirum per imputationem, *after that manner whereby that may be communicated which is transcient and gone, to wit by imputation.* Omnibus enim imputatur, &c. *for it is imputed to all who are borne of Adam, be-cause wee all being then in the loynes of Adam, when hee sinned, in him and by him wee sinned.* Yea, and farther hee rightly disputeth,[12] that if *Adams* sinne were not ours by imputation, neither the guilt of it, nor the corruption following upon it, had belonged to us. This assertion of *Bellarmine* confirmeth our assumption and contradicteth his own, alleaging that wee are made sinners through the disobedience of *Adam* by injustice inherent, and not imputed: which also he con-tradicteth in other places. For he granteth[13] the *sinne of Adam so to be imputed to all his posterity, as if they all had committed that sinne,* and to the same purpose citeth *Bernard.*[14] Our is *Adams* fault, because though in another, yet we sinned; and to us it was imputed by the just, though secret judgement of God. And againe, taking upon him to prove that the propagation of sinne may bee defended without maintaining the propagation or traduction of the soule: he saith,[15] that *nothing else is required to the traduction of sinne, but that a man be descended from Adam by true and ordinary generation.* For gen-eration not being of a part,[16] but of the person, or whole man (for *homo generat hominem*) therefore the person descending from *Adam* (though his soule be from God) was in the loynes of *Adam,* and being in him originally, as in the roote, in him, and with him hee sinned; the actuall sinne of *Adam* being communicated unto him *by imputation.* For as *Augustine* saith, *definita est sententia,* &c. it is a resolved case by the Apostle, that in *Adam* we all sinned.

III. But what shall wee say to the inherent corruption, which *Adam* by his transgression contracted? By this assertion, it seemeth not to be traducted otherwise, than as the fruit and consequent of the actuall disobedience: which was the opinion of *Pighius* and

---

11. *Ibid.* §. *itaque.*

12. *Ibid. c.18. Reatus cum sit relatio consequens actionem, qua ratione sieri potist, ut existat in eo, qui non est particeps actionis? iaversio habitualis, nisi precesserit actualis, ne intelligi qu dem potest.*

13. *De amissi. gratiae & statu peccat. l.4. c.10.*

14. *Serm. de Dominica. I. post octavas Epiphaniae.*

15. *De amis. gr. & stat. pec. l.4. c.12. § est aliaex Anselm de conceptu. c.7. Virg. & 10. & ex Th. in I.2. q.81 art.1. & ex Scote Durando, &c. in 2. Sent. dist. 51.*

16. *Ibid.* §. *porro vere.*

Catharinus. For as *Adam* by his first transgression, which was the sinne of mankind, contracted not onely the guilt of death, but also the corruption of his nature, being both a privation of originall righteousnesse, and also an evill disposition and pronenesse to all manner of sinne, which is that *macula peccati* remaining in the sinner after the act is gone: so wee having sinned in *Adam* are not onely made guilty of death, and void of originall righteousnesse; but also are defiled with that habituall disposition and pronenesse to all manner of sinne. So that, according to this assertion, it may be defended, that nothing in our generation is communicated unto us with the humane nature but the disobedience of *Adam,* which is communicated by imputation. As for the guilt of death and the inherent coruption, they are not derived from *Adam,* but contracted by our sinning in him. And hereunto we may apply *Bellarmines* distinction of sinne so properly called:[17] that it is either a voluntary transgression, or that blemish which remaineth in the soule, caused and contracted by the transgression, being of the same nature with it, differing no otherwise from it, than as heat from the act of heating. For in the former sense originall sinne is the voluntary transgression of *Adam* imputed unto us, and is one and the same in all men; in *Adam* actuall and personall, in us originall. For onely he by actuall will committed it, but to us it is communicated, after that manner, by which, that which is past and gone, may bee communicated, to wit, *by imputation.* In the latter sense it is the corruption inherent contracted and caused, as in *Adam* by his personall sinne, so in us by our sinning originally in him, which though it bee alike and equall in all, yet it is every mans owne.

IV. But supposing originall sinne, according to the received opinion, to be wholly communicated unto us from *Adam* in our *generation:* yet we must distinguish betwixt *Adams* first transgression or actuall disobedience, which we call his fall; and the corruption or depravaation of his nature, which thereupon followed. For though we be partakers of both, yet not after the same manner. Of the transgression we can be no otherwise partakers than by imputation. For *Adams* transgression being an action, and actions continuing, or having a being, no longer than they are in doing, cannot bee traducted or transmitted from *Adam* to his posterity. But the corruption being habituall, is derivable by propagation. Now the Apostle, *Rom.* 5. speaketh of *Adams* actuall disobedience once committed by him, by which he saith we are made sinners, that sinne of his being communicated

---

17. *De amiss. gra. & statu. pec. l.5. c.17.*

unto us by imputation; and not of the corruption thereupon following. So by the like reason we are made just by the obedience of Christ, which hee performed for us in the daies of his flesh, which can no otherwise be communicated unto us, than by imputation.

Object, Yea, but wee are truly made sinners by the disobedience of *Adam,* and truly made righteous by the obedience of Christ. *Answ.* As we are truly made sinners by imputation of *Adams* disobedience; so we are as truly made righteous by imputation of Christs obedience. *Iust.* Yea, but we are made sinners by injustice inherent through *Adams* disobedience, and therefore wee are made just by inherent justice, through the obedience of Christ. *Answ.* We are not made sinners in respect of inherent justice by *Adams* disobedience formally, as *Bellarmine* saith,[18] *(Inobedientia Adami nos constituit peccatores, non formaliter sed efficienter)* for that only is imputed, but by the corruption which followeth and is caused by that transgression, committed by *Adam,* and imputed to us. In like manner, wee are not made just in respect of inherent justice, by the obedience of Christ, whether active or passive formally, for that is onely imputed; but by the graces of the Spirit merited by the obedience of Christ, performed by him, and imputed to us.

V. Thus then standeth the comparison betwixt the first and the second *Adam.* As by the actuall disobedience or transgression of the first *Adam* all his off-spring were made guilty of sinne, and subject to death, his disobedience being not inherent in them, but imputed to them, as if it were their owne, because they were in him originally: so by the obedience of the second *Adam* all his off-spring[19] are or shall be justified from sinne and accepted to life, his obedience not being inherent in them, but imputed to them, as if it were their owne, because by faith they are in him. And this is our justification by imputation of Christs righteousnesse. And further as *Adams* fall deserved, as a just punishment, the defacing of Gods image by inherent corruption in all his posterity, to whom the same corruption is by naturall generation transfused: so the obedience of Christ merited, as a just reward, the restoring of Gods image in us by inherent righteousnesse in all the faithfull, into whom the said righteousnesse is in their Spirituall regeneration infused. And this is our Sanctification by the Spirit of Christ, of which the Apostle speaketh not untill the next *Chapter,* where he sheweth, that our justification is alwayes accompanied with Sanctification. In a word from either of the two

---

18. *De iustif. l.2. c.9. §. Quartum.*
19. *Heb.* 2:13.

Adams we receive two things, which are contrary each to other. From the first *Adam,* his disobedience is communicated unto us by imputation, whereby wee are made sinners, that is, guilty of sinne and damnation; which guilt is opposite to justification, and secondly the corruption, which he contracted, is transfused unto us by carnall generation, which corruption is contrary to sanctification. From the second *Adam,* his obedience is communicated to us by imputation, whereby wee are constituted just, that is, absolved from the guilt of sinne and damnation, and accepted in Christ as righteous and as heires of eternall life which is the benefit of justification, and secondly, the graces of his holy Spirit, which hee received without measure, are, in some measure as it were by influence infused into us by our spirituall regeneration.

VI. Whereas therefore hee would prove out of this place, that justification is the obtayning of righteousnesse inherent. I answer, first, that to be constituted sinners by *Adams* disobedience, is to be made guilty of sinne and subject to death and damnation: and so contrariwise, to be constituted just or justified by Christs obedience, is to be acquitted from the guilt of sinne and damnation, and to bee accepted unto life: secondly, that wee are constituted sinners by *Adams* personall sinne, which is not inherent in us, but once, and that long since committed by him: so we are justified by Christs personall obedience, which is not inherent in us, but long since performed by him: thirdly, that as wee are truely made sinners by imputation of *Adams* transgression which is not inherent in us: so we are truly made just by imputation of Christs obedience, which is not inherent in us: fourthly, that the disobedience of the first *Adam* is imputed to all his children, because they were in him originally, as the root; so in him they sinned, and therefore when he did fall, they fell: so the second *Adams* obedience is imputed to all the sonnes of God, because by faith they are in him, as his members, the head and the members making but one body. This place therefore alleaged by *Bellarmine,* maketh wholly against him. Neither doth that, which he addeth concerning perfect, absolute and abundant righteousnesse communicated unto us by Christ, agree to that righteousnesse, which is inherent in us, unperfect and but begunne, as being the first fruits of the Spirit; but to the absolute and most perfect righteousnesse of Christ communicated unto us by imputation. On this place I have insisted the longer, because, though *Bellarmine* alleage it as a prime place to prove his purpose; is notwithstanding a most pregnant testimony to prove justification by imputation of Christs righteousnesse, as hereafter shall further appeare.

George Downame

VII. His second Testimony is, *Rom*. 3:24 which I have also heretofore fully proved to make wholly against him, *Lib. 3. Cap. 3. & 4.*

His third allegation is out of I *Cor*. 6:11. to which also I have
answered before[20] where I acknowledged the benefit of baptisme to
be here described, according to that which here he alleageth out of
Chrysost. Ambrose, Theophylact and others which is noted first, generally in the word *washed,* and then particularly in the words *Sanctified,* and *Iustified;* the former, signifying the cleansing of the Soule
from the pollution of sinne; the latter, from the guilt of sinne: the
former wrought by the *Spirit of our God;* the latter, by faith in the
name of the Lord Iesus. And these two distinct benefits the Scriptures
ascribe to Baptisme, *viz.* remission of sinnes, and regeneration, as I
shewed before. And therefore these benefits which the Holy Ghost
hath accurately distinguished, ought not to be either ignorantly or
Sophistically confounded. And whereas he saith, that these benefits
(as here it is noted) are wrought by the invocation of the name of
Christ, and by the power of his Spirit, neither of which is needfull
to justification, by declaration or imputation: he saith, he knoweth not
what. For to justification (as we conceive of it) to be granted and
sealed in Baptisme, both these are as needfull; as to Sanctification.
For to the obtayning of the remission of sinnes to be sealed unto us
in Baptisme, invocation of the name of God is required, *Acts* 22:16.
and it is the Spirit of Adoption, which by Baptisme sealeth unto us
the remission of our sinnes.

VIII. His fourth testimony is *Titus* 3:1, 6, 7. whence hee argueth
to this effect:

*Regeneration or renovation is formally wrought by some inherent
gift: Iustification according to the Apostle in this place is regeneration or renovation. Therefore justification is formally wrought by
some inherent gift.*

The proposition, which no man denieth, he laboreth to prove by
three arguments, which he might very well have spared; but that he
would have the world to thinke, that we deny sanctification to be
inherent. The assumption (which we do deny) he proveth by his
own authority; alleaging, that in the fifth and the sixth *verses, The
Apostle describeth justification* (which indeed he doth not) *to be
regeneration and renovation wrought in us out of the bounty of God
by the laver of Baptisme, and effusion of the holy Ghost.* This we

deny: first, because the word *justifie*, never in the whole Scriptures is used in that sense: secondly, here the Apostle in plaine termes saith, that we are justified and saved not by works of righteousnesse, whereby is excluded all justice inherent, but by Gods grace. How then doth he prove it? because in these words, *vers.* 7, that being justified by his grace wee might bee heires in hope of eternall life, the Apostle rendreth a reason, why God by the laver, and by the Holy Ghost did regenerate and renew us, and faith *the cause was, that being justified, that is,* saith he, *that being by that regeneration and renovation justified, we might deserve*[21] *to be made heires of the kingdome, and of life everlasting. Answ.* This glosse, maketh the Apostle not like himselfe, but like a popish merit-monger, corrupteth the text, which indeed doth paralell that, I *Cor.* 6:11. shewing how men converted from Gentilisme to Christianity should be exhorted to the performance of Christian duties. For howsoever whiles they were Gentiles, they were addicted to many vices and sinnes: yet after they were called (which the Apostle expresseth thus; after that the bounty and humanity of God was manifested, *viz* by the preaching of the Gospel) God, not out of any desert of theirs, but out of his meere mercy, saved them by Baptisme (as Saint *Peter* also speaketh)[22] that is, justified them, for that is the salvation we have here, to bee intitled to salvation, or saved in hope; that being justified by his grace, that is, (as he said before) by his undeserved mercy, they should be made heires, according to hope of eternall life, that is, they might be saved in hope. Of this sentence therefore stripped of its amplifications, as it were its garments, the naked substance is this. But after we were called, God by Baptisme justified us, that being justified by his grace, we might be saved in hope. The amplifications which are added, are to set forth and describe Baptisme unto us: which as hee had noted to be the seale of that righteousnesse which is by faith,[23] when he saith, that God justified or saved us by it: so he calleth it the laver of regeneration and of the renovation wrought by the Spirit, which God hath plentifully bestowed upon us. So that these words are not a description of justification, as *Bellarmine* dreameth waking, but of Baptisme. And they are added according to the purpose of the Apostle in this place, as arguments to move men to Christian duties. Why? Because Baptisme, as it was a seale unto them of their justification, so also a Sacrament of their regeneration and renovation

---

21. *Effici mereamur.*
22. I *Peter* 3:21.
23. *Rom.* 4:11.

of the Spirit; which Spirit God hath poured forth plentifully upon the faithfull: which he speaketh to this end, that the faithfull which are Baptized, should make this use of their Baptisme, not onely as of a seale to assure them of their justification and salvation: but also to be a Sacrament, token, memoriall of their regeneration and renovation wrought by the Spirit plentifully poured upon them. (To which purpose the Apostle telleth the *Romans*,[24] that so many as were baptized into Christ, were baptized into the similitude of Christs death and resurrection) whereupon the Apostle inferreth in the next words *vers.* 8. this is a faithfull saying, and these things I will thou shouldest affirme and confirme, that they which have beleeved in God, ought to bee carefull precedents of good workes. The Apostle therefore doth not say (as *Bellarmine* maketh him speake) that we are justified, or saved, or made heires of salvation by regeneration or renovation, and much lesse that thereby we merit our inheritance: but that God hath justified, or saved us Sacramentally by Baptisme, which as it is the seale of our justification and salvation; so it is also the laver of regeneration and renovation wrought by the Spirit, that being justified by his grace we might, according to hope, bee made heires of eternall life. For howsoever we are neither justified nor saved, nor made heires of eternall life, by our Sanctification: yet Sanctification is, both the way, wherein from our justification wee are to walke unto glorification.[25] For God hath chosen us to salvation through the sanctification of the Spirit, II *Thess.* 2:13. and therefore sanctification, as it is a necessary consequent of our justification, so it is a necessary fore-runner of glorification,[26] a necessary marke and cognizance of all that are justified and to be saved. And therefore our Saviour saith,[27] that by faith in him wee receive remission of sinnes, and inheritance *among them that are sanctified* and so the Apostle also, *Acts* 20:32.

IX. His fifth testimony is, *Heb.* 11. and some other places of the Scripture, which doe give testimony to some men, that they were truly, and perfectly just, and that not by an imputative justice, but inherent: his reason is, because the Scriptures would not call them absolutely just, if they were not absolutely just. *Answ.* To omit, that it is one thing to be absolutely called just, and another to be

---

24. *Rom.* 6:4, 6.
25. *Eph.* 2:10.
26. *Heb.* 12:14.
27. *Acts* 26:18.

just absolutely and perfectly: I answere, that the faithfull, who are commended in the Scriptures for righteous, were righteous, by a twofold justice, both imputative and inherent. The former, being the righteousnesse of justification; the latter, of sanctification: the former, absolute and perfect; the latter, inchoated and unperfect. By the former they were justified before God: in respect of the latter, though they were also called just, yet they were not justified thereby: that is, they were neither absolved thereby from their sinnes past, nor intitled to the kingdome of heaven; as may appeare by all those Arguments which before I produced against justification by inherent righteousnesse. As for those examples, which hee alleageth out of *Heb.* 11 (which is the *Chapter* of faith,) namely of *Abel, vers.* 4. and *Noah, vers.* 7. &c. it is evident, that they were justified by the righteousnesse which is of faith (as is expresly said of *Noah, vers.* 7) that is, by the righteousnesse of Christ apprehended by faith, and imputed to them that beleeve: for the righteousnesse, which is of faith, is imputative, *Rom.* 4:5. And when it is said, that without faith they could not possibly have pleased God,[28] it is plainely intimated that by faith they pleased God, and that they being before justified by faith, brought forth the fruits of faith acceptable unto God, by which their faith was approved. But as they were just by imputation, that is to say, justified; so also by infusion, that is, sanctified. For the justifying faith, being a lively and effectuall faith, purifieth the heart,[29] and worketh by love[30] and may be demonstrated by good works.[31] And where is not inherent righteousnesse concurring with faith, there is no justifying faith at all. But although sanctification doe alwaies accompany justification; yet wee are not justified by the righteousnesse of sanctification, which is inherent: because it is unperfect, and wee are sanctified but in part, whiles we have the flesh, that is, the body of sinne remaining in us. Neither was there ever any man since the fall absolute or perfect in respect of inherent righteousnesse, Christ only excepted.

X. Yea; but saith *Bellarmine the Scripture acknowledgeth some men to have been perfect, Gen.* 6:9. *immaculate, Ps.* 119:1. *just before God, Luke* 1:6.

I answere, that this perfection is not legall, as being a perfect conformity with the Law, which is the perfect rule of righteousnesse;

---

28. *Heb.* 11:6.
29. *Acts* 15:9.
30. *Gal.* 5:6.
31. *James* 2:18.

but evangelical, as being one of the properties of our new obedience, which is not to bee measured by the perfect performance, but by the sincere and upright desire and purpose of the heart. For this uprightnesse goeth under the name of perfection; and what is done with an upright heart, is said to be done with a perfect heart, and with the whole, that is entire heart. And likewise those men who were upright, are said to have been perfect. And yet notwithstanding all those men, who are said in the Scriptures to have been perfect and to have walked before God with a perfect heart, as *Noah, Iacob, Iob, David, Ezekias, &c.* had their imperfections. *Ezekias* is said to have been a perfect man, and to have served God with a perfect heart: notwithstanding when God left him a little to try him he discovered his imperfections, II *Chron.* 32:25, 31. Of *Asa* it is said, II *Chron.* 15:17. that his heart was perfect all the dayes of his life, and yet in the very next chapter[32] there are three faults of his recorded; where *Zachary* is said to have beene just before God, and to have walked in all the Commandments and Ordinances of God blamelesse: in the same chapter[33] his incredulity is registred, for which hee was stricken with dumbnesse and deafnesse for the space of tenne moneths. So that all that are sincere and upright, that is to say, no hypocrits, are notwithstanding their imperfections called perfect, and so the word which is translated immaculate, *Ps.* 119:1. signifieth upright; and to be righteous before God is all one with upright. Thus the holy Ghost teacheth us to expound the word, which is translated perfect, *viz. thamin* and *tham,* that to be upright is to walke before God and to walke before God is to be perfect, *Gen.* 17:1. Let perfection and uprightnesse preserve me, *Ps.* 25:21. *Ps.* 37:37. Observe the perfect man, and behold the upright, for the end of that man is peace.

XI. Yea but *Bellarmine* will prove, *that these men which are in the Scriptures called just, were endued with inherent righteousnesse, because they brought forth good workes, which were the fruits and effects of their inward righteousnesse: for he that doth righteousnesse is righteous:*[34] whom doth he now confute? wee doe not deny them, who are commended in the Scriptures for righteous persons, to have been endued with righteousnesse inherent: but wee deny, that they, or any of them, were justified before God thereby. As for example, *Abraham,* who abounded with good workes, was justified by faith

32. II *Chron.* 16:7, 10, 12.
33. *Luke* 1:20, 62.
34. I *John* 3:7.

without workes, *Rom.* 4:2, 3. and as hee was justified, so are all the faithfull. *Rom.* 4:23, 24. *David,* though a man according to God's own heart, walking before him in truth,[35] and righteousnes, and uprightnesse of heart; yet professeth, that neither he, nor any man living,[36] could be justified, if God should enter into judgement with them, and therefore placeth his happinesse and justification, not in his vertues or good works, but in the not imputing of sin, and imputation of righteousnesse without workes, *Rom.* 4:6. *Paul,* though hee knew nothing by himselfe, yet professeth, that hee was not thereby justified, I *Cor.* 4:4. Yea, in the question of justification, hee esteemeth his owne righteousnesse of no worth, *Phil.* 3:8, 9. But as wee doe not deny the faithfull to bee endued with inherent righteousnesse; so we affirme, that whosoever is justified by imputative righteousnesse, is also sanctified in some measure with righteousnesse infused and inherent. In respect whereof, though they bee also sinnes in themselves, by reason of their habituall corruptions, and actuall transgressions, being in part carnall and sold under sinne, and by the Law,[37] which is in the members, led captive to the Law of sinne: yet they have their denomination from the better part. Even as a wedge of metall, wherein much drosse is mingled with Gold, is called a wedge of Gold, though not of pure Gold; and an heape of Corne, wherein is as much chaffe as Wheate, is called an heape of Wheate, though not of pure Wheate: So the faithfull man in whom there is the flesh and body of sinne, as well as the Spirit and regenerate part, is called of the better part a righteous man, though not perfectly, absolutely, purely, just in respect of his righteousnesse inherent. Indeed every true beleever, so soone as he is indeed with a true justifying faith, is perfectly just, by righteousnesse imputed; but at the best he is sanctified onely in part.

XII. His sixth testimony is taken out of *Rom.* 8:29. and I *Cor.* 15:49. where it is said, that the just are conformable to the image of Christ, and doe beare the image of the second *Adam,* as they have borne the image of the first *Adam,* from whence hee collecteth three reasons: The first,

As Christ was just, so are wee; and as hee was not just, so are not we. But Christ was just by inherent righteousnesse, and not by imputation:

---

35. I *Kings* 3:6.
36. *Ps.* 143:2.
37. *Rom.* 7:14, 23.

Therefore we are just by inherent righteousnesse, and not by imputation.

The proposition he proveth by the places alleaged.

First I answer to the proofe of the proposition; that the places alleaged are impertinent: For the question being of the righteousnesse of justification, never any understood the Apostle in these places to speake thereof: But either of filiation, as *Chrysostome* and others understand the former place, because as Christ is the Sonne of God, so also are wee: or of afflictions, because whom God hath predestinated to bee like his Sonne in glory, they shall bee conformable to the image of his Sonne in bearing the Crosse (which sense is given by our Writers and is agreeable to the scope of the Apostle in that place to the *Romans*) or of Glory, that when he shall appeare wee shall bee like him in glory: of which as *Ambrose, Sedulius* and others understand, *Rom.* 8:19. so the other place[38] being read in the future, as it ought to bee in the latter branch (as wee have borne the image of the earthy, so wee shall beare the image of the heavenly) is necessarily to be understood. Or of holinesse as *Oecumenius* understandeth that place, that as hee is holy, so we should be holy also. Neither is it to be doubted, but that the image of God, according to which we are renewed, consisteth in true holines and righteousnes but that is the righteousnes of sanctification, whereby we resemble the image of Christ in true righteousnes & holines. But the righteousnes of justification is Christs righteousnes it self, not the image of it.

XIII. As touching the proposition it selfe; wee must distinguish betwixt the thing, and the manner. In respect of the thing, it is true, that Christ is righteous, and so are all his members. But in respect of the manner, it is not true, neither generally, nor *adequate* or reciprocally, as *Bellarmine* understandeth it: who from thence argueth negatively, as well as affirmatively. For things that be like are not like altogether, and in all respects: as may appeare by other resemblances, in respect whereof wee are said to beare the image of Christ. As first in respect of filiation. Christ is the Sonne of God, and so are wee. True, in respect of the thing, but not true in respect of the manner. For hee is the Sonne of God by nature, and by eternall generation: but wee are the Sonnes of God in him by grace of regeneration and adoption. Secondly, in regard of the Crosse. Christ did beare the Crosse, and so do wee. True in respect of the thing, but not true in respect of the manner. For Christs sufferings were the λύτρον

---

38. I *Cor.* 15:49.

the price of ransome which hee as our Redeemer laid downe for us. But wee doe not suffer as redeemers, neither are our sufferings λύτρον a price of ransome, but either παιδεία chastisements for sinne,[39] or δοκιμασία trialls for our good,[40] or μαρτύριον our sufferings for Christ,[41] or τιμωρία that is such chastisements or corrections as the Lord laieth upon his children having scandalously offended, to vindicate his owne honour.[42] Thirdly, in respect of glory; Christ is glorified, and so shall we, who beare his image, true in respect of the thing, but not in respect of the manner: for he as the head, we as the members, according to our proportion. Fourthly, in respect of holinesse or sanctification. Christ was holy, and so are wee, true in respect of the thing, for whosoever is in Christ hee is a new creature,[43] renewed according to his image in true holinesse, but not in respect of the manner. Christ was holy from his conception, and originally, so are not wee. Christ in himselfe was perfectly just and holy without blemish of sinne, so are not wee.

XIV. But as touching the righteousnesse of justification, we are not said to beare Christs image. Neither can Christ bee said truely and properly to be justified as we are. For justification properly is of a sinner, and it consisteth partly in remission of sin. But if in respect thereof wee did beare Christs image, then in imitation of *Bellarmine* wee might conclude: As Christ was not just, nor made just, so neither are wee. But Christ was not just, nor made just by the benefit of justification; in like manner neither are wee just or made just by the benefit of jutsification, which is evidently false. But in respect of our justification we may rather use that similitude of the Apostle, II *Cor.* 5:21. As Christ was made sinne or a sinner for us, so wee are made righteous with the righteousnesse of God in him. Christ was made a sinner for us, not by inherencie (God forbid?) but by imputation of our sinne. Therefore we are made righteous in our justification, not by inherencie, but by imputation of his righteousnesse.

XV. Secondly, he reasoneth thus: *If wee bee not just by inherent righteousnesse, but by imputation onely,* or as hee speaketh (like a cavilling Sophister) putative, *and not indeed, being indeed unjust, then doe we beare the image of the Devill rather than of Christ. For*

39. I *Cor.* 11:32.
40. *Deut.* 8:16.
41. *Phil.* 1:29.
42. II *Sam.* 12:14.
43. II *Cor.* 5:17.

more rightly have wee our denomination from that which we are, than from that which we are onely supposed to bee. I answer, first, that whosoever is just by imputation, he is not *putative* onely just, but truely and indeed. For though he bee a sinner in himselfe (as all but Papists are) yet hee is righteous, or as the Apostle speaketh the righteousnesse of God in him, II *Cor.* 4:21. Secondly, that the faithfull are just, not onely by righteousnesse imputed, which is the righteousnesse of justification: but also in respect of justice inherent, which is the righteousnesse of sanctification, in regard whereof all the faithfull are called Saints, as *Rom.* 1:7, &c.[44] Thirdly, although the faithfull bee sinners in themselves, yet being regenerate and sanctified in part, they have their denomination from their better part, and are called just, though not purely and perfectly just, as I have shewed before.

XVI. His third reason: *Of the earthy Adam, who was a sinner, wee have borne the true image; because sinne was not in us putative but truely and indeed: so the true image of Christ wee shall beare, if justice bee inherent in us not putative; but truely and indeed.*

Answer. As wee receive two things from the first *Adam, viz.* the guilt of his sinne communicated, as *Bellarmine* himselfe confesseth, by imputation, by which we were truely made sinners, and truly obnoxious to death and damnation, which is opposite to justification, and by it is taken away: and secondly, the corruption of his nature which hee drew upon himselfe, being propagated by carnall generation, which is opposite to sanctification, and by it in some measure, and by degrees is taken away: so from the second *Adam* we receive also two things, the merits of Christs sufferings and obedience communicated by imputation, by which we are truely made just, and heires of eternall life; and the vertue of his death and resurrection derived unto us by spirituall regeneration; by which wee beare the image of the second *Adam,* as truely, though not so fully in this life, as by carnall generation wee did beare the image of the first *Adam.* But this withall is to bee observed, that as we doe beare the image of the first *Adam* in respect of the corruption derived unto us by generation, and not in respect of the participation of his transgression, for in him we sinned and were guilty of the same transgression with him, it being communicated unto us by imputation: so we do beare the image of the second *Adam* in respect of holinesse and righteousnesse derived unto us from him in our regeneration, by which we are renewed according to his image in true righteousnesse and holinesse and not in respect of our justification, wherein the same righteous-

---

44. *Rom.* 16:15; I *Cor.* 1:2; II *Cor.* 1:1; *Phil.* 1:1; 4:22; I *Tim.* 5:10.

nesse and obedience which hee performed in the daies of his flesh is communicated unto us by imputation, and accepted of God in our behalfe as if we had performed the same in our own persons. To conclude therefore, it is not the image of Christs righteousnesse and obedience by which we are justified: But we are justified by the righteousnesse and obedience of Christ it selfe.

XVII. His seventh Allegation of *Rom.* 6:4, 6. is scarce worth the answering, wherein hee proveth, which no man denieth, *that the godly doe truly, and not putative dye unto sinne, and rise unto righteousnesse; even as Christ whose death and resurrection is represented in Baptisme, did truly dye and rise againe.*

For this dying unto sinne, and rising unto righteousnesse are the two parts of our sanctification; which never any denied to bee inherent. But that justification and sanctification are not to bee confounded, I have before proved at large.[45] If hee would have said any thing to the purpose, he should have proved, that our justification consisteth in our mortification and vivification: and then might he well have concluded, that we are not justified by imputation, but by inherent righteousnesse. But I cannot sufficiently wonder at the blind malice of these men, who either would perswade themselves, or would goe about to perswade others, that we hold the righteousnesse of sanctification and the parts thereof, which we acknowledge to be wrought in us by the holy Spirit, not to bee inherent, but imputative. As for these words *vers.* 7. he that is dead is justified from sinne: the meaning is, as I have shewed before,[46] that he is freed from sinne, as our translation readeth, and as *Chrysostome* and *Oecumenius* expound it: the speciall sense of freeing from guilt opposed to condemnation, which is the proper sense of the word, *Acts* 13:38, 39. extended to the generall signification of freedome: he that is dead is freed from committing of sinne, according to that place of *Peter*, I *Epist.* 4:1. which *Bellarmine* paralelleth with this, he that hath suffered in the flesh hath ceased from sinne.

XVIII. In his eighth allegation hee patcheth divers places of Scripture together, as it were *invita Minerva*, out of which nothing can be concluded, but that the Papists have not one sound Argument to prove their justification by inherent righteousnesse. The places which he patcheth together are these, *Rom.* 8:15. *That wee now by Christ*

---

45. *Lib.* 2.
46. *Lib.* 2. *c.*2. §.8.

have received the Spirit of Adoption of the sonnes of God, quoad
animam, saith he, *in respect of the Soule, the which, as it is there said,*
(viz. vers. 10.) *liveth by reason of justification, although the body
be dead, (that is, be mortall as yet) by reason of sinne.* But (saith he)
a little after, (viz. vers. 23.) *he added, that wee having the first fruits
of the Spirit, doe groane within our selves, expecting the adoption
of the sonnes of God, even the redemption of our body. For as the
same Apostle saith Phil.* 3:20, 21. *wee expect our Saviour who shall
reforme the body of our humility, configured to the body of his glory.
But the adoption of sonnes, which wee expect in the redemption of
the body shall be most true and inherent in the body it selfe, that is
to say immortality and impassibility, not putative, but true. Therefore
the adoption, which now we have in the spirit by justification, must
also be true, not putative, otherwise as we expect the redemption of
the body, so also wee should expect the redemption of the soule.*
Answ. See what poore shifts so learned a man is put unto, according
to the ancient profession of *Sophistres* noted by *Plato,* τὸν ἥττω λόγον
κρείττω ποιεῖν to make good a bad cause. This is *Bellarmines* whole
dispute word for word: where with much travell he hath brought
forth this conclusion that our adoption, which now we have by justification is true, and not in conceit onely: which we freely confesse.
For whoever denied, that our adoption is as true, as our justification?
But doth it from hence follow, that wee are justified by inherent
righteousnesse? A good syllogisme concluding that assertion from those
premisses had beene worth his labour. The most that can bee said
in this matter, as I suppose, is this. That when our gracious God by
his holy Spirit doth regenerate us, he doth beget in us the grace of
faith. As soone as faith is wrought in us, wee are engrafted into
Christ: to us being in Christ, the Lord communicateth the merits
of his Sonne; by imputation of whose righteousnesse unto us, hee,
remitting our sinnes, doth not onely accept of us, as righteous in
Christ; but also in him hee adopteth us to bee his Sons and heires
of eternall life.

XIX. Let this proposition then *tanquam commune principium* bee
agreed upon betweene us. *Such as is our adoption, such is our justification:* and let us see, what either of us can inferre thereupon. *Bellarmine* assumeth thus: but our adoption is not imputative, for that
I suppose is his meaning by that odious word *putative,* as though if
it were imputative, it were but putative, which is most false. For he
that either is a sinner by imputation of *Adams* transgression, is as
truely a sinner, as by transfusion of the corruption: yea, if he had not
beene truely a sinner by imputation of *Adams* guilt, hee should never

have beene punished, either with the transfusion of the corruption, or with death, unto which by the guilt he was bound over: or hee that is righteous by imputation of Christs righteousnesse, is as truely righteous before God; yea, more truely, than by infusion of inherent righteousnesse. For that is perfect; this is stained with the flesh, and therefore is but a sinnefull righteousnesse, which cannot stand in judgment before God, judging according to the sentence of his Law. But *Bellarmines* assumption, as I was saying, is this. *Our adoption is not imputative, but by grace inherent:* therefore our justification is not imputative, but by righteousnesse inherent. The assumption, which is utterly false, hee endevoreth to prove, because the Apostle, *Rom.* 8:15 saith, that now by Christ wee have received the Adoption of the sonnes of God, *quoad animam,* (saith *Bellarmine,* that he might patch with it, *vers.* 10.) in respect of the soule, which, as it is there said, liveth *propter justificationem,* although the body bee dead, that is to say, *mortall,* by reason of sinne. These places *Bellarmine* alleaged before, to prove that the grace by which wee are justified is inherent, and namely charity: because charity is that, by which wee cry in our hearts Abba Father. Secondly, because it is said, that the Spirit liveth by reason of justification, though the body bee dead by reason of sinne: to both which I have before answered.[47]

XX. But here *Bellarmine* maketh a twofold Adoption; the one of the soule, patched out of *Rom.* 8:10, 15. the other of the body pieced out of *Rom.* 8:23. and *Phil.* 3:20, 21. when as indeed Adoption is not of either part, but of the person or of the whole man, who is Adopted to be the sonne of God. Neither doth the Apostle speake of the adoption of the soule, nor yet of the adoption of the body, but of the redemption of the body from the servitude of corruption into the glorious liberty of the sonnes of God, which is not the adoption of the body, but the fruite of the adoption of the whole man, which here by a Metonymy is called adoption. The former he proveth by the latter not to be imputative, but inherent. *The adoption of sonnes which we expect in the redemption of the body, shall be most true and inherent in the body it selfe, that is to say, immortality and impassibility not putative but true: therefore the adoption which now we have in the spirit by justification, is also true, not putative but inherent. Ans.* In this similitude he should rather have said, that as the adoption of sonnes which we doe expect at the redemption of our bodies, that is, at the resurrection, is the everlasting inheritance whereunto wee were adopted as sonnes, which a true and glorious

---

47. *Lib.* 3. *c.*5. §.5.6.

inheritance, though not inherent, in the body but enjoyed by the whole man as adherent unto him: so the adoption which we now have in the Spirit by justification, which is the entituling of us to this inheritance, is a true adoption, though not inherent, but wrought by imputation of Christs merits unto us. But suppose the adoption of the body as hee calleth it, were inherent: how doth it follow, that the adoption of the soule, as hee calleth it, should also be inherent? he saith, it must bee so: *Otherwise,* saith he, *as wee expect the redemption of the body: so also we should expect the redemption of the soule* (which the Papists had neede to doe whose soules shall be in purgatory at the last day, but from thence to be delivered at that day by a gaole-delivery) but I say, it followeth not; for the adoption which is imputative is a most true adoption: and wee need no other, but the accomplishment thereof, which is our full redemption. As for that adoption, which he supposeth to bee inherent, it is a meere fancie.

XXI. Now let us see, what may from that proposition, which was agreed upon betweene us, be truly inferred on our part. Such as is our adoption, such is our justification: but our Adoption is imputative, and not by inherencie. For as I have shewed heretofore[48] these foure benefits, reconciliation, redemption, justification and adoption doe not import any reall mutation in the subject but relative and imputative: for when God imputing to a beleever the merits of his Sonne forgiveth his sinnes, which made him an enemy to God, a bondslave of sinne and Satan, guilty of sinne and damnation, the childe of the Devill; and receiveth him into his favour, maketh him Christs freeman, accepteth of his as righteous, admitteth him to bee his sonne: he is said to reconcile, to redeeme, to justifie, and to adopt him, not by working any reall or positive change in the party, but relative, or in respect of relation. To be a father, and to be a sonne are relatives: when a man therefore hath first a sonne, hee becommeth a father, which hee was not before, not by any reall change in himselfe, but by a new relation which before he had not. When a man is adopted, he becommeth the sonne of another man, whose sonne he was not before; not by any reall mutation, but onely in regard of relation. For if the party adopted by God should by adoption bee really changed, then God, who adopteth should also seeme to bee really changed, which is impossible, because he is immutable. For as he which is adopted becommeth the sonne of God, which hee was not before: so God, when he first adopteth any man, becommeth his father, which

---

48. *Lib.* 1. *c.*1. and *lib.* 2. *c.*6.

hee was not before. Here therefore seemeth to bee a change as well in God adopting, as in the party adopted: not reall, for that is not possible, but relatively onely, which is a manifest evidence, that as our Adoption, so our justification is not any reall change wrought in us by infusion of any inherent quality, but a relative change wrought without us by imputation of Christs righteousnesse.

John Bunyan
1628-1688

11

Sanctification

John Bunyan was born at Elstow (near Bedford), England, of poor and uneducated parents. He joined the army at age sixteen or seventeen and began a life of godless revelry. After his military service he returned to Elstow and took up his father's trade of tinker. In 1647 he married a poor Christian girl whose prayers brought him to Christ, and in 1655 he was baptized at the Baptist church in Bedford. That same year, however, his wife died, leaving him with four small children. Bunyan was made a deacon the same year, and he began to preach. His sermons drew great crowds and were used of God to convert many people.

In 1659 John Bunyan married Elizabeth, a woman sent by God to care for his children, one of whom was blind. During the Restoration in 1660, Bunyan was arrested while preaching in a farmhouse at Lower Samsell. Though it was not yet unlawful to preach the evangelical message when Bunyan was arrested, he remained in prison for twelve years! Thus, as a Baptist and a Puritan, he became one of the first nonconformists to suffer for his faith.

While in the Bedford prison, Bunyan wrote his famous *Pilgrim's Progress*, which became the most popular and influential book next to the Word of God. During his imprisonment Bunyan poured forth dozens of other books as well. Some of them were *Profitable Meditations* (1664), *Prayer* (1664), *Christian Behaviour* (1664), *One Thing Needful* (1665), *The Holy City* (1665), *Resurrection of the Dead* (1665), and *Grace Abounding to the Chief of Sinners* (1666).

In 1672 the Bedford congregation appointed Bunyan, who was still in prison, their pastor, and after several months the king's Declaration of Religious Indulgence secured Bunyan's release. Early in his ministry he wrote a treatise in which he disputed with London Baptists who closed communion to nonimmersionists. The Test Act of 1674 put Bunyan back in prison, and during this confinement he wrote *The Strait Gate* and *Saved by Grace*. Also at this time he began writing *Pilgrim's Progress*. Meanwhile John Owen, who is said to have been willing to exchange all his learning for the tinker's power to move men's hearts, began working to secure Bunyan's release. Once free, Bunyan showed his manuscript of *Pilgrim's Progress* to Owen, and Owen urged him to print it. It appeared in 1678 and was reprinted the same year; within ten years 100,000 copies were in print! God had used two great Puritan preachers to bring the "dream" of one of them into reality. The book was especially popular among the common people, due to the vivid and realistic struggles of its characters.

In 1680 the Baptist minister wrote *The Life and Death of Mr. Badman,* and in 1682 he produced his second great allegory, *The Holy War. Christiana's Progress* appeared in 1685, and in his last years he wrote *Come and Welcome to Christ, The Work of Jesus Christ as an Advocate,* and *The Acceptable Sacrifice.* Bunyan died in 1688 of a severe cold while traveling to London. He was buried at Bunhill Fields.

Following is an essay on practical Christian holiness. In it Bunyan gives several reasons why those who profess Christ should depart from sin. One need not point out the need of such teaching today when liberal attitudes and "easy-believism" have captured the majority of professing Christians. Holy living is not a relic from Puritan days, but something that is essential to all true Christians of every age; it results from the normal and necessary working of the Spirit of God in their hearts.

...I come now to another observation with which I will present you, and that is this, namely, "that every one that in way of profession and religion names the name of Christ, should depart from iniquity."

I say, that every one that in a way of profession and religion, nameth the name of Christ, should depart from iniquity. This truth needs more practice than proof: for I think there are none that have either scripture or reason by them, but will freely consent to this.

Nor is there anything ambiguous in the observation that we need now to stand upon the explaining of. For,

What iniquity is, who knows not?

That it cleaves to the best, who knows not?

That it is disgraceful to profession, who knows not? and therefore that it ought to be departed from, who knows not?

But because the motives in particular may not be so much considered as they ought, and because it is Satan's design to tempt us to be unholy, and to keep iniquity and the professing man together; therefore I will in this place spend some arguments upon you that profess, and in a way of profession do name the name of Christ, that you depart from iniquity; to wit, both in the inward thought, and in the outward practice of it. And those arguments shall be of four sorts, some respecting Christ, some his Father, some ourselves....

Our Relation to Christ

First. The Christ, whom you profess, whose name you name, and whose disciples you pretend to be, is holy. "Be ye holy, for I am holy." (I Peter 1:16) This is natural to our discourse: for if Christ be holy, and if we profess him, and in professing of him, declare that we are his disciples, we ought therefore to depart from iniquity, that we may show the truth of our profession to the world.

Second. They that thus name the name of Christ should depart from iniquity, because this Christ, whose name we name is loving. Those that have a loving master, a master that is continually extending his love unto his servants, should be forward in doing of his will, that thereby they may show their sense, and acceptation of the love of their master. Why, this is his will, "that we depart from iniquity, that we throw sin away; that we fly every appearance of evil." (I Thess. 5:22)

Third. They that thus name the name of Christ should depart from iniquity, because of the honour and reputation of the Lord. It is a disparagement to Christ, that any of his servants, and that any that name his name, should yet abide by, and continue with iniquity. "A son honoureth his father, and a servant his master: if then I be a Father, where is mine honour? and if I be a Master, where is my fear? saith the Lord of Hosts, unto you, O priests, that despise my name; and ye say, Wherein have we despised thy name?" (Mal. 1:6)

Fourth. They that name the name of Christ should depart from iniquity, because of his name, that his name may not be evil spoken of by men; for our holiness puts a lustre and a beauty upon the name of Christ, and our not departing from iniquity draws a cloud upon it. Wherefore we ought to depart from iniquity, that the name of the Lord Jesus may be glorified, and not reproached through us.

Fifth. They that name the name of Christ should depart from iniquity, because of the gospel of the Lord Jesus Christ. That the gospel of our Lord Jesus Christ, which they profess, may not be evil spoken of by our neighbours. "The gospel is called holy, therefore let them be holy that profess it." (II Peter 2:21) The which they can by no means be, if they depart not from iniquity. Men cannot serve the designs of the gospel, and their own worldly and fleshly designs. But they that profess the name of Christ, they should be tender of his gospel, that they keep that in good esteem and reputation in the world. The which they can by no means do, unless they depart from iniquity.

Sixth. They that name the name of Christ should depart from iniquity, because the very profession of that name is holy. The profession is an holy profession. Be ye clean that bear the vessels of the Lord; the vessels, that is, the profession, for by that is, as it were, carried about the name and gospel of Jesus Christ. We must, therefore, lay aside all iniquity, and superfluity of naughtiness, and do as persons professing godliness, as professing a profession, that Christ is the priest of, the high-priest of. (I Tim. 2:10; Heb. 3:1) It is a reproach to any man to be but a bungler at his profession, to be but a sloven in his profession. And it is the honour of a man to be excellent in the managing of his profession. Christians should be excellent in the management of their profession, and should make that which is good in itself, good to the church and to the world, by a sweet and cleanly managing of it.

Seventh. They that profess the name of Christ, or that name it religiously, should to their utmost depart from iniquity, because of the church of Christ which is holy. He that religiously professeth the name of Christ, has put himself into the church of Christ, though not into a particular one, yet, into the universal one. Now that is holy. What agreement then hath the temple of God with idols? or any pillar, or post, or pin, or member of that temple? (II Cor. 6:16) One black sheep is quickly espied among five hundred white ones, and one mangey one will soon infect many. One also among the saints, that is not clean, is a blemish to the rest, and, as Solomon says, "one sinner destroyeth much good." (Eccles. 9:18)

Eighth. They that profess the name of Christ, or that name that name religiously, should depart from iniquity, because of the ordinances of Christ, for they are holy. Men of old, before they went in to meddle with holy things, were to wash their hands and their feet in a vessel prepared for that purpose. (Exod. 30:17-21) Now since they that name that name religiously do also meddle with Christ's appointments, they must also wash and be clean; cleanse your hands ye sinners if you mean to meddle with Christ in his appointments; wash, lest God cut you off for your not departing from iniquity.

Ninth. They that name the name of Christ religiously, should depart from iniquity, because of Christ's observers. There are many that keep their eye upon Christ, and that watch for an opportunity to speak against him, even through the sides of those that profess him. "Behold, this child is set for the fall and rising again of many in Israel: and for a sign that shall be spoken against." (Luke 2:34) Some take occasion to speak against him, because of the meanness of his person; here some again speak against him, because of the plainness of his doctrine; also some speak against him, because of the meanness of his followers; and some speak against him, because of the evil deeds of some that profess him. But if he that gives just occasion of offence to the least of saints had better be drowned in the sea with a millstone about his neck; what, think you, shall his judgment be, who, through his mingling of his profession of Christ's name with a wicked life, shall tempt or provoke men to speak against Christ?

Our Relation to God the Father

I come now to those arguments that respect God the Father.

First. Then, they that profess the name of Christ should depart from iniquity because of God the Father; because God the Father has made Christ to be to us what he is; to wit, the apostle and high-priest of our profession. "He that honoureth not the Son, honoureth not the Father, which hath sent him." (I Cor. 1:30; John 5:23; 15:8) Nor can the Father be honoured by us, but by our departing from iniquity. All our talk and profession of Christ adds no glory to his Father, who has made him our King, and Priest, and Prophet, if it be not joined to an holy conversation. Wherefore, if you profess the name of Christ, and would hold the word in hand, that you have believed in him, depart from iniquity, for the Father's sake that hath sent him.

Second. As it is the Father which hath made Christ to us what he is; so it is the Father, who hath called us to partake of Christ and all his benefits. "Wherefore we must depart from iniquity, that profess the name of Christ, that we may glorify him for his call." (I Cor. 1:9; Heb. 3:14) He has called us to the fellowship of his Son Jesus Christ; that is, to partake of all that good that is in him, as Mediator, and to be done by him for those that trust in him. Nor had we ever come out of a cursed and condemned condition, to Christ for life and blessedness, but by the call of the Father; for it is "not of works, but of him that calleth." (Rom. 9:11) Now since he has called us to this privilege (even us whom he has called) and left others in their sins to perish by his judgments, it is meet, we should depart from iniquity. Especially since the call by which he called us, is heavenly, and holy, and because he has not only called us to glory, but to virtue. (Heb. 3:1; II Peter 1:2, 3)

Third. We that religiously name the name of Christ, should depart from iniquity, because God the Father of our Lord Jesus Christ has commanded us so to do. Wherefore gird up the loins of your minds, be sober, and hope to the end, for the grace that is to be brought unto you at the revelation of Jesus Christ. As obedient children, not fashioning yourselves according to your former lusts in your ignorance; but as he that has called you is holy, so be ye holy in all manner of conversation: because it is written, "Be ye holy, as I am holy." (I Peter 1:13-16)

Fourth. They that religiously name the name of Christ, should depart from iniquity, that they may answer the end for which they are called to profess his name. The Father has therefore called them to profess his name, that they might be trees of righteousness, the planting of the Lord, that he might be glorified. Dost thou then profess the name of Christ; bring forth those fruits that become that holy profession, that you may be called trees of righteousness, and that God may be glorified for, and by your professed subjection to the gospel of his Son. (Isa. 61:3)

Fifth. They that name, as afore, the name of the Lord Jesus Christ, should depart from iniquity, that they may show to the world the nature and power of those graces, which God the Father has bestowed upon them that do religiously name the name of Christ. And the rather, because, he that religiously nameth that name, declareth even by his so naming of him, that he has received grace of the Father, to enable him so to do. Now he cannot declare this by deeds, unless he depart from iniquity; and his declaring of it by words alone, signifies little to God or man. (Titus 1:16)

Sixth. We, therefore, that religiously name the name of Christ, should also depart from iniquity, because the Spirit of the Father will else be grieved. (Eph. 4:30) The countenancing of iniquity, the not departing therefrom, will grieve the holy Spirit of God, by which you are sealed to the day of redemption; and that is a sin of an higher nature than men commonly are aware of. He that grieveth the Spirit of God shall smart for it here, or in hell, or both. And that Spirit that sometimes did illuminate, teach and instruct them, can keep silence, can cause darkness, can withdraw itself, and suffer the soul to sin more and more; and this last is the very judgment of judgments. He that grieves the Spirit, quenches it; and he that quenches it, vexes it; and he that vexes it, sets it against himself, and tempts it to hasten destruction upon himself. (I Thess. 5:19) Wherefore take heed, professors, I say take heed, you that religiously name the name of Christ, that you meddle not with iniquity, that you tempt not the Spirit of the Lord to do such things against you, whose beginnings are dreadful, and whose end in working of judgments is unsearchable. (Isa. 63:10; Acts 5:9) A man knows not whither he is going, nor where he shall stop, that is but entering into temptation; nor whether he shall ever turn back, or go out at the gap that is right before him. He that has begun to grieve the Holy Ghost, may be suffered to go on until he has sinned that sin which is called the sin against the Holy Ghost. And if God shall once give thee up to that, then thou art in the iron cage, out of which there is neither deliverance nor redemption. Let every one therefore that nameth the name of Christ, depart from iniquity, upon this second consideration.

Our Relation to Ourselves

In the next place, I come now to those arguments that do respect thyself.

First. Those that religiously name the name of Christ should, must, depart from iniquity, because else our profession of him is but a lie. "If we say we have fellowship with him, and walk in darkness, we lie." (I John 1:6) "And walk in darkness"; that is, and walk in iniquity, and depart not from a life that is according to the course of this world. "He that saith, I know him, and keepeth not his commandments, is a liar, and the truth is not in him." (I John 2:4) The truth that he professes to know, and that he saith he hath experience of, is not in him. Every man that nameth the name of Christ, is not therefore a man of God, nor is the word in every man's mouth, truth; though he makes profession of that worthy name. (I Kings 17:24) It is then truth in him, and to others with reference to him, when his mouth and his life shall agree. (Rev. 2:2, 9; 3:9) Men may say they are apostles, and be liars: they may say they are Jews, that is, Christians, and lie, and be liars, and lie in so saying. Now this is the highest kind of lying, and certainly must therefore work the saddest sort of effects. Thus man's best things are lies. His very saying, I know him, I have fellowship with him, I am a Jew, a Christian, is a lie. His life giveth his mouth the lie: and all knowing men are sure he lies. 1. He lies unto God: he speaks lies in the presence, and to the very face of God. Now this is a daring thing: I know their lies, saith he: and shall he not recompense for this? (See Acts 5:4; Rev. 21:8, 27; 22:15; and take heed.) I speak to you that religiously name the name of Christ, and yet do not depart from iniquity. 2. He lies unto men; every knowing man; every man that is able to judge of the tree by the fruit, knows that that man is a liar, and that his whole profession as to himself is a lie, if he doth not depart from iniquity. Thus Paul called the slow bellies, the unsound professors among the Cretians, liars. They were so in his eyes, for that their profession of the name of Christ was not seconded with such a life as became a people professing godliness. (Titus 1:12-16) They did not depart from iniquity. But again, 3. Such a man is a liar to his own soul. Whatever such an one promiseth to himself, his soul will find it a lie. There be many in the world that profess the name of Christ, and consequently promise their soul the enjoyment of that good that indeed is wrapt up in him, but they will certainly be mistaken hereabout, and with the greatest terror, will find it so, when they shall hear that direful sentence, "Depart from me, all ye workers of iniquity." (Luke 13:27) Christ is resolved that the loose-lived professor shall not stand in the judgment, nor any such sinners in the congregation of the righteous. They have lied to God, to men, and to themselves; but Jesus then will not lie unto them: he will plainly tell them that he hath not known them, and that they shall not abide in his presence. But,

Second. Those that religiously name the name of Christ should depart from iniquity, else, as they are liars in their profession, so they are self-deceivers. I told you but now such lie to themselves, and so, consequently, they deceive themselves. "But be ye doers of the word, not hearers only, deceiving your ownselves." (James 1:22) It is a sad thing for a man, in, and about eternal things, to prove a deceiver of others; but for a man to deceive himself, his ownself of eternal life, this is saddest of all: yet there is in man a propenseness so to do. Hence the apostle says, "be not deceived, and let no man deceive himself." And again (ver. 26), "If any man among you seem to be religious, and bridleth not his tongue, but deceiveth his own heart, this man's religion is vain." These words "but deceiveth his own heart" I have much mused about: for they seem to me to be spoken to show how bold and prodigiously desperate some men are, who yet religiously name the name of Christ: desperate I say at self-deceiving. He deceiveth his own heart; he otherwise persuadeth it, than of its ownself it would go: ordinarily, men are said to be deceived by their hearts, but here is a man that is said to deceive his own heart, flattering it off from the scent and dread of those convictions, that by the word sometimes it hath been under: persuading of it that there needs no such strictness of life be added to a profession of faith in Christ, as by the gospel is called for: or that since Christ has died for us, and rose again, and since salvation is alone in him, we need not be so concerned, or be so strict to matter how we live. This man is a self deceiver; he deceives his own heart. Self-deceiving and that about spiritual and eternal things, especially when men do it willingly, is one of the most unnatural, unreasonable, and unaccountable actions in the world. 1. It is one of the most unnatural actions. For here a man seeks his own ruin, and privily lurks for his own life. (Prov. 1:18) We all cry out against him that murders his children, his wife, or his own body, and condemn him to be one of those that has forgot the rules and love of nature. But behold the man under consideration is engaged in such designs as will terminate in his own destruction: he deceiveth his own soul. 2. This is also the most unreasonable act; there can no cause, nor crumb of cause that has the least spark or dram of reason, or of anything that looks like reason, be shown why a man should deceive himself, and bereave his soul of eternal life. Therefore, 3. Such men are usually passed over with astonishment and silence. "Be astonished, O ye heavens at this, and be horribly afraid, for my people have committed two evils; they have forsaken me the fountain of living waters, and hewed them out cisterns, broken cisterns that can hold no water." (Jer. 2:12, 13)

But above all this, as to this head, is the most amazing place, where it is said, that the self-deceiver makes his self-deceiving his sport: "Sporting themselves with their own deceivings." (II Peter 2:13) These are a people far gone to be sure, that are arrived to such a height of negligence, carelessness, wantonness, and desperateness of spirit, as to take pleasure in, and make a sport of, that which will assuredly deceive them for ever. But this is the fruit of professing of Christ, and of not departing from iniquity. The wisdom and judgment of God is such, as to give such over to the sporting of themselves in their own deceivings.

Third. Those that religiously name the name of Christ, should depart from iniquity, because of the scandal that will else assuredly come upon religion, and the things of religion through them. Upon this head I may begin to write, with a sigh; for never more of this kind than now. There is no place where the professors of religion are, that is clean and free from offence and scandal. Iniquity is so entailed to religion, and baseness of life to the naming of the name of Christ, that one may say of the professors of this age, as it was said of them of old, "All tables are full of vomit and filthiness, so that there is no place clean." (Isa. 28:8) Where are they, even amongst those that strive for the rule, that mind it at all, when it pinches upon their lusts, their pride, avarice, and wantonness? Are not now-a-days, the bulk of professors like those that strain at a gnat and swallow a camel? (Matt. 23:24) Yea, do not professors teach the wicked ones to be wicked? (Jer. 2:33) Ah! Lord God, this is a lamentation, and will be for a lamentation. What a sore disease is now got into the church of God, that the generality of professors should walk with scandal!

No fashion, no vanity, no profuseness, and yet no niggardliness, but is found amongst professors. They pinch the poor, and nip from them their due, to maintain their own pride and vanity. I shall not need to instance particulars, for from the rich to the poor, from the pastor to the people, from the master to his man, and from the mistress to her maiden, all are guilty of scandal, and of reproaching, by their lives, the name of the Lord. For they profess, and name that worthy name of Christ, but are not, as they should be, departed from iniquity.

1. Hence the name of God is polluted and reproached, even till God is weary and cries out, "Pollute ye my name no more with your gifts, and with your idols." (Ezek. 20:39) O do not pollute my name, says God; rather leave off profession, and go every one to his wickedness. Tell the world, if you will not depart from iniquity, that Christ and you are parted, and that you have left him, to be embraced by them to whom iniquity is an abomination. It would far better secure the name of God from scandal and reproach, than for you to name the name of Christ, and yet not to depart from iniquity. Then, though you sin as now you do, the poor world would cry out, Ay, this is

your religion! Then they would not have occasion to vilify religion because of you, since you tell them that Christ and you are parted. But,

2. If you will not leave off to name the name of Christ, nor yet depart from iniquity, you also scandal the sincere professors of religion; and that is a grievous thing. There are a people in the world that have made it their business ever since they knew Christ, to cleanse themselves from all filthiness of flesh and spirit, and that desire to perfect holiness in the fear of God; and you scandalous professors mixing yourselves with them, "make their gold look dim." You are spots and blemishes to them, you are an evil mixing itself with their good, and a scandal to their holy profession. (II Peter 2:13; Jude 12) You are they that make the heart of the righteous sad, whom God would not have sad. You are they that offend his little ones. Oh! the millstone that God will shortly hang about your necks, when the time is come that you must be drowned in the sea and deluge of God's wrath.

3. If you will not leave off to name the name of Christ, nor yet depart from iniquity, you continue to extend your scandal also to the word and doctrine of God. They that name the name of Jesus religiously, should so carry it in the world, that they might adorn the doctrine of God their Saviour; but thou that professest and yet departest not from iniquity, thou causest the name and doctrine which thou professest to be blasphemed and reproached by the men of this world; and that is a sad thing, a thing that will bring so heavy a load upon thee, when God shall open thine eyes, and he will open them either here or in hell-fire, that thou wilt repent it with great bitterness of soul. (I Tim. 6:1; Titus 2:5, 10) The Lord smite thee to the making of thee sensible to thy shame and conversion, if it be his blessed will. Amen. But,

4. If thou wilt not leave off to name the name of Christ, nor yet depart from iniquity, thou wilt bring reproach, scorn, and contempt upon thyself. For "sin is a reproach to any people." (Prov. 14:34) 1. These are they that God will hold in great contempt and scorn: (see the first of Isaiah.) 2. These are they that his people shall have in great contempt. "Therefore," saith he, "have I also made you contemptible and base before all the people, according as you have not kept my ways, but have lifted up the face against my law." (Mal. 2:9; Jer. 25:9, 18) 3. Such shall also be contemned, and had in derision of the men of this world. They shall be an hissing, a bye-word, a taunt, and a reproach among all people. "For him that honoureth me," saith God, "I will honour, but he that despiseth me shall be lightly esteemed." (I Sam. 2:30) I remember that Philpot used to

tell the papists that they danced bare-buttocked in a net, because of the evil of their ways; and the Lord bids professors have a care, "that the shame of their nakedness does not appear," or lest they walk naked, and their shame be discovered. For those professors that depart not from iniquity, however they think of themselves, their nakedness is seen of others. And if it be a shame to the modest to have their nakedness seen of others, what bold and brazen brows have they who are not ashamed to show their nakedness, yea, the very shame of it, to all that dwell about them? And yet thus doth every one that religiously names the name of Christ, and yet doth not depart from iniquity.

Fourth. Those that religiously name the name of Christ, and do not depart from iniquity; "they are the cause of the perishing of many." "Woe," saith Christ, "to the world because of offences." (Matt. 18:7) And again, "woe to that man by whom the offence cometh." These are they that cause many to stumble at sin, and fall into hell. Hark, you that are such, what God says to you. "You have caused many to stumble at the law, and at religion." (Mal. 2:8) Men that are for taking of occasion, you give it them; men that would enter into the kingdom, you puzzle and confound them with your iniquity, while you name the name of Christ, and do not depart therefrom. One sinner destroyeth much good; these are the men that encourage the vile to be yet more vile; these be the men that quench weak desires in others; and these be the men that tempt the ignorant to harden themselves against their own salvation. A professor that hath not forsaken his iniquity is like one that comes out of the pest-house, among the whole, with his plaguey sores running upon him. This is the man that hath the breath of a dragon, he poisons the air round about him. This is the man that slays his children, his kinsmen, his friend, and himself. What shall I say? A man that nameth the name of Christ, and that departeth not from iniquity; to whom may he be compared? The Pharisees, for that they professed religion, but walked not answerable thereto, unto what doth Christ compare them, but to serpents and vipers? what does he call them, but hypocrites, whited walls, painted sepulchres, fools, and blind? and tells them that they made men more the children of hell than they were before. (Matt. 23) Wherefore such an one cannot go out of the world by himself: for as he gave occasion of scandal when he was in the world, so is he the cause of the damnation of many. "The fruit of the righteous is a tree of life." (Prov. 11:30) But what is the fruit of the wicked, of the professors that are wicked? why, not to perish alone in their iniquity. (Job 22:20) These, as the dragon, draw many of the stars of heaven, and cast them to the earth with their most stinking tail (Rev. 12:4); cast many a professor into earthly and carnal delights, with their most filthy conversations.

The apostle did use to weep when he spake of these professors, such offence he knew they were and would be in the world. (Acts 20:30; Phil. 3:18, 19)

These are the chief of the engines of Satan, with these he worketh wonders. One Balaam, one Jeroboam, one Ahab, O how many fish bring such to Satan's net! These are the tares that he strives to sow among the wheat, for he knows they are mischief to it. "Wherefore let every one that nameth the name of Christ depart from iniquity."

Fifth. Those that religiously name the name of Christ, and do not depart from iniquity; how will they die, and how will they look that man in the face, unto the profession of whose name they have entailed an unrighteous conversation? or do they think that he doth not know what they have done, or that they may take him off with a few cries and wringing of hands, when he is on the throne to do judgment against transgressors? Oh! it had been better they had not known, had not professed: yea, better they had never been born. For as Christ said of Judas, so may it be said of these; it had been good for that man if he had never been born. And as Christ says it had been good, so Peter says it had been better. (Mark 14:22; II Peter 2:20, 21) Good they had not been born, and better they had not known and made profession of the name of Christ....

Richard Baxter
1615-1691

12

The Church

Richard Baxter, the most voluminous writer of his era, had no formal university education. Born in Rowton (near Shrewsbury), England, he studied under a John Owen and Richard Wickstead. In his early years he was greatly influenced by Richard Sibbes's *Bruised Reed* and William Perkins's *Repentance*. After the death of his mother in 1634, Richard pursued four years of private study and was ordained to the Anglican ministry at the age of twenty-three.

In 1640 Baxter became vicar of Kidderminster. For fourteen years there he enjoyed a very fruitful ministry, which led to his writing *The Reformed Pastor*. When the Restoration came, he left Kidderminster and went to London, preaching at St. Dunstans, Pinners Hall, and Fetter Lane. His ministry flourished there after the Act of Uniformity of 1662.

At this point, he married Margaret Charlton and ministered at Acton until, after an imprisonment, he fled to Totteridge. When James II came to the throne in 1685, Baxter was charged with heresy and again imprisoned; he was released by pardon from the king. His final years were spent quietly at Charterhouse Square, preaching occasionally and finishing his literary works.

Baxter published 168 separate titles. His *Practical Works* were published in 1707 in four folio volumes and reprinted in 1830 in twenty-three regular volumes. He also wrote several controversial volumes in Latin. His main English works were *The Saint's Everlasting Rest* (1650), *The Reformed Pastor* (1657), *A Call to the Unconverted* (1658), *Reasons for the Christian Religion* (1672), *A Christian Directory* (1673), *Autobiography* (1696), *A Paraphrase on the New Testament* (1685), and *Dying Thoughts* (1687).

Baxter's importance as a writer rests in ecclesiology and practical devotion. In the following excerpt he discusses the true nature of the church and defines the true Christian. He contrasts the Puritan concept of the church with the Catholic and Anabaptist concepts of a "pure church," pointing out that the visible and invisible church are never in fact identical, but that this must remain the goal. Thus, one must never assume that all church members are true Christians simply because they are members, or have been baptized, or have responded to an altar call.

I Corinthians 12:12—For as the body is one, and hath many members, and all the members of that one body, being many, are one body: so also is Christ.

It is a pitiful case with the poor afflicted church of Christ, that almost all the members cry out against division, and yet cause and increase it, while they speak against it. And that all cry up unity, and yet very few do any thing that is very considerable to promote it; but multitudes are destroying unity, while they commend it: and those few that would heal and close the wounds, are not able by the clearest reasons, and most importunate requests, to hold the hands of others from opposing it; and to get leave of the rest to do that work, which they will not do themselves while they extol it. You would think this were rather the description of a bedlam, than of a Christian! to set all on fire, and furiously to rail at all that would quench it, and at the same time to rail as much at incendiaries, and cry out for concord, and against division, and call other men all that is naught, for doing that which they do themselves, and will not be persuaded from! But to the injurious dishonour of Christianity itself it is thus with millions of professed Christians! thus is the church used: the sin and shame is made so public, that no charity can much excuse it, and no shift can cover it from the reproachful observation of those that are without. Alas, our flames do rise so high, that Turks, and Jews, and

Heathens stand looking on them, and ask, "What is the matter that these Christians thus irreconcileably worry one another?" Do we need any proof, when we feel the smart? When we see the blood? When we hear the noise of revilers at home, and see the scornful laughters of those abroad? When almost all Christendom is up in arms? When the churches are so many by-names, and broken into so many odious fractions; and so many volumes fly abroad, containing the reproaches and condemnations of each other? And (which is enough to break an honest heart to think or speak of) that all this hath continued so long a time! And they be not so wise as the passionate, or the drunken, that in time will come to themselves again; and that it hath continued notwithstanding the greatest means that are used for the cure: Mediation prevaileth not: pacificatory endeavours have done almost nothing: nay, sin gets advantage in point of reputation, and dividing is counted a work of zeal, and ministers themselves are the principal leaders of it; yea, and ministers of eminent parts and piety; and piety itself is pretended for this, which is the poison of piety; and pacification is become a suspected or derided work; and the peace-makers are presently suspected of some heresy; and perhaps called dividers for seeking reconciliation. It made my heart ache with grief, the other day, to read over the narrative of the endeavours of one man (Mr. John Dury), to heal the Protestant churches themselves, and to think that so much ado should be necessary to make even the leaders of the Christian flocks to be willing to cease so odious a sin, and come out of so long and doleful a misery; yea, and that all should do so little good, and get from men but a few good words, while they sit still and suffer the flames to consume the deplorable remnant: yea, such havock hath division made, and cut the church into so many pieces, that it is become one of the commonest questions among us, which of these pieces it is that is the Church; one saith, "We are the catholic church"; and another saith, "No, but it is we!" and a third contendeth that it is "only they": and thus men seem to be at a loss; and when they believe the holy catholic church, they know not what it is, which they say, they believe. Though I dare not presume to hope of much success in any attempts against this distraction, after the frustration of the far greater endeavours of multitudes that have attempted it with far greater advantage, yet I have resolved by the help of Christ to bear witness against the sin of the dividers, and leave my testimony on record to posterity, that if it may not excite some others to the work, yet at least it may let them know, that all were not void of desires for peace in this contentious age.

To which purpose I intend, 1. To speak of the unity and concord of the catholic church. 2. Of the unity and concord of Christians in their particular churches, and in their individual state. And the first discourse I shall ground upon this text, which from the similitude of a natural body doth assert, 1. The multiplicity of the members: and 2. The unity of the body or church of Christ, notwithstanding the multiplicity of the members. The members are here said to be many for number, and it is intimated (which after is more fully expressed) that they are divers for office, and use, and gifts. The church here spoken of is the universal church, as it is both in its visible and mystical state: It is not only a particular church that is here meant; nor is it the catholic church only as mystical, or only as visible, but as it containeth professors and believers, the body and soul, which make up the man, having both ordinances and spirit in their possession. That it is the catholic church is apparent: 1. In that it is denominated in the text from Christ himself, "So also is Christ." And the universal church is more fitly denominated from Christ as the Head, than a particular church. It is not easy to find any text of Scripture that calleth Christ the Head of a particular congregation (as we use not to call the king the head of this, or that corporation, but of the commonwealth), though he may be so called, as a head hath respect to the several members: but he is oft called the Head of the catholic church. (Eph. 1:22; 4:15; Col. 1:18; 2:19; Eph. 5:23) The head of such a body is a commoner phrase than the head of the hand or foot. 2. Because it is expressly called "the body of Christ," which title is not given to any particular church, it being but part of the body, verse 27. 3. It is such a church that is here spoken of, to which was given apostles, prophets, teachers, miracles, healings, helps, governments, tongues, &c. verse 28, 8, 9, 10. But all particular churches had not all these; and it is doubtful whether Corinth had all that is here mentioned. 4. It is that church which all are baptized into, Jews and Gentiles, bond and free: but that is only into the universal church. The Spirit doth not baptize, or enter men first or directly into a particular church; no, nor the baptism of water neither always, nor primarily. The scope of the chapter, and of the like discourse of the same apostle (Eph. 4), do shew that it is the catholic church that is here spoken of.

The sense of the text then lyeth in this doctrine.

Doct. The universal church being the body of Christ is but one, and all true Christians are the members of which it doth consist.

Here are two propositions; first, that the catholic church is but one. Secondly, that all Christians are members of it, even all that by the one spirit are baptized into it. These are both so plain in the text, that were not men perverse or very blind, it were superfluous to say any more to prove them. And for the former propositions, that the catholic church is but one, we are all agreed in it. And therefore I will not needlessly trouble you with answering such objections as trouble not the church, which are fetched from the difference of the Jewish church, and the Gentile church, (or strictly catholic) or between the called (the true members) and the elect uncalled; or between the church militant and triumphant.

And as for the second proposition, that the catholic church consisteth of all Christians, as its members, it is plain in this text, and many more. It is all that (heartily) say "Jesus is the Lord" (verse 3), and all that "are baptized by one Spirit into the body" (verse 13), and all that Paul wrote to, and such as they: and yet some of them were guilty of division, or schism itself, and many errors and crimes, which Paul at large reprehendeth them for. The Galatians were members of this church (Gal. 3:26-29); for all their legal conceits and errors, and for all that they dealt with Paul as an enemy for telling them the truth. This church consisteth of all that have the "one Spirit, one faith, one baptism, one God and Father of all, &c." and of all that "have so learned Christ, as to put off the old man, and to be renewed in the spirit of their minds, and put on the new man, which after God is created in righteousness and true holiness." (Eph. 4:4-6, 20-24) This church consisteth of all that "Christ is a Saviour of," and that are "subject" unto Christ, and for "whom he gave himself, that he might sanctify and cleanse them by the washing of water by the word." (Eph. 5:23-26) It containeth all such as the Romans then were to whom Paul wrote (Rom. 12:4, 5), however differing among themselves to the censuring of each other. It containeth in it all "such as shall be saved." (Acts 2:47) These things are beyond all just dispute.

When I say, that all Christians are members of the catholic church, I must further tell you that men are called Christians, either because they are truly and heartily the disciples of Christ; or else because they seem so to be by their profession. The first are such Christians as are justified and sanctified, and these constitute the mystical body of Christ, or the church as invisible: professors of this inward true Christianity doth constitute the church as visible to men. Professors of some pieces only of Christianity, leaving out or denying any essential part of it, are not professors of Christianity truly, and therefore are no members of the visible church: and therefore we justly exclude the Mahometans.

And whereas it is a great question, Whether heretics are members of the catholic church? The answer is easy: contend not about a word. If by a heretic you mean a man that denieth or leaves out any essential part of Christianity, he is no member of the church: but if you extend the word so far as to apply it to those that deny not, or leave not out any essential part of Christianity, then such heretics are members of the church. It is but the perverseness of men's spirits, exasperated by disputation, that makes the Papists so much oppose our distinction of the fundamentals of religion from the rest: when at other times they confess the thing in other words themselves. By the fundamentals we mean the essentials of the Christian faith, or religion: And do they think indeed that Christianity hath not its essential parts? Sure they dare not deny it, till they say, "it hath no essence, and so is nothing, which an infidel will not say?" Or do they think that every revealed truth, which we are bound to believe, is essential to our Christianity? Sure they dare not say so, till they either think that no Christian is bound to believe any more than he doth believe, or that he is a Christian that wants an essential part of Christianity, or that Christianity is as many several things, as there be persons that have several degrees of faith or knowledge in all the world. For shame therefore, lay by this senseless cavil, and quarrel not with the light by partial zeal, lest you prove your cause thereby to be darkness. But if you perceive a difficulty (as who doth not, though it be not so great as some would make it) in discerning the essential parts from the integrals, do not therefore deny the unquestionable distinction, but join with us for a more full discovery of the difference.

In a few words, every man that doth heartily believe in God the Father, Son, and Holy Ghost, by a faith that worketh by love, is a true Christian. Or every one that taketh God for his only God, that is his Creator, Lord, Ruler, and felicity, or end, and Jesus Christ for his only Redeemer, that is, God and man; that hath fulfilled all righteousness, and given up himself to death on the cross in sacrifice for our sins, and hath purchased and promised us pardon, and grace, and everlasting life; and hath risen from the dead, ascended into heaven, where he is Lord of the church, and intercessor with the Father, whose laws we must obey, and who will come again at last to raise and judge the world, the righteous to everlasting life, and the rest to everlasting punishment: and that taketh the Holy Ghost for his Sanctifier, and believeth the Scriptures given by his inspiration, and sealed by his work, to be the certain word of God. This man is a true Christian, and a member of the catholic church; which will be manifested when he adjoineth a holy, sober and righteous life, using all known means and duties, especially baptism at first, the Lord's-supper afterward, prayer, confession, praise, meditation, and hearing the word of God, with a desire to know more, that his obedience may be full: living under Christ's ministers, and in communion of saints, denying himself, mortifying the flesh and world, living in charity and justice to man; he that doth this is a true Christian, and shall be saved, and therefore a member of the catholic church as invisible; and he that professeth all this, doth profess himself a true Christian, and if he null not that profession, is a member of the catholic church as visible. These things are plain, and in better days were thought sufficient.

He that hath all that is contained but in the ancient Creed, the Lord's-prayer and Ten Commandments, with baptism and the Lord's-supper, in his head, and heart, and life, is certainly a member of the catholic church. In a word, it is no harder to know who is a member of this church, than it is to know who is a Christian. Tell me but what Christianity is, and I will soon tell you how a Church member may be known.

But because it will tend both to the further clearing of this, and the text itself, I shall next shew you in what respects the members of the church are divers, and then in what respects they are all one, or in what they are united.

The Diversity of the Church

And as the text tells you, that the members are many numerically, so they are divers in their respects.

1. They are not of the same age or standing in Christ. Some are babes, and some are young men, and some are fathers. (I John 2:12-14) Some are novices, or late converts, and raw Christians (I Tim. 3:6), and some are of longer standing, that have "borne the burden and heat of the day." (Matt. 20:12)

2. The members are not all of the same degree of strength. Some are of small understanding, that reach little further than the principles of holy doctrine, and have need to be fed with milk, being unskilful in the word of righteousness: Yea, they have need to be taught the very principles again, not as being without a saving knowledge of them (for they are all taught of God, and these laws and principles are written in their hearts); but that they may have a clearer, more distinct and practical knowledge of them, who have but a darker, general, less effectual apprehension. (Heb. 5:11-13; 6:1) And some being at full age, are fit for "stronger meat," that is harder of digestion.

(Heb. 5:14) Who by reason of use have their senses exercised to discern both good and evil. Some have faith and other graces but as a "grain of mustard-seed," and some are thriven to a greater strength. (Matt. 18:20; 12:31) Some grow in grace, and are able to resist a temptation, and do or suffer what they are called to (II Peter 3:18), being "strengthened with might by the Spirit in the inner man, according to the glorious power of grace" (Eph. 3:17; Col. 1:11), being "strong in faith, giving glory to God" (Rom. 4:20), having accordingly "strong consolation." (Heb. 6:18) And some are "weak in the faith," apt to be offended, and their consciences to be wounded, and themselves in greater danger by temptations, whom the stronger must receive, and take heed of offending, and must support them, and bear their infirmities. (Rom. 14:1, 2, 21; 15:1; I Cor. 8:7, 10-12; 9:22; I Thess. 5:14; Acts 20:35)

3. Moreover the members have not all the same stature or degree of gifts; nor in all things the same sort of gifts; some excel in knowledge, and some in utterance; some in one sort of knowledge, and some in another; and some are weak in all. But of this the chapter speaks so fully, that I need say no more but refer you thither.

4. The members are not altogether of the same complexion. Though all God's children be like the Father, being holy as he is holy, yet they may be known from one another. Some are naturally more mild, and some more passionate: some of colder and calmer temper, and some so hot, that they seem more zealous in all that they say or do: some of more orderly, exact apprehensions, and some of more confused: some of quick understanding, and some dull. (Heb. 5:11)

5. The members are not all of the same degree of spiritual health. Some have much quicker and sharper appetites to the bread of life than others have: some are fain to strive with their backward hearts before they can go to secret duties, or hold on in them, and before they can get down the food of their souls: and some go with cheerfulness, and find much sweetness in all that they receive: some are of sounder understandings, and others tainted with many errors and corrupt opinions: as appears in Paul's writings to the Romans, Corinthians, Galatians, and others. Some relish only the food that is wholesome, and some have a mind of novelties, and vain janglings, and contentions, needless disputes, like stomachs that desire coals and ashes, or hurtful things. Some in their conversations maintain their integrity, and walk blamelessly, and without offence. (Luke 1:6; Phil. 2:15) And some are overcome by temptations, and give offence to others and grievously wound themselves....

6. Hence also it follows, that the members are not all of the

same usefulness and seviceableness to the church and cause of Christ. Some are as pillars to support the rest (Gal. 2:9; I Thess. 5:14), and some are a trouble to others, and can scarce go any further than they are guided and supported by others. Some lay out themselves in the helping of others: and some are as the sick, that cannot help themselves, but trouble the house with their complaints and necessities, which call for great and continual attendance. Some are fit to be teachers of others, and to be pastors of the flock, and guide the Lord's people in the way of life, and give the children their meat in season, rightly dividing the word of truth. And some are still learning, and never come to much knowledge of the truth, and do no great service to God in their generations: yea, too many weary their teachers and brethren by their frowardness and unfruitfulness: and too many do abundance of wrong to the church, and Gospel, and the world by their offensive miscarriages: yea, too many prove as thorns in our sides, and by some error in their understandings, cherished and used by the too great remnant of pride, self-conceitedness, passion and carnality, are grievous afflicters of the church of Christ, and causes of dissention; one saying I am of Paul, and another I am of Apollos, and another I am of Christ, as if Christ were divided, or else appropriated to them, and Paul or Apollos had been their saviours. (I Cor. 3:1-5) Some live so as that the church hath much benefit by their lives, and much loss by their death: and some are such troublers of it, by their weakness and corrupt distempers, that their death is some ease to the places where they lived. And yet all these may be truly godly, and living members of the catholic church.

7. Moreover, the members are not all the same in regard of office. Some are appointed to be pastors, teachers, elders, overseers, to be stewards of God's mysteries, and to feed the flock, taking heed to them all, as being over them in the Lord, as their rulers in spiritual things. (Eph. 4:11; Acts 14:23; Titus 1:5; I Cor. 4:1; Acts 20:17, 28; I Thess. 5:12; Heb. 13:7, 17) And some are the flock, commanded to learn of them, to have them in "honour, and highly esteem them for their work sake, and to obey them." (I Thess. 5:12; Heb. 13:17; I Tim. 5:17) In this chapter saith Paul, "If the whole body were an eye, where were the hearing? If the whole were hearing, where were the smelling? Are all apostles? Are all prophets? Are all teachers?" (I Cor. 12:17, 29) As there are diversity of gifts, so also of offices: for God hath designed men to use the gifts they have in such order and manner as may edify the church. All the body is not the bonds, or nerves, and ligaments, by which the parts are joined together.

(Eph. 4:16) All are not "pastors and teachers, given for perfecting of the saints, the work of the ministry, and edifying of the body of Christ" (Eph. 4:11-13). . . .

10. To conclude, from all this imparity it will follow, that the members will not have an equal degree of glory, as not having an equal preparation and capacity. All are not in Abraham's bosom, as Lazarus was. "To sit on Christ's right hand and left in his kingdom will not be the lot of all, but of those to whom the Father will give it." (Matt. 20:23) All are not to sit on thrones, in full equality with the apostles. (Luke 20:30) There are of the first for time of coming in, that shall be last of dignity, and of the last that shall be first. (Matt. 19:30; 20:16) All shall not be rulers of five cities, but only they that have double five talents. (Matt. 25) And thus I have shewed you the disparity of the members, wherein they differ.

The Unity of the Church

Secondly, I am now to shew you the unity of them, and of the body which they constitue. The members of the catholic church are united in all these following respects:

1. They have all but one God, the fountain of their being and felicity, and are all related to him as children to one Father, reconciled to them, and adopting them in Jesus Christ. (John 1:12) "Ye are all the children of God by faith in Christ Jesus." (Gal. 3:26) "There is one God and Father of all," &c. (Gal. 4:5, 6; Eph. 4:6)

2. The members of the church have all one Head, the Redeemer, Saviour, Mediator, Jesus Christ. (Eph. 4:5) As the commonwealth is denominated from the unity of the sovereign power that heads it; so the church is hence principally denominated one from Christ, who is the Head, the Sovereign, and the Centre of it. And therefore it is called frequently his body, and he the Head of it. (Eph. 4:15; 1:22; Col. 1:18; 2:19; Eph. 5:23; Col. 3:15; Rom. 12:4, 5; I Cor. 10:17; Eph. 2:16) He is the foundation, and the church is the building that is erected upon him, "and other foundation can no man lay." (I Cor. 3:11, 12) "From this head the whole body fitly joined together, and compacted by that which every joint supplieth, according to the effectual working of the measure of every part, maketh increase of the body to the edifying of itself in love." (Eph. 4:16) All therefore are members of the catholic church that are members of Christ. He is "the chief corner-stone that is laid in Zion, elect and precious, and he that believeth on him shall not be confounded; to whom coming as to a living stone, we also as lively stones are built up a spiritual

house." (I Peter 2:4-6) As this "One died for all" (II Cor. 5:14), because all were dead, so by the righteousness of this One, the free gift cometh on all to justification of life, and by the obedience of this One shall many be made righteous." (Rom. 5:18, 19) "And by one Jesus Christ we shall reign in life." (Rom. 5:17) "In him the church of Jews and Gentiles are made one." (Eph. 2:14, 15) "To this one Husband we are all espoused." (II Cor. 11:2) So that we "are all one in Christ Jesus." (Gal. 3:28) And "to us there is but one God the Father, of whom are all things, and we in him; and one Lord Jesus Christ, by whom are all things, and we in him." (I Cor. 8:6)

3. The whole catholic church (strictly taken, as comprehending only the living members) have only one Holy Ghost dwelling in them, illuminating, sanctifying and guiding them, and are animated as it were by this one Spirit. "By this one Spirit we are all baptized into one body, and have been all made to drink into one Spirit." (I Cor. 12:13) And "whoever hath not this Spirit of Christ, the same is none of his." (Rom. 8:9) "By this one Spirit we have all access to the Father." (Eph. 2:18) And through this Spirit we are "one habitation of God." (Eph. 2:22) And therefore, "he that is joined to the Lord is called one Spirit." (I Cor. 6:17) And it is said of Christ, so may it be of the Spirit in a sort, "He that sanctifieth, and they that are sanctified are all one." (Heb. 2:11) This is the scope of the chapter that my text is in.

4. The church is *one* as to their principal, ultimate end. The same God is their end who is their beginning. The same eternal glory with him, is purchased and prepared for them, and intended by them through their Christian course. The wicked have a lower end, even flesh and self: but all the members of Christ are united in the true intention of this end. They are all the "heirs of life, and partakers of the inheritance of the saints in light, and have all lain up their treasure in heaven." (Matt. 6:20, 21; Col. 1:12; Gal. 4:7; Rom. 8:17; I Peter 3:7; Titus 3:7; Gal. 3:29; Heb. 1:14; Eph. 3:6) "All that are risen with Christ, do seek the things that are above" (Col. 3:1), "and have their conversation with him in heaven." (Phil. 3:20, 21)

5. All the members of the catholic Gospel-church have one Gospel to teach them the knowledge of Christ. (Gal. 1:10, 11) And one word of promise to be the charter of their inheritance (I Tim. 4:8; Heb. 9:15; Gal. 3:22, 29), and one holy doctrine to be the instrument of their regeneration, and the "seed of God abiding in them." (I Peter 1:23, 25; Luke 8:11) It is but one that God hath appointed

for them; and it is one in the substance that is the instrument of their change.

6. It is one kind of faith, that by this one holy doctrine is wrought upon their souls. Though the degrees be various, yet all believe the same essential points of faith, with a belief of the same nature. There is "one faith" (Eph. 4:5); and in all these essentials the church is of "one mind" (John 17:21; Acts 4:32; I Peter 3:8; I Cor. 15:2-4), though in lesser things there be exceeding great diversity.

7. There is one new disposition, or holy nature wrought by the Spirit of God in every member of the catholic church. This is called their holiness, and the new creature, and the divine nature, and the image of God. (I Peter 1:16; II Peter 1:4; John 3:6) "That which is born of the Spirit, is spirit." (Col. 3:10; II Cor. 5:17)

8. The affections which are predominant in all the members of the church, have one and the same object. Sin is the chiefest thing that all of them hate, and the displeasure of God the chief thing they fear, and God in Christ is the prime object of their love; and they have all the same object of their desires and hopes, even the favour of God, and everlasting life: and they all chiefly rejoice in the same hopes and felicity; as were easy to manifest and prove in the particulars, as to all the essentials of Christianity that are the objects of the will. (Phil. 1:27; 2:3; Eph. 4:4; Matt. 22:37, 38; Rom. 8:28; I Cor. 2:9) And thus they are all of one heart and soul, as uniting in the same objects.

9. They have also one rule or law to live by, which is the law of faith, of grace, of liberty, of Christ. (Rom. 3:27; 8:2; James 1:25; Gal. 6:2) And as one law is appointed for them all, so one law in the points of absolute necessity is received by them all; for "it is written in their hearts," and put into "their inward parts." (Jer. 31:32; Heb. 8:10, 16) Though in the other points of the law of Christ there be much diversity in their reception and obedience. All of them are sincerely obedient to what they know, and all of them know that which God hath made of necessity to life.

10. Every member of the church is devoted to God in one and the same covenant. As the covenant on Christ's part is one to them all; so is it one on their part. They all renounce the world, the flesh and the devil, and give up themselves to God the Father, Son, and Holy Ghost. And this being used by God's appointment, to be solemnly done in baptism, therefore baptism is called the principle or foundation. (Heb. 6:1) And there is said to be one baptism (Eph. 4:5), and baptism is said to save us; "Not the putting away the filth of the flesh (that is, not the outward washing), but the answer of

a good conscience to God" (I Peter 3:21), that is, the sincere, internal covenant of the heart, and delivering up ourselves to Christ. So also the fathers, when they (usually) speak of the necessity of baptism, they mean principally our becoming Christians, and entering into the holy covenant, which was done by baptism. Though if any be so weak as to think that this outward baptism is to be delayed (as Constantine and many of the fathers did), if in the meantime he make and profess his covenant with Christ, he is to be taken as a Christian and church-member: but as a soldier without colours, or a king not crowned; he is a Christian not orderly admitted, which is his sin. . . .

13. Every member of the church hath an habitual love to each particular member of the same church. Though mistakes and infirmities may occasion fallings out, even as with Paul and Barnabas, to a parting; and there may be dislikes and bitterness against one another upon misunderstandings, and not discerning God's graces in each other; yet still, as Christians, they are heartily loved by each other; and did they know more of the truth of each other's Christianity, they would love each other more. Every member is united by love to the rest; for this is a lesson that is taught us inwardly of God: "And by this we know that we are translated from death to life" (I Peter 1:22; I John 3:11, 14, 23; 4:12, 20, 21, 8: I Thess. 4:9; John 13:34, 35). . . .

16. All members have an inward inclination to hold communion with fellow members, so far as they discern them to be members indeed. As fire would to fire, and water would to water, and earth to earth, and every thing to its like; so Christians would have actual communion with Christians, as delighting in each other, and loving Christ in each other, and finding benefit by each other's communion. Though I know that this inclination may be much kept from execution, and communion much hindered, by mistakes about the nature, and manner, and requisites of it, and by infirmities and passions of our own. Brethren may fall out, but there is naturally in them a brotherly love, and when the mistake or passion is over, they will get together again (Acts 9:32, 33; 2:42, 44; Heb. 10:25; Ps. 16:3). . . .

19. And every member hath an inward enmity to that which is destructive to itself, or to the body, so far as he knoweth it, that is, 1. To sin in general. 2. To all known sin in particular. And, 3. Specially to divisions, distractions, and diminution of the church. These things their inward disposition is against; and when they are led to them, it is by temptation producing mistakes and passions against the bent of their hearts and lives. They abhor that which is de-

structive to the body, as such.

20. Lastly. They shall all at the end of their course obtain the same crown of glory, and see and enjoy the same blessed God and glorified Redeemer, and be members of the same celestial Jerusalem, and be employed everlastingly in the same holy love, and joy, and praise, and glorify and please the Lord in all, and centre, and be united perfectly in him. (John 17:21, 23, 24) "For of him, and through him, and to him are all things, to whom be glory for ever, Amen." (Rom. 11:36)

And thus I have shewed you in twenty particulars the unity of the saints; though it is not from every one of these that they are called one church, yet all these are inseparable as to possession from the true members, and as to profession from the seeming members that are adult. . . .

I beseech you therefore, poor, peevish, quarrelsome souls, give others leave to live in the same house with you: Do not disown your brethren, and say, they are bastards, because they somewhat differ from you in complexion, in age, in strength, in health, in stature, or any of the points wherein I told you a little before that the members of the church do usually differ in. Shew not yourselves so ignorant or froward as to make a wonder of it, that God should be the Father both of infants, and men at age, of weak and strong, and that the sick and sound should both be in his family. Doth such cruelty beseem the breast of a Christian, as to wish God to cast out all his children from his family that are weak and sick? Do not make it such a matter of wonder, that God's house should have so many rooms in it; and think it not a reproach to it, that the kitchen or the coal-house is a part of the house. Wonder not at it as a strange thing, that all the body is not a hand or eye; and that some parts have less honour and comeliness than the rest. Hath God told you so plainly and fully of these matters, and yet will you not understand, but remain so perverse? I pray hereafter remember better that the catholic church is one, consisting of all true Christians as the members. . . .

Jonathan Edwards
1703-1758

13

Eschatology

Jonathan Edwards, the great American Puritan theologian, was born at Windsor Farms, Connecticut, where his father was a Congregational minister for over sixty years. His mother's father was Solomon Stoddard, who pastored the church at Northfield, Massachusetts, for fifty-seven years. With this heritage, Edwards began studying Latin at age six, tutored by his father and four older sisters. When he entered Yale College just before turning thirteen, he already knew Latin, Greek, and Hebrew. He graduated with highest honors just before his seventeenth birthday. He was converted while seventeen and two years later became a preacher in a small Presbyterian church in New York.

In the fall of 1723, Edwards became a tutor at Yale, but four years later he was ordained at the Northampton church and became his celebrated grandfather's assistant. Edwards's preaching was rhetorically neither powerful nor dynamic, but it did exhibit deep thought and strong feeling. After Stoddard's death, Edwards succeeded him as pastor of the church, and it was during his tenure there that the Great Awakening began in 1734. Edwards's strong Calvinistic sermons led to many conversions, overwhelming his listeners with their spiritual power. During this awakening Edwards became a close friend of George Whitefield, a Calvinistic evangelist. During the Northampton years his writings included *God Glorified in Man's Dependence* (1731), *A Divine and Supernatural Light Imparted to the Soul by the Spirit of God* (1734), *A Narrative of Surprising Conversions* (1736), *Sinners in the Hands of an Angry God* (1741), *Thoughts on the Revival in New England* (1742), *A Treatise Concerning Religious Affections* (1745), and the *Life and Diary of the Rev. David Brainerd* (1749).

An old controversy arose in the church over the requirements for admission to membership and to the Lord's Supper. Edwards opposed what had been Stoddard's practice, that of giving communion to people who were moral but unconverted. As a result of his faithfulness to the Scriptures, Edwards was dismissed in June 1750 after twenty-three years of service. His principles eventually prevailed among American evangelical churches, however.

Left with no congregation and no income to provide for his large family, Edwards lived on gifts from friends until he was called to pastor the small Congregational church at Stockbridge, Massachusetts, in 1751. Here he also preached, through an interpreter, to the Housatonic Indians. During these years he became ill with fever from the uncivilized conditions of the wilderness. In 1754 he published his most controversial work, *Essay on the Freedom of the Will*. It was a defense of the doctrines of divine foreordination, original sin, and eternal punishment.

In 1757 Edwards was elected president of Princeton College in New Jersey, beginning to exercise his office in January and being inaugurated on 16 February 1758. On 23 February he was inoculated for small pox, and on 22 March he died from a resulting fever. His father and son-in-law had died only months before, and his wife died just six months later. Thus, the sharpest philosophical and theological mind in colonial America was silenced—except for his written legacy.

Samuel Hopkins, Edwards's former student, edited and published eighteen of his sermons in 1764. In 1777 his valuable work *History of Redemption* was published. Samuel Austin published an eight-volume collection of his published works in 1809. Finally, in 1829 a ten-volume edition was published, edited by S. E. Dwight. Some of Edwards's greatest sermons were on the theme of final judgment, and the present selection deals with the final state of the righteous and the wicked. Interestingly, most of the discourse deals with the portion of the righteous and their eternal glories in Christ. The value of this treatise is that it illustrates the Puritan eschatological emphasis on judgment and the eternal states of the blessed and the damned. One finds very little speculation concerning the exact fulfillment of events prophesied of the "last days." Though teaching about the events related to the return of Christ is certainly valid and important, speculation as to how soon Christ will return engenders far less spiritual revival than does the Puritan emphasis upon final judgment and blessing.

The Portion of the Wicked

Romans 2:8, 9—*But unto them that are contentious, and do not obey the truth, but obey unrighteousness, indignation and wrath, tribulation and anguish, upon every soul of man that doeth evil, of the Jew first, and also of the Gentile.*

It is the drift of the apostle in the three first chapters of this epistle to show, that both Jews and Gentiles are under sin, and therefore cannot be justified by works of law, but only by faith in Christ. In the first chapter he had shown that the Gentiles were under sin: in this he shows that the Jews also are under sin, and that however severe they were in their censures upon the Gentiles, yet they themselves did the same things; for which the apostle very much blames them: "Therefore, thou art inexcusable, O man, whosoever thou art that judgest, for wherein thou judgest another, thou condemnest thyself; for thou that judgest, doest the same things." And he warns them not to go on in such a way, by forewarning them of the misery to which they will expose themselves by it, and by giving them to understand that instead of their misery being less than that of the Gentiles, it would be the greater, for God's distinguishing goodness to them above the Gentiles. The Jews thought that they should be exempted from future wrath, because God had chosen them to be his peculiar people. But the apostle informs them that there should be indignation and wrath, tribulation and anguish, to every soul of man; not only to the Gentiles, but to every soul; and to the Jews first and chiefly, when they did evil, because their sins were more aggravated.

In the text we find,

1. A description of wicked men. . . .

Those qualifications of wicked men here mentioned that have the nature of a cause, are their being *contentious,* and *not obeying the truth,* but *obeying unrighteousness.* By their being contentious, is

251

meant their being contentious against the truth, their quarrelling with the gospel, their finding fault with its declarations and offers. Unbelievers find many things in the ways of God at which they stumble, and by which they are offended. They are always quarrelling and finding fault with one thing or another, whereby they are kept from believing the truth and yielding to it. Christ is to them a stone of stumbling, and rock of offence. They do not obey the truth, that is, they do not yield to it, they do not receive it with faith. That yielding to the truth and embracing it, which there is in saving faith, is called *obeying,* in scripture. Rom. 6:17. "But God be thanked that ye were the servants of sin; but ye have obeyed from the heart that form of doctrine which was delivered you." Heb. 5:9. "And being made perfect, he became the author of eternal salvation unto all them that obey him." Rom. 1:5. "By whom we have received grace and apostleship, for obedience to the faith among all nations for his name": But they obey unrighteousness instead of yielding to the gospel, they are under the power and dominion of sin, and are slaves to their lusts and corruptions.

It is in those qualifications of wicked men that their wickedness radically consists; their unbelief and opposition to the truth, and their slavish subjection to lust, are the foundation of all wickedness.

Those qualifications of wicked men, which have the nature of an effect, are their doing evil. This is the least of their opposition against the gospel, and of their slavish subjection to their lusts; that they do evil. Those wicked principles are the foundation, and their wicked practice is the superstructure; those were the root, and this is the fruit.

2. The punishment of wicked men....

Those things mentioned in their punishment that have the nature of a cause are *indignation* and *wrath;* i.e. the indignation and wrath of God. It is the anger of God that will render wicked men miserable; they will be the subjects of divine wrath, and hence will arise their whole punishment.

Those things in their punishment that have the nature of an effect, are *tribulation* and *anguish.* Indignation and wrath in God, will work extreme sorrow, trouble, and anguish of heart, in them.

Doctrine. Indignation, wrath, misery, and anguish of soul, are the portion that God has allotted to wicked men.

Every one of mankind must have the portion that belongs to him. God allots to each one his portion; and the portion of the wicked is nothing but wrath, and distress, and anguish of soul. Though they may enjoy a few empty and vain pleasures and delights, for a few days while they stay in this world, yet that which is allotted to them by the Possessor and Governor of all things to be their portion, is only indignation and wrath, tribulation and anguish. This is not the portion that wicked men choose; the portion that they choose is worldly happiness, yet it is the portion that God carves out for them; it is the portion that they in effect choose for themselves. For they choose those things that naturally and necessarily lead to it, and those that they are plainly told, times without number, will issue in it. Prov. 8:36. "But he that sinneth against me, wrongeth his own soul; all they that hate me love death." But whether they choose it or not, this will and must be the portion to all eternity of all who live and die wicked men. Indignation and wrath shall pursue them as long as they live in this world, shall drive them out of the world, and shall follow them into another world; and there wrath and misery shall abide upon them throughout eternity.

The method that I shall take in treating this subject, is to describe the wrath and misery of which wicked men shall be the subjects, both here and hereafter, in the successive parts and periods of it, according to the order of time.

I. I shall describe the wrath that often pursues wicked men in this life. Indignation and wrath often begin with them here.

1. God oftentimes in wrath leaves them to themselves. They are left in their sins, and left to undo themselves, and work out their own ruin; he lets them alone in sin. Hos. 4:17. "Ephraim is joined to his idols; let him alone." He often leaves them to go great lengths in sin, and does not afford them that restraining grace that he does to others. He leaves them to their own blindness, so that they always remain ignorant of God and Christ, and of the things that belong to their peace. They are sometimes left to hardness of heart, to be stupid and senseless, so that nothing will ever thoroughly awaken them. They are left to their own hearts lusts, to continue in some wicked practices all their days. Some are left to their covetousness, some to drunkenness, some to uncleanness, some to a proud, contentious, and envious spirit, and some to a spirit of finding fault and quarrelling with God. God leaves them to their folly, to act exceedingly foolishly, to delay and put off the concerns of their souls from time to time, never to think the present time the best, but always to keep it at a distance, and foolishly to continue flattering themselves with hopes of long life, and to put far away the evil day, and to bless themselves in their hearts, and say, "I shall have peace, though I add drunkenness to thirst." Some are so left that they are miserably hardened and senseless, when others all around them are awakened,

and greatly concerned, and inquire what they shall do to be saved.

Sometimes God leaves men to a fatal backsliding for a misimprovement of the strivings of his spirit. They are let alone, to backslide perpetually. Dreadful is the life and condition of those who are thus left of God. We have instances of the misery of such in God's holy word, particularly of Saul and Judas. Such are, sometimes, very much left to the power of Satan to tempt them, to hurry them on in wicked courses, and exceedingly to aggravate their own guilt and misery.

2. Indignation and wrath are sometimes exercised towards them in this world, by their being cursed in all that concerns them. They have this curse of God following them in every thing. They are cursed in all their enjoyments. If they are in prosperity, it is cursed to them; if they possess riches, if they have honour, if they enjoy pleasure, there is the curse of God that attends it. Psalm 92:7. "When the wicked spring as the grass, and when all the workers of iniquity do flourish; it is that they may be destroyed for ever."

There is a curse of God that attends their ordinary food: every morsel of bread which they eat, and every drop of water which they drink. Psalm 69:22. "Let their table become a snare before them; and that which should have been for their welfare let it become a trap." They are cursed in all their employments, in whatsoever they put their hands to; when they go into the field to labour, or are at work at their respective trades. Deut. 28:16. "Cursed shalt thou be in the city, and cursed shalt thou be in the field." The curse of God remains in the houses where they dwell, and brimstone is scattered in their habitations. Job 18:15. The curse of God attends them in the afflictions which they meet with, whereas the afflictions that good men meet with, are fatherly corrections, and are sent in mercy. The afflictions which wicked men meet with are in wrath, and come from God as an enemy, and are the foretaste of their everlasting punishment. The curse of God attends them also in their spiritual enjoyments and opportunities, and it would have been better for them not to have been born in a land of light. Their having the Bible and the sabbath, is only to aggravate their guilt and misery. The word of God when preached to them is a savour of death unto death. Better would it be for them, if Christ had never come into the world, if there had never been any offer of a Saviour. Life itself is a curse to them; they live only to fill up the measure of their sins. What they seek in all the enjoyments, and employments, and concerns of life, is their own happiness; but they never obtain it; they never obtain any true comfort, all the comforts which they have are worthless and unsatisfying. If they lived a hundred years with never so much of the world in their possession, their life is all filled up with vanity. All that they have is vanity of vanities, they find no true rest for their souls, they do but feed on the east wind, they have no real contentment. Whatever outward pleasures they may have, their souls are starving. They have no true peace of conscience, they have nothing of the favour of God. Whatever they do, they live in vain, and to no purpose; they are useless in the creation of God, they do not answer the end of their being. They live without God, and have not the presence of God, nor any communion with him. But on the contrary, all that they have and all that they do, does but contribute to their own misery, and render their future and everlasting state the more dreadful. The best of wicked men live but miserable and wretched lives, with all their prosperity; their lives are most undesirable, and whatever they have, the wrath of God abides upon them.

3. After a time they must die. Eccles. 9:3. "This is an evil among all things that are done under the sun, that there is one event unto all: yea, also the heart of the sons of men is full of evil, and madness is in their heart while they live, and after that they go to the dead."

Death is a far different thing when it befals wicked men, from what it is when it befals good men; to the wicked it is in execution of the curse of the law, and of the wrath of God. When a wicked man dies, God cuts him off in wrath, he is taken away as by a tempest of wrath, he is driven away in his wickedness. Prov. 14:32. "The wicked is driven away in his wickedness: but the righteous hath hope in his death." Job 18:18. "He shall be driven from light into darkness, and chased out of the world." Job 27:21. "The east wind carrieth him away, and he departeth, and as a storm, hurleth him out of his place." Though wicked men while they live, may live in worldly prosperity, yet they cannot live here always, but they must die. The place that knoweth him, shall know him no more; and the eye that hath seen him shall see him no more in the land of the living. . . .

4. Wicked men are oftentimes the subjects of much tribulation and anguish of heart on their death beds. Sometimes the pains of body are very extreme and dreadful; and what they endure in those agonies and struggles for life, after they are past speaking, and when body and soul are rending asunder, none can know. Hezekiah had an awful sense of it; he compares it to a lion's breaking all his bones. Isaiah 38:12, 13. "Mine age is departed, and is removed from me as a shepherd's tent: I have cut off as a weaver my life; he will cut me off with pining sickness; from day even to night, wilt thou make an end of me. I reckoned till morning, that, as a lion, so will he break

255

all my bones: from day even to night, wilt thou make an end of me."
But this is but little to what is sometimes undergone by wicked
men in their souls when they are on their death beds. Death appears
sometimes with an exceedingly terrible aspect to them; when it comes
and stares them in the face, they cannot bear to behold it. It is always
so, if wicked men have notice of the approach of death, and have
reason and conscience in exercise, and are not either stupid or dis-
tracted. When this king of terrors comes to show himself to them,
and they are called forth to meet him, O how do they dread the
conflict! But meet him they must: "There is no man that hath power
over the spirit to retain the spirit; neither hath he power in the day
of death: and there is no discharge in that war; neither shall wickedness deliver those that are given to it." Death comes to them
with all his dreadful armour, and his sting not taken away; and it is
enough to fill their souls with torment that cannot be expressed. It
is an awful thing for a person to be lying on a sick bed, to be given
over by physicians, to have friends stand weeping round the bed
as expecting to part with him; and in such circumstances as those,
to have no hope, to be without an interest in Christ, and to have
the guilt of his sins lying on his soul, to be going out of the world
without his peace being made with God, to stand before his holy
judgment-seat in all his sins, without any thing to plead, or answer....

II. I shall describe the wrath that attends wicked men hereafter.

1. The soul, when it is separated from the body, shall be cast
down into hell. There is without doubt a particular judgment by
which every man is to be tried at death, beside the general judgment:
for the soul, as soon as it departs from the body, appears before God
to be judged. Eccles. 12. "Then shall the dust return to the earth,
as it was; and the spirit shall return unto God, who gave it": that is,
to be judged and disposed of by him. Heb. 9:27. "It is appointed
unto men once to die, but after this the judgment." But this particular judgment is probably no such solemn transaction, as that which
will be at the day of judgment; the soul must appear before God,
but not in the manner that men shall appear at the end of the world.
The souls of wicked men shall not go to heaven to appear before
God, neither shall Christ descend from heaven for the soul to appear
before him; neither is it to be supposed, that the soul shall be
carried to any place where there is some special symbol of the divine
presence, in order to be judged. But as God is every where present,
so the soul shall be made immediately sensible of his presence. Souls
in a separate state shall be sensible of the presence of God and
of his operations in another manner than we now are. All separate

spirits may be said to be before God: the saints are in his glorious presence, and the wicked in hell are in his dreadful presence; they are said to be tormented in the presence of the Lamb. Rev. 14:10. "The same shall drink of the wine of the wrath of God, which is poured out without mixture into the cup of his indignation; and he shall be tormented with fire and brimstone in the presence of the holy angels, and in the presence of the Lamb." So the soul of a wicked man, at its departure from the body, will be made immediately sensible that it is before an infinitely holy and dreadful God and his own final Judge; and will then see how terrible a God he is, he will see how holy a God he is, how infinitely he hates sin; he will be sensible of the greatness of God's anger against sin, and how dreadful is his displeasure. Then will he be sensible of the dreadful majesty and power of God, and how fearful a thing it is to fall into his hands. Then the soul shall come naked with all its guilt, and in all its filthiness, a vile, loathsome, abominable creature, an enemy to God, a rebel against him, with the guilt of all its rebellion and disregard of God's commands, and contempt of his authority, and slight of the glorious gospel, before God as its Judge....

2. Here the souls of wicked men shall suffer extreme and amazing misery in a separate state, until the resurrection. This misery is not indeed their full punishment; nor is the happiness of the saints before the day of judgment their full happiness. It is with the souls of wicked men, as it is with devils. Though the devils suffer extreme torment now, yet they do not suffer their complete punishment; and therefore it is said, that they are cast down to hell, and bound in chains. II Peter 2:4. "God spared not the angels that sinned, but cast them down to hell, and delivered them into chains of darkness, to be reserved unto judgment." ...

But yet they are there in extreme and inconceivable misery; they are there deprived of all good, they have no rest nor comfort, and they are subject to the wrath of God; God there executes wrath on them without mercy, and they are swallowed up in wrath. Luke 16:24. "And he cried, and said, father Abraham, have mercy on me; and send Lazarus, that he may dip the tip of his finger in water, and cool my tongue; for I am tormented in this flame." Here we are told that, when the rich man died, he lifts up his eyes being in torment, and he tells Abraham that he is tormented in a flame; and it seems that the flame was not only about him, but in him; he therefore asks for a drop of water to cool his tongue. This doubtless is to represent to us that they are full of the wrath of God as it were with fire, and they shall there be tormented in the midst of devils and damned spirits; and they shall have inexpressible torment from their own consciences. God's wrath is the fire that never shall be quenched, and conscience is the worm that never dies. How much do men suffer from horror of conscience sometimes in this world, but how much more in hell! . . .

3. The separate souls of the wicked, besides the present misery that they suffer, shall be in amazing fear of their more full punishment at the day of judgment. Though their punishment in their separate state be exceedingly dreadful, and far more than they can bear, though it be so great as to sink and crush them, yet this is not all; they are reserved for a much greater and more dreadful punishment at the day of judgment; their torment will then be vastly augmented, and continue in that augmentation to all eternity. Their punishment will be so much greater then, that their misery in this separate state is but as an imprisonment before an execution; they, as well as the devils, are bound in chains of darkness to the judgment of the great day. . . .

4. When the day of judgment comes they shall rise to the resurrection of damnation. When that day comes, all mankind, that have died from off the face of the earth shall arise; not only the righteous, but also the wicked. Dan. 12:2. "And many of them that sleep in the dust of the earth, shall awake; some to everlasting life, and some to shame and everlasting contempt." Rev. 20:13. "And the sea gave up the dead which were in it, and death and hell delivered up the dead which were in them: and they were judged, every man according to his works." The damned in hell know not the time when the day of judgment will be, but when the time comes it will be made known, and it will be the most dreadful news that ever was told in that world of misery. It is always a doleful time in hell; the world of darkness is always full of shrieks and doleful cries; but when the news is heard, that the day appointed for judgment is come, hell will be filled with louder shrieks and more dreadful cries than ever before. When Christ comes in the clouds of heaven to judgment, the news of it will fill both earth and hell with mourning and bitter crying. We read that all the kindreds of the earth shall wail because of him, and so shall all the inhabitants of hell, and then must the souls of the wicked come up to be united to their bodies, and stand before the Judge. They shall not come willingly, but shall be dragged forth as a malefactor is dragged out of his dungeon to execution. They were unwilling when they died to leave the earth to go to hell; but now they will be much more unwilling to come out of hell to go to the last judgment. . . .

5. Then must they appear before their judge to give up their account. They will find no mountains or rocks to fall upon them, that can cover them, and hide them from the wrath of the Lamb. Many of them will see others at that time, who were formerly their acquaintance, who shall appear with glorious bodies, and with joyful countenances and songs of praise, and mounting up as with wings to meet the Lord in the air, while they are left behind. Many shall see their former neighbours and acquaintance, their companions, their brothers, and their wives taken and they left. They shall be summoned to go and appear before the judgment seat; and go they must, however unwilling; they must stand at Christ's left hand, in the midst of devils, and wicked men. This shall again add still further amazement, and will cause their horror still to be in a further degree than ever. With what horror will that company come together! and then shall they be called to their account; then shall be brought to light the hidden things of darkness; then shall all the wickedness of their hearts be made known; then shall be declared the actual wickedness they have been guilty of; then shall appear their secret sins that they have kept hid from the eye of the world; then shall be manifested in their true light those sins that they used to plead for, and to excuse and justify. . . .

6. Then the sentence of condemnation shall be pronounced by the Judge upon them. Matt. 25:41. "Depart from me, ye cursed, into everlasting fire, prepared for the devil and his angels." This sentence will be pronounced with awful majesty; and there shall be great indignation, and dreadful wrath shall then appear in the Judge, and in his voice, with which he shall pronounce the sentence; and what a horror and amazement will these words strike into the hearts of the wicked, on whom they shall be pronounced! Every word and syllable shall be like the most amazing thunder to them, and shall pierce their souls like the fiercest lightning. The Judge will bid them depart from him; he will drive them from his presence, as exceedingly abominable to him, and he shall give them the epithet *accursed*; they shall be an accursed company, and he will not only bid them depart from his presence, but into everlasting fire, to dwell there as their only fit habitation. And what shows the dreadfulness of the fire, is, that it is prepared for the devil and his angels: they shall lie for ever in the same fire in which the devils, those grand enemies of God, shall be tormented. When this sentence shall be pronounced, there shall be in the vast company at the left hand tremblings, and mourning, and crying, and gnashing of teeth, in a new manner, beyond all that ever was before. If the devils, those

proud and lofty spirits, tremble many ages beforehand at the bare thoughts of this sentence, how will they tremble when it comes to be pronounced! And how, alas! will wicked men tremble! Their anguish will be aggravated by hearing that blessed sentence pronounced on those who shall be at the right hand: "Come, ye blessed of my Father, inherit the kingdom prepared for you from the foundation of the world." . . .

8. In this condition [i.e., in those everlasting burnings to which they are sentenced] they shall remain throughout the never-ending ages of eternity. Their punishment shall be then complete, and it shall remain in this completion for ever. Now shall all that come upon them which they so long trembled for fear of, while their souls were in a separate state. They will dwell in a fire that never shall be quenched, and here they must wear out eternity. Here they must wear out one thousand years after another, and that without end. There is no reckoning up the millions of years or millions of ages; all arithmetic here fails, no rules of multiplication can reach the amount, for there is no end. They shall have nothing to do to pass away their eternity, but to conflict with those torments; this will be their work for ever and ever; God shall have no other use or employment for them; this is the way that they must answer the end of their being. And they never shall have any rest, nor any atonement, but their torments will hold up to their height, and shall never grow any easier by their being accustomed to them. Time will seem long to them, every moment shall seem long to them, but they shall never have done with the ages of their torment. . . .

The Portion of the Righteous

Romans 2:10—*But glory, honour, and peace, to every man that worketh good.*

The Apostle, having in the preceding verses declared what is the portion of wicked men; viz. indignation and wrath, tribulation and anguish; in this verse declares what is the portion assigned to good men. In the words of the text we should observe,

1. The description of a good man; viz. *the man that worketh good.* Such men are here described by the fruit which they bring forth. Christ has taught us that the tree is known by its fruit. Paul here describes them by that which most distinguishes them; not by the external privileges which they enjoy, or the light under which they live; but by the fruits which they bring forth. For as the Apostle says, in verse 13, "Not the hearers of the law are just before God,

but the doers of it shall be justified." That which distinguishes good men from bad, is not that they *hear* good, or that they *profess* good, or that they *intend* good; but that they *do* good. They are *workers* of good.

2. The reward of such a man; viz. *"glory, honour, and peace"*; in which are mentioned three sorts of good that are assigned to them as their portion. 1. Their moral good, expressed by the word *glory*. Glory shall be given them; i.e. they shall be made excellent and glorious. They shall be endued with those excellent and glorious qualifications, which will render them beautiful and lovely. They shall have the image of God, and be partakers of his holiness. Thus the word glory is used by St. Paul, II Cor. 3:18, We are changed into the same image from glory to glory. 2. Their relative good; *Honour*. They shall be in most honourable circumstances. They shall be advanced to great dignity, receive a relation to God, and Christ, and the heavenly inhabitants, and God shall put honour upon them. 3. Their natural good; *Peace*: which, as it is used in the scriptures, signifies happiness; and includes all comfort, joy and pleasure.

I shall endeavour to show from the text, that glory, honour, and peace are the portion which God has given to all good men. In describing their happiness, I shall consider the successive parts of it; both here and hereafter.

First. I propose to treat of their happiness in this world. Those who are truly good men have been the subjects of a real, thorough work of conversion, and have had their hearts turned from sin to God. Of such persons it may be said, that they are truly blessed. They are often pronounced blessed by God. He is infinitely wise, and sees and knows all things. He perfectly knows who are blessed, and who are miserable. He hath said, "Blessed is the man that walketh not in the counsel of the ungodly."—"Blessed is he whose sins are forgiven."—"Blessed is the man that maketh the Lord his trust."—"Blessed are the poor in spirit"—"the meek"—"the merciful"—"the pure in heart." . . .

Secondly. I proceed to consider the happiness of the saints in Death. It may seem a mystery to the world that men should be happy in death, which the world looks upon as the most terrible of all things; but thus it is to the saints. Their happiness is built upon a rock, and it will stand the shock of death: when the storm and floods of death come with their greatest violence, it stands firm, and neither death nor hell can overthrow it. . . .

Thirdly. Let us next consider the happiness of the saints, in their state of Separation from the Body.

1. When the soul departs from the body, it is received by the blessed angels and conducted by them to the third heavens. On the eve of its departure there is a guard of angels standing round the dying bed; and the devils, though eager to seize upon it as their prey, shall by no means be suffered to come nigh. The holy angels shall be a guard to the soul, to keep off all its enemies. We are taught that this is part of the office in which God employs them. Psalm 34:7. "The angel of the Lord encampeth round about them that fear him, and delivereth them." Psalm 91:11. "For he shall give his angels charge over thee, to keep thee in all thy ways."... There are some who say that there is no such place as heaven; but this is evidently a mistake, for the heaven, into which the man Christ Jesus entered with his glorified body, is certainly some place. It is absurd to suppose that the heaven where the body of Christ is, is not a place. To say that the body of Christ is in no place, is the same thing as to say he has no body. The heaven where Christ is, is a place; for he was seen ascending, and will be seen descending again; and the heaven where the departed souls of the saints are, is the same heaven where Christ has ascended. And therefore Stephen, when he was departing this life, saw heaven opened, and the Son of man standing on the right hand of God. And he prayed to that same Jesus whom he he saw, that he would receive his spirit; i.e. that he would receive it to him, where he saw him, at the right hand of God. And the apostle Paul signifies, that if he should depart, he should be with Christ. Phil. 1:23. "For I am in a strait betwixt two, having a desire to depart, and to be with Christ, which is far better": II Cor. 5:8. "We are confident, I say, and willing rather to be absent from the body, and to be present with the Lord." Besides there are some of the saints there already with their bodies, as Enoch and Elijah....

3. They shall remain there in a state of exceeding glory and blessedness, till the resurrection. They shall remain there in the enjoyment of God, dwelling with Jesus Christ in a state of perfect rest, without the least disturbance or molestation. Rev. 4:13. "And I heard a voice from heaven saying unto me, Write, Blessed are the dead which die in the Lord, from henceforth: Yea, saith the spirit, that they may rest from their labours; and their works do follow them." There they shall dwell in habitations of sweet delight and pleasure in Paradise; there they shall drink of those rivers of pleasures for evermore; there they shall dwell in perfect light and perfect love; there they shall see and converse with God and Christ, and with angels and glorious spirits, and shall contemplate the wonderful love of God to men in sending his only Son; there shall they

contemplate the glorious love of God to them, the love he had to them before the foundation of the world. There shall they see and know what love Christ had to them, that influenced him to lay down his life for them: and shall behold the beauty and excellency of Christ, and see face to face, and know even as they are known. . . .

4. They remain in a joyful expectation of their more full and complete blessedness at the resurrection. As the wicked have not their full punishment until after the resurrection, so neither have the saints their complete happiness. Though they have attained to such exceeding glory, yet they are not yet arrived at its highest degrees, for that is reserved for their final state. The reward which the saints receive after the resurrection, is often spoken of as their chief reward. This is the reward that Christ has promised. John 6:40. "And this is the will of him that sent me, that every one which seeth the Son, and believeth on him, may have everlasting life; and I will raise him up at the last day." This is the chief reward that the saints seek and wait for. Rom. 8:23. "And not only they, but ourselves also, which have the first fruits of the spirit, even we ourselves groan earnestly within ourselves, waiting for the adoption, to wit, the redemption of our body." Phil. 3:11. "If by any means I might attain unto the resurrection of the dead." "Women received their dead raised to life again: and others were tortured, not accepting deliverance, that they might obtain a better resurrection." So the happiness, that shall be given at Christ's second coming, is spoken of as the principal happiness. Titus 2:13. "Looking for that blessed hope, and the glorious appearing of the great God and our Saviour Jesus Christ."

This the saints will be in joyful expectation of in heaven; they shall rest in sweet repose on God's promise that it shall be so, their desires of it bringing no uneasiness; they rejoicing in it most in the consideration that it will be in God's time, in the fittest and best time.

Fourthly. I shall consider the glory, honour, and peace, which the godly shall receive at the Resurrection and the Day of Judgment.

1. When the time appointed comes, notice shall be given of it in heaven, which will be to their exceeding joy. God has in his own eternal counsels fixed the time, but now it is kept secret; it is not only not known by any on the earth, but neither is it known in heaven by either saints or angels there, and the man Christ Jesus himself, in his state of humiliation, did not himself know it: Matt. 24:36. "But of that day and hour knoweth no man; no not the angels of heaven, but my Father only." The saints and angels in heaven have a joyful expectation of it, but they know not when it is; but

when the time comes, God's eternal counsels concerning it shall be made known; the joyful tidings shall be proclaimed through all heaven, that all may prepare to attend the Lord Jesus Christ in his descent to the earth.

2. They shall descend with Christ from the highest heaven towards the earth. When notice is given to the heavenly host, they shall all gather themselves together to attend on this most joyful and glorious occasion; and then the glorious Son of God shall descend, and the holy angels with him, and not only the angels, but the souls of the saints shall come with Christ. I Thess. 4:14. "For if we believe that Jesus died, and rose again, even so them also which sleep in Jesus will God bring with him." Christ shall descend with the glory of his Father; he shall appear in a glory becoming the Supreme Lord and Judge of heaven and earth. Now heaven will for a time be left empty of its inhabitants; those glorious and blessed abodes will be deserted by those that dwelt there, to attend the Judge of the world. . . .

4. The dead in Christ shall arise at the sound of the last trumpet with glorified bodies, and the living saints shall see them. The holy and blessed souls of saints that descended from heaven with Christ, shall then be re-united to those bodies that shall be prepared by infinite wisdom and skill to be fit organs for a holy and happy soul. The body shall not rise as it was before; there shall be a vast difference in it. I Cor. 15:42, 43, 44. "It is sown in corruption, it is raised in incorruption; it is sown in dishonour, it is raised in glory; it is sown in weakness, it is raised in power; it is sown a natural body, it is raised a spiritual body. There is a natural body, and there is a spiritual body." The glory of that body that the saints shall rise with is what we now cannot conceive of. It shall not be such a dull and heavy moulded thing as it is now: it shall be active and vigorous as a flame of fire fit for the use of a glorified soul. . . .

6. Then shall the good works, which the saints have done, be declared to their peace and glory. We are often told that every man shall be judged according to his works, and Christ keeps a book of remembrance of the good works of the saints as well as of the sins of the ungodly. And however mean and polluted that which the saints do, is in itself, yet all the pollution that attends it is hid, and every thing they do for God that has the least sincerity in it is precious in God's eyes. Through his infinite grace it shall in no case lose its reward, neither shall it in any wise lose its honour. At the day of judgment they shall receive praise and glory in reward for it. Christ will declare all the good they have done to their honour; what

they did secretly and the world knew it not, and when they did not let their left hand know what their right hand did. Then shall they receive praise and honour for all their labour, for all their self-denial, and all their suffering in the cause of Christ; and those good works of theirs that were despised, and for which they were condemned, and suffered reproach, shall now be set in true light; and however they were reproached and slandered by men, they shall receive praise of God in the sight of angels and men. I Cor. 4:5....

7. The saints shall sit on thrones with Christ, to judge wicked men and devils. Christ will put that honour upon them on that day, he will cause them to sit on his right hand as judges with him, and so the saints shall judge the world. Matt. 19:28. "And Jesus said unto them, Verily I say unto you, that ye which have followed me, in the regeneration, when the Son of man shall sit on the throne of his glory, ye also shall sit upon twelve thrones judging the twelve tribes of Israel." I Cor. 6:2, 3. "Do ye not know that the saints shall judge the world? and if the world shall be judged by you, are ye unworthy to judge the smallest matters? Know ye not that we shall judge angels? how much more things that pertain to this life?" They shall judge kings and princes who were their persecutors, and the devils, who were their tempters.

8. At the finishing of the judgment Christ shall pronounce the blessed sentence upon them, "Come, ye blessed of my Father, inherit the kingdom prepared for you from the foundation of the world."

This blessed sentence Christ shall pronounce on them with inexpressible manifestations of grace and love. Every word of it will be ravishing to them, and will cause raptures of joy in their hearts; that this glorious person, though he orders with such indignation the wicked to depart from him, yet will so sweetly invite them to come with him, and that he should accost them after such a manner, saying, "ye blessed of my Father." Christ will pronounce them blessed in the sight of men and angels; and blessed indeed, because blessed by his Father. There will not only be a manifestation of Christ's love to them in this sentence, but a declaration of the Father's love, for they are declared to be blessed of him. Christ shall invite them to come with him, and for no less a purpose then to inherit a kingdom. Christ gives them a glorious kingdom; the wealth to which he invites them is the wealth of a kingdom; and the honour he gives them is the honour of kings; and what yet adds to the blessedness is this, that it is a kingdom prepared for them from the foundation of the world. God loved them from all eternity, and therefore he has prepared a kingdom for them. God had respect to them in the creation of the world, and then prepared this glorious kingdom for them, and out of love to them. They have therefore a right to it, and now therefore they are invited to come to possess it; and not only to possess it, but to *inherit* it, that is, to possess it as *heirs,* as those that have a right to the kingdom by virtue of their being his children....

...to sum up this whole description, there shall never be any end to their glory and blessedness. Therefore is it so often called eternal life, and everlasting life. We are told that at the day of judgment, when the wicked shall go away into everlasting punishment, the righteous shall enter into life eternal. Matt. 25:46. The pleasures which there are at God's right hand, are said to be for evermore; Psalm 16:11: And that this is not merely a long duration, but an absolute eternity, is evident from that which Christ has said, that those who believe on him shall not die. John 6:50; Rev. 22:5. In the description of the New Jerusalem it is said, "And they shall reign for ever and ever." The eternity of this blessedness shall crown all. If the saints knew that there would be an end to their happiness, though at never so great a distance, yet it would be a great damp to their joy. The greater the happiness is, so much the more uncomfortable would the thoughts of an end be, and so much the more joyful will it be to think that there will be no end. The saints will surely know that there will be no more danger of their happiness coming to an end, than there will be that the being of God will come to an end. As God is eternal, so their happiness is eternal; as long as the fountain lasts, they need not fear but they shall be supplied....

Bibliography

Primary Sources

Adams, Thomas. *Works*. London, 1630.

Alleine, Joseph. *An Alarm to the Unconverted*. London, 1671.

Ames, William. *An Analytical Exposition of Both the Epistles of the Apostle Peter*. London, 1641.

———. *Conscience, with the Power and Cases Thereof*. London, 1639.

———. *The Marrow of Sacred Divinity*. London, 1641.

Andrewes, Lancelot. *Ninety-six Sermons*. 5 vols. Oxford, 1841-1865.

Ball, John. *The Power of Godliness*. London, 1657.

———. *A Short Catechism Containing the Principles of Religion*. London, 1642.

———. *A Treatise of the Covenant of Grace*. London, 1645.

Baxter, Richard. *An Apology for the Nonconformist's Ministry*. London, 1681.

———. *A Call to the Unconverted to Turn and Live*. Kidderminster, 1658.

———. *A Christian Directory: or, A Sum of Practical Theology*. London, 1673.

———. *Directions and Persuasions to a Sound Conversion*. Kidderminster, 1658.

———. *Methodus Theologiae Christionae*. London, 1681.

———. *The Reformed Pastor*. Kidderminster, 1657.

———. *Reliquiae Baxterianae*. Edited by Matthew Sylvester. London, 1696.

————. *Richard Baxter and Puritan Politics.* Edited by Richard Schlatter. New Brunswick, N.J., 1957.

————. *The Saint's Everlasting Rest.* Kidderminster, 1650.

————. *The Scripture Gospel Defended.* London, 1690.

Baynes, Paul. *An Entire Commentary upon the Whole Epistle of the Apostle Paul to the Ephesians.* London, 1643.

Bedford, Thomas. *An Examination of the Chief Points of Antinomianism.* London, 1646.

Bolton, Samuel. *The Sinfulness of Sin.* London, 1646.

————. *The True Bounds of Christian Freedom.* London, 1645.

Bradford, John. *Writings.* Edited by Aubrey Townsend. 2 vols. Cambridge, 1848, 1853.

Bradshaw, William. *English Puritanism.* Dort(?), 1605.

————. *The Unreasonableness of the Separation.* Dort, 1614.

Bridge, William. *Works.* 5 vols. London, 1845.

Brooks, Thomas. *Apples of Gold for Young Men and Women.* London, 1657.

————. *The Crown and Glory of Christianity.* London, 1662.

————. *Heaven on Earth.* London, 1654.

————. *Paradise Opened.* London, 1675.

————. *Works.* Edited by Alexander B. Grosart. 6 vols. Edinburgh, 1866-1867.

Bunyan, John. *Christian Behaviour.* London, 1664.

————. *Grace Abounding to the Chief of Sinners.* London, 1666.

————. *The Life and Death of Mr. Badman.* London, 1680.

————. *The Pilgrim's Progress from This World to That Which Is to Come.* London, 1678.

————. *Prayer.* London, 1664.

Burgess, Anthony. *Spiritual Refining.* 2 vols. (*A Treatise of Grace and Assurance* and *A Treatise of Sin*). London, 1652, 1654.

————. *The True Doctrine of Justification.* London, 1648.

Burroughs, Jeremiah. *A Treatise of the Evil of Evils: or, The Exceeding Sinfulness of Sin.* London, 1654.

Burton, Henry. *The Law and the Gospel Reconciled.* London, 1631.

Caryl, Joseph. *The Nature and Principles of Love, as the End of the Commandment.* London, 1673.

Charnock, Stephen. *On the Existence and Attributes of God.* London, 1682.

————. *Discourse on the Nature of Regeneration.* London, 1683.

————. *Necessity of Regeneration.* London, 1683.

————. *Works.* Edited by Thomas Smith. 5 vols. Edinburgh, 1864-1866.

Chauncy, Charles. *Seasonable Thoughts on the State of Religion in New England*. Boston, 1743.

Clarkson, David. *Justification by the Righteousness of Christ*. London, 1675.

The Confession of Faith: Agreed upon by the Assembly of the Divines at Westminster. London, 1647.

Cotton, John. *A Brief Exposition with Practical Observations upon the Whole Book of Ecclesiastes*. London, 1654.

———. *The Way of Life*. London, 1641.

Cranmer, Thomas. *Work*. Edited by G. E. Duffield. Appleford, Berkshire, 1964.

Crisp, Tobias. *Works*. 2 vols. 7th ed. London, 1832.

Dod, John. *A Plain and Familiar Exposition of the Lord's Prayer*. London, 1625.

———. *A Plain and Familiar Exposition of the Ten Commandments*. London, 1603.

Downame, George. *The Christian's Freedom*. Oxford, 1635.

———. *The Covenant of Grace*. Dublin, 1631.

———. *A Treatise of Justification*. London, 1639.

Edwards, Jonathan. *Essay on the Freedom of the Will*. London, 1754.

———. *History of Redemption*. Boston, 1777.

———. *Images or Shadows of Divine Things*. Edited by Perry Miller. New Haven, 1948.

———. *Life and Diary of the Rev. David Brainerd*. Boston, 1749.

———. *Puritan Sage: Collected Writings of Jonathan Edwards*. Edited by Vergilius Ferm. New York, 1953.

———. *Selections from the Unpublished Writings of Jonathan Edwards of America*. Edited by Alexander B. Grosart. Published privately, 1865.

———. *Treatise on Grace, and Other Posthumously Published Writings*. Edited by Paul Helm. Cambridge, 1971.

———. *A Narrative of Surprising Conversions*. London, 1736.

———. *Sinners in the Hands of an Angry God*. London, 1741.

———. *Thoughts on the Revival in New England*. London, 1742.

———. *A Treatise Concerning Religious Affections*. London, 1745.

Flavel, John. *The Method of Grace in the Holy Spirit's Applying to the Souls of Men the Eternal Redemption Contrived by the Father, and Accomplished by the Son*. London, 1681.

———. *The Mystery of Providence*. London, 1671.

———. *The Reasonableness of Personal Reformation and the Necessity of Conversion*. London, 1691.

Goodwin, Thomas. *Exposition of Ephesians*. London, 1681.

———. *The Objects and Acts of Justifying Faith*. London, 1697.

———. *An Unregenerate Man's Guiltiness Before God*. London, 1692.

———. *The Work of the Holy Ghost in Our Salvation*. London, 1703.

Greenham, Richard. *Faith, Justification, and Feeling.* London, 1599.

————. *The Marks of a Righteous Man.* London, 1599.

————. *Of Conscience.* London, 1599.

————. *Of Quenching the Spirit.* London, 1599.

————. *Works.* Edited by Henry Holland. London, 1599.

Hinde, William. *The Office and Use of the Moral Law of God in the Days of the Gospel.* London, 1622.

Hooker, Richard. *Of the Laws of Ecclesiastical Polity.* 2 vols. London, 1593-1597.

Hooker, Thomas. *The Application of Redemption by the Effectual Work of the Word and Spirit of Christ, for the Bringing of Lost Sinners to God.* London, 1656.

————. *The Soul's Preparation for Christ.* London, 1632.

————. *A Survey of the Sum of Church Discipline.* London, 1648.

Hopkins, Ezekiel. *A Discourse of the Nature, Corruption, and Renewing of the Conscience.* London, 1701.

————. *Exposition of the Ten Commandments.* London, 1692.

————. *Practical Christianity.* London, 1701.

————. *A Practical Exposition on the Lord's Prayer.* London, 1692.

Hopkins, Samuel. *System of Doctrine.* 3 vols. Boston, 1782.

Howe, John. *The Blessedness of the Righteous.* London, 1668.

————. *Man's Creation in an Holy but Mutable State.* London, 1660.

————. *Works.* Edited by J. P. Hewlett. 3 vols. London, 1848.

Jewel, John. *An Apology in Defence of the Church of England.* London, 1562.

————. *A Defence of the "Apology."* London, 1565.

————. *A Treatise on the Holy Scriptures.* London, 1582.

————. *A Treatise on the Sacraments.* London, 1583.

Manton, Thomas. *Exposition of the Epistle of James.* London, 1651.

————. *Exposition of the Epistle of Jude.* London, 1658.

————. *A Practical Exposition of the Lord's Prayer.* London, 1684.

————. *Works.* Edited by Thomas Smith. 22 vols. London, 1870-1875.

Marshall, Walter. *Gospel Mystery of Sanctification.* London, 1692.

Mather, Cotton. *Ratio Discipline Fratrum Nov-Anglorum.* Boston, 1726.

Mather, Increase. *The Divine Right of Infant-Baptism Asserted and Proved from Scripture and Antiquity.* Boston, 1680.

————. *The Doctrine of Divine Providence.* Boston, 1684.

————. *The Order of the Gospel, Professed and Practiced by the Churches of Christ in New England.* Boston, 1700.

Mather, Samuel. *All Men Will Not Be Saved Forever.* Boston, 1782.

Milton, John. *Complete Poetical Works.* Edited by Henry Stebbing. New York, 1853.

Owen, John. *Works*. Edited by William Orme. 23 vols. London, 1820.

Pemple, William. *A Treatise of Justification by Faith*. Oxford, 1625.
———. *A Treatise of Justification by Grace*. London, 1627.

Perkins, William. *Complete Works*. Edited by I. Breward. Appleford, Berkshire, 1970.
———. *A Discourse of Conscience*. Cambridge, 1596.
———. *The Foundation of Christian Religion, Gathered into Six Principles*. London, 1590.
———. *A Golden Chain: or, The Description of Theology, Containing the Order of the Causes of Salvation and Damnation According to God's Word*. London, 1591.
———. *Of the Calling of the Ministry*. London, 1606.
———. *A Reformed Catholic*. Cambridge, 1598.
———. *Works*. Cambridge, 1603.

Preston, John. *A Heavenly Treatise of the Divine Love of Christ*. London, 1640.
———. *The Law Out Lawed: or, The Charter of the Gospel*. Edinburgh, 1631.
———. *The New Covenant*. London, 1629.
———. *The Saint's Daily Exercise*. London, 1633.

Prince, Thomas, Jr., ed. *The Christian History, Containing Accounts of the Revival and Propagation of Religion in Great Britain and America*. 2 vols. Boston, 1744, 1745.

Rutherford, Samuel. *Christ Dying and Drawing Sinners to Himself*. London, 1647.
———. *The Covenant of Life Opened*. Edinburgh, 1655.
———. *Letters*. Edited by A. A. Bonar. London, 1891.
———. *A Survey of the Spiritual Antichrist*. London, 1648.
———. *The Trial and Triumph of Faith*. London, 1645.

Sibbes, Richard. *The Bruised Reed and Smoking Flax*. London, 1630.
———. *The Christian Work*. London, 1639.
———. *The Demand of a Good Conscience*. London, 1640.
———. *Exposition of Philippians 3*. London, 1639.
———. *The Spouse: Her Earnest Desire after Christ Her Husband*. London, 1638.
———. *Works*. Edited by Alexander B. Grosart. 6 vols. Edinburgh, 1861-1864.

Smith, Henry. *Sermons*. London, 1615.

Stennett, Joseph. *Hymns in Commemoration of the Sufferings of Our Blessed Saviour Jesus Christ*. London, 1733.

Taylor, Thomas. *The Principles of Christian Practice*. London, 1635.
———. *The Progress of Saints to Full Holiness*. London, 1630.

Traill, Robert. *Sermons Concerning the Throne of Grace.* London, 1696.
————. *A Vindication of the Protestant Doctrine Concerning Justification.* London, 1692.

Tyndale, William. *Works.* Edited by G. E. Duffield. Appleford, Berkshire, 1964.

Ussher, James. *A Body of Divinity.* London, 1645.

Watson, Thomas. *A Body of Divinity.* London, 1692.

Zanchius, Hieronymus. *The Doctrine of Absolute Predestination.* Translated by A. M. Toplady. 2nd ed. London, 1779.

Secondary Sources

Babbage, Stuart Barton. *Puritanism and Richard Bancroft.* London: SPCK, 1962.

Bartlett, Robert M. *The Pilgrim Way.* Philadelphia: Pilgrim, 1971.

Bennet, Benjamin. *A Memorial of the Reformation Chiefly in England.* 2nd ed. London: Clark, 1721.

Benoit, Jean Daniel. *Direction spirituelle et Protestantisme: Étude sur la legitimité d'une direction Protestante.* Paris: Alcan, 1940.

Blunt, John Henry. *The Reformation of the Church of England.* 2 vols. London: Longmans and Green, 1892, 1896.

Bolam, Charles Gordon, et al. *The English Presbyterians: From Elizabethan Puritanism to Modern Unitarianism.* Boston: Beacon, 1968.

Brook, Benjamin. *The Lives of the Puritans.* 3 vols. London: Black, 1813.

Brown, John. *The English Puritans.* Cambridge: University, 1910.

Burnet, Gilbert. *The History of the Reformation of the Church of England.* 2 vols. London: Smith, 1841.

Burrage, Champlin. *The Early English Dissenters in the Light of Recent Research (1550-1641).* 2 vols. Cambridge: University, 1910.

Cadier, Jean. *The Man God Mastered: A Brief Biography of John Calvin.* Translated by O. R. Johnston. Grand Rapids: Eerdmans, 1960.

Calamy, Edmund. *An Account of the Ministers Ejected or Silenced After the Restoration in 1660.* 2 vols. London: Lawrence, 1713.

Campbell, Douglas. *The Puritan in Holland, England, and America.* 3rd ed. New York: Harper, 1893.

Carruthers, Samuel William. *The Everyday Work of the Westminster Assembly.* Philadelphia: Presbyterian Historical Society, 1943.

Choisy, Eugène. *Études sur Calvin et le Calvinisme.* Paris, 1935.

Clark, Henry W. *A History of English Nonconformity from Wiclif to the Nineteenth Century.* 2 vols. London: Chapman and Hall, 1911, 1913.

Clark, William. *The Anglican Reformation.* Ten Epochs of Church History, edited by John Fulton, vol. 10. New York: Christian Literature, 1897.

Coolidge, John S. *The Pauline Renaissance in England: Puritanism and the Bible.* Oxford: Clarendon, 1970.

Cragg, Gerald R. *Puritanism in the Period of the Great Persecution, 1660-1688.* New York: Harper, 1957.

Dale, R. W. *History of English Congregationalism.* Edited by A. W. W. Dale. 2nd ed. London: Hodder and Stoughton, 1907.

Davies, Horton. *The Worship of the English Puritans.* London: Oxford University, 1948.

De Jong, Peter Y. *The Covenant Idea in New England Theology, 1620-1847.* Grand Rapids: Eerdmans, 1945.

Elliott, Emory. *Power and the Pulpit in Puritan New England.* Princeton: Princeton University, 1975.

Eusden, John D. *Puritans, Lawyers and Politics in Early Seventeenth-Century England.* New Haven: Yale University, 1958.

Faust, Clarence H., and Johnson, Thomas H. *Jonathan Edwards.* American Century Series, edited by Harry Hayden Clark. New York: Hill and Wang, 1935.

Foster, Frank Hugh. *A Genetic History of the New England Theology.* Chicago: University of Chicago, 1907.

Gaustad, Edwin Scott. *The Great Awakening in New England.* New York: Harper, 1957.

Gould, George, ed. *Documents Relating to the Settlement of the Church of England by the Act of Uniformity of 1662.* London: Kent, 1862.

Haller, William. *The Rise of Puritanism.* New York: Columbia University, 1938.

Henson, Herbert Hensley. *Studies in English Religion in the Seventeenth Century.* London: Murray, 1903.

Hill, Christopher. *The World Turned Upside Down: Radical Ideas During the English Reformation.* New York: Viking, 1972.

Hughes, Philip Edgcumbe. *Theology of the English Reformers.* Grand Rapids: Eerdmans, 1965.

Kevan, Ernest F. *The Grace of Law: A Study in Puritan Theology.* Grand Rapids: Baker, 1965.

Latourette, Kenneth Scott. *A History of Christianity.* New York: Harper, 1953.

Loane, Marcus L. *Makers of Religious Freedom in the Seventeenth Century.* Grand Rapids: Eerdmans, 1961.

———. *Masters of the English Reformation.* London: Church Book Room, 1954.

———. *Pioneers of the Reformation in England.* London: Church Book Room, 1964.

McGiffert, Arthur Cushman. *Jonathan Edwards.* New York: Harper, 1932.

Marsden, J. B. *The History of the Early Puritans.* London: Hamilton and Adams, 1850.

———. *The History of the Later Puritans.* London: Hamilton and Adams, 1852.

Martin, Hugh. *Puritanism and Richard Baxter.* London: SCM, 1954.

Miller, Perry. *Errand into the Wilderness.* New York: Harper, 1966.

———. *The New England Mind: The Seventeenth Century.* Cambridge: Harvard University, 1954.

———, and Johnson, Thomas H. *The Puritans.* 2 vols. New York: American Book, 1938.

Monk, Robert C. *John Wesley: His Puritan Heritage.* Nashville: Abingdon, 1966.

Neal, Daniel. *The History of the Puritans.* 4 vols. London: 1732-1738.

Nuttall, Geoffrey F. *The Holy Spirit in Puritan Faith and Experience.* Oxford: Blackwell, 1946.

Palmer, Edwin H.; Cohen, Gary G.; and Hughes, Philip Edgcumbe: eds. *The Encyclopedia of Christianity.* 4 vols. Wilmington: National Foundation for Christian Education, 1964-1972.

Paul, Robert S. *The Lord Protector: Religion and Politics in the Life of Oliver Cromwell.* Grand Rapids: Eerdmans, 1955.

Plooij, Daniël. *The Pilgrim Fathers from a Dutch Point of View.* New York: New York University, 1932.

Porter, H. C. *Puritanism in Tudor England.* Columbia: University of South Carolina, 1971.

Prall, S. E. *The Puritan Revolution: A Documentary History.* Garden City, N.Y.: Doubleday, 1968.

Price, Thomas. *The History of Protestant Nonconformity in England.* London: Ball, 1836.

Robinson, William Childs. *The Reformation: A Rediscovery of Grace.* Grand Rapids: Eerdmans, 1962.

Rupp, E. G. *Studies in the Making of the English Protestant Tradition (Mainly in the Reign of Henry VIII).* Cambridge: University, 1947.

Schneider, Herbert Wallace. *The Puritan Mind.* New York: Holt, 1930.

Simpson, Alan. *Puritanism in Old and New England*. Chicago: University of Chicago, 1955.

Smyth, Charles H. *Cranmer and the Reformation Under Edward VI*. London: SPCK, 1973.

Thomas, I. D. E., ed. *The Golden Treasury of Puritan Quotations*. Chicago: Moody, 1975.

Toon, Peter. *God's Statesman: The Life and Work of Dr. John Owen*. London: Paternoster, 1972.

———. *Puritans and Calvinism*. Lancashire, Pa.: Reiner, 1973.

Tracy, Joseph. *The Great Awakening: A History of the Revival of Religion in the Time of Edwards and Whitefield*. Boston: Tappan and Dennet, 1842.

Wakefield, Gordon Stevens. *Puritan Devotion: Its Place in the Development of Christian Piety*, 1957.

Walker, Williston. *A History of the Christian Church*. New York: Scribner, 1918.

Whiting, C. E. *Studies in English Puritanism from the Restoration to Revolution, 1660-1688*. London: SPCK, 1931.

Index of Scripture References

…